WOMAN OF THE HOUSE

WOMAN OF THE HOUSE

HOUSE

The Rise of Nancy Pelosi

Vincent Bzdek

palgrave
macmillan

WOMAN OF THE HOUSE
Copyright © Vincent Bzdek, 2008.

First published in 2008 by
PALGRAVE MACMILLAN™
175 Fifth Avenue, New York, N.Y. 10010 and
Houndmills, Basingstoke, Hampshire, England RG21 6XS
Companies and representatives throughout the world.

PALGRAVE MACMILLAN is the global academic imprint of the Palgrave Macmillan division of St. Martin's Press, LLC and of Palgrave Macmillan Ltd. Macmillan® is a registered trademark in the United States, United Kingdom and other countries. Palgrave is a registered trademark in the European Union and other countries.

ISBN-13: 978–0–230–60319–6
ISBN-10: 0–230–60319-X

Library of Congress Cataloging-in-Publication Data is available from the Library of Congress.

A catalogue record for this book is available from the British Library.

Design by Newgen Imaging Systems (P) Ltd., Chennai, India.

First edition: January 2008

10 9 8 7 6 5 4 3 2 1

Printed in the United States of America.

To my wife and my life, Kelsey

CONTENTS

Nancy Pelosi with children on the day she became Speaker.
(Richard A. Lipski/*Washington Post)*

INTRODUCTION

She had to do everything Fred Astaire had to do, only backward and in high heels.

—An old saying about Ginger Rogers

As the House chamber begins to fill with its usual gray flannel and navy blue, it isn't immediately apparent this morning on Capitol Hill will be so different from all the others. The first members of the 110th Congress are trickling in from the marble corridors, greeting each other with the same fraternal bonhomie and jackhammer handshakes they've used for much of the 200-year history of the place. It's always been more informal and boisterous—more macho—than its upscale, prissy counterpoint on the other side of the Hill. But as more and more dark suits amass today, it is hard not to notice from high up in the galleries that there are quite a few reds and whites spangling the vast field of gray. Look, there's a yellow, a paisley, and a beige. And one baby blue for good measure. Compared to 20 years ago, this semicircle of Brooks Brothers suits is positively popping with color.

Since all the congress*men* are clad in pretty much the same uniform—dark suit, white shirt, red or yellow tie—it is the congress*women* who stand out like firecrackers just lit. Seventy-four firecrackers amid the blue and gray, the largest assemblage of womanly ordnance in the history of Congress. In fact, the "gentlewomen" bursting into smiles as they throw open the doors and waltz into the room like they own it account for one third of all of the women who have ever served in the House. It took 231 years before this single day to accumulate the other two thirds. The 16 women serving in the Senate at the beginning of 2007 represent just under half of all the women senators elected in U.S. history: 35.

No question about it, today is the most historic day ever for women in Congress, the result of decades of steady, painstaking gains. The woman right at the heart of all those gains, both as beneficiary and engine, is Nancy Pelosi, here today to become the first-ever woman Speaker of the House, the highest political office ever held by a woman in the United States. In two hours she will be two heartbeats away from the presidency. If the president and vice president are both incapacitated for some reason—by illness, death, or indictment—the Constitution says Pelosi is in charge.

And now Pelosi enters the room, a biblical Esther in a cloud of children, her smile on high beam. In her royal purple suit, or bipartisan purple, or Armani violet, depending on how a person looks at it, Pelosi stands out in the blue gray, as well, but also complements it. The elegant, energetic "gentle-lady" from San Francisco has a kind of star quality about her as she makes her entrance. "There's excitement across the country," said longtime colleague Anna Eshoo. "I've seen her in the airport, and there's spontaneous applause for her." Camera phones come popping out when she strolls by. Aides who travel with her have taken to carrying Sharpies because of all the autograph requests. Brendan Daly, her communications director, said her name and face recognition have gone up "a hundredfold" since her inauguration. To many women across the country Pelosi is something rare in American history, a genuine national heroine.

The symbolism of her inauguration, her steady rise to Speaker, and the women she has lifted up and brought along with her on her long skirts have transformed the American political and cultural landscape. Many historians see it as a signal moment, a pivotal point in the country's history. Pelosi and her fellow gentleladies have built up such a strong network of powerful women that it's beginning to reach critical mass, several political analysts believe, spurring a new kind of women's political movement that may clear the way for many more women to enter public service. As the first female leader of her party in the House in 2003, Pelosi used her high profile to raise millions of dollars for women candidates and encouraged others to run in the 2006 elections, as she had in many elections before that. She has installed many women in key leadership positions within Congress through committee appointments, positioning them to move into committee chairs. Women now lead two Senate committees and four House panels that hold sway over ethics; environment and public works; small business; and the rules of Congress. Nine states chose women as governors in 2006, including the first woman chief for the rugged male bastion of Alaska. Other women in Congress such as Barbara Boxer and Dianne Feinstein have tried for years to get a range of so-called women's issues or family issues to the top the country's agenda; now Pelosi is doing it wholesale.

Representative Rosa DeLauro (D-Conn.) calls Pelosi "the most powerful person in Washington."

"What's happened with Pelosi . . . what you've got, at the top and bottom, is a serious new look in women in politics," said Marie Wilson, author of *Closing the Leadership Gap: Why Women Can and Must Help Run the World.*

Pelosi sees even larger possibilities ahead. "We have to believe it's easier now for women in every field," she commented after the 2006 election that won her the right to take the Speaker's chair. "Becoming the first woman Speaker will send a message to young girls and women across the country that anything is possible for them, that women can wield power and breathe the air at that altitude. As the first woman Speaker of the House, I will work to make certain that I will not be the last."

Some scholars of American politics see Pelosi's election as a quantum leap: from now on it will seem normal to have women serving in the country's highest offices. Yet the United States is still far behind other countries when it comes to gender equity in politics. Dozens of other nations have had women leaders and can boast a much better balance between men and women in their bodies politic, including Iraq and Afghanistan. In Iraq, 31 percent of the representatives in its national legislature are women, compared to 16 percent in the U.S. House of Representatives. France now mandates that parties run an equal number of men and women candidates on their tickets for all elections. Scholars argue that the imbalance in America's political bodies has led to an imbalance in the country's overall priorities. But if Pelosi's rise marks the end of America's cultural allergy to women leading the country, then the winds of history have shifted forever.

Back in 1992, after the midterm congressional vote in November, pundits talked of a Year of the Woman. A record number of female candidates, angered by the Anita Hill hearings, had risen up and demanded a few more seats at the table. But that Year of the Woman was but an opening act for 2006. Back then, 24 new women were elected to the House, bringing the total number of women to 48. Today the total is 74. Five women were newly elected to the Senate in 1992, upping the total there to 7. Today there are 16. Shortly after this *new,* unchristened year of the woman got under way, the first female anchor of one of the three major broadcast networks took her seat, and Harvard named its first woman president. Yet the gains for women were so expected, so overdue, so mainstream, and the country so accustomed to women's faces in leadership that no Year of Woman II was ever declared in the media. Perhaps 2006 was the Year We Got Past the Need for a Year of the Woman. Or perhaps it was the start of a Decade of Women, a pump primer for more substantial gains to come. The 2008 elections, with a woman presidential contender and the inspiration of a woman Speaker driving them, could very well tell us whether this is new, permanent, higher ground in our history or a one-year peak with more gender valleys ahead.

The 74 disruptions in the congressional monochrome aren't the only anomalies today. There are many other small signs a cataclysm has occurred, that things will never be the same. One of those is a pink dress with stuffed animals clinging to the shoulder straps. Another is a two-toned T-shirt with a giant black Deutschland eagle on the front. The one garnering the most attention, however, is the one in Nancy Pelosi's arms: an infant wrapped in its white receiving blanket whose name is the same as his granddad's: Paul. It's not every day in the House that the Speaker's six-week-old grandchild takes the floor.

The gray-blue sea of Congress is white-capped with children today. In a chamber weary of war, the symbolism of rebirth and new priority is hard to miss. Children are everywhere—the accessory of the day, quipped several observers. And as children are wont to do, they play. A young man of six engages in a robust game of peek-a-boo around the side of a chair with the Speaker-designate. A future congresswoman, aged eight, tries out one of the giant leather chairs for size, swinging her legs vigorously beneath her. Bouncing on Heath Schuler's lap is Island, the two-year-old daughter of the former Redskin and brand-new congressman from North Carolina, one of 60 candidates recruited personally by Pelosi and her campaign commander Rahm Emanuel. Schuler's daughter probably won't remember being here, but when her dad reminds her, she'll always know that she was.

Today at least, this is not your father's Congress. "Surely once every 10,000 years you could try new ways of doing things," said Berkeley professor Robin Lakoff. It's a long tradition in the House that children are allowed on the floor for swearing-in day, but there are more children today than ever before, and they've made themselves at home. Great scads of these children on the carpet belong to the extended Pelosi family itself. But many others, the daughters and granddaughters of congressmen, have been brought to the floor specially today, to see history being made.

In the galleries that hang high above the proceedings, more women and children. Pelosi's entire life story is gathered up there as well—she's got

66 years of history packed to the rafters. Her story is best told in people, really, and people from all chapters of her life are in the hall today. Pelosi might be best described as a collector of people; it's her identity, her gift, her strongest skill. She's a builder of coalitions and communities, a human homepage with thousands of hyperlinks. That is who she is and why she has gotten here. Her talent lies in assembling and maintaining an ever-widening circle of friends and loyalists. By one count, Nancy Pelosi has more than 2,000 friends she keeps in touch with regularly, asking their advice, sending them notes, checking up on their children.

Her staff keeps a careful database of the more than 29,000 donors who have contributed to her and her causes. Certainly even more people than that *consider* themselves her friend, even if it was a friendship of a day or an hour. Five hundred Californians alone are crammed into the Capitol, for Nancy is the first from the Golden State to serve as Speaker as well. Her own family is bursting at the seams: four siblings and six grandchildren, the prototypical big Catholic family. Pelosi said the glue that holds all this together, the bond for this great web of benefactors and advisers and voters and emotional struts, is simple: R-E-S-P-E-C-T.

Who are the people that represent the pages of her story? Certainly her husband, Paul, up there in the gallery, directly facing the dais. His good-natured support for this Italian mom's second chapter as a politician, not to mention his $25 million fortune, have been crucial to Pelosi's rise. ("Thank God for Paul Pelosi," Nancy likes to say before meals.) Pelosi didn't run for office until age 46, when her last daughter was in high school. Her first career was motherhood; her second is politics. Pelosi often notes the similar skills required of the two disciplines: multitasking, maintaining discipline, making sure everyone has done their homework.

Sitting with Paul are the living products of her first career: daughters Nancy Corinne, Alexandra, Jacqueline, Christine, and son Paul, each with a few of their own hyperlinks spread around. It's a safe bet in San Francisco circles that Christine will follow her mother's footsteps into political office someday, as might her son, Paul Jr.

Sitting not far away is Tommy D'Alesandro, Nancy's oldest brother and patriarch of the Baltimore family she grew up in. Tommy the Third is probably Pelosi's closest personal adviser and her chief image counselor. He critiques every one of her television appearances. The night the Democrats took back Congress, Tommy was the first person she called. Tommy also served as mayor of Baltimore, as did Nancy's dad, who is something of a legend in Maryland politics. Before he was elected mayor three times, Pelosi's father spent a few years on the House floor where Pelosi now treads. More than anyone else, he taught Pelosi the nuts-and-bolts political lessons she employed to reach the high-backed leather speaker's chair. He's not here today, but he did visit the House floor to see Pelosi take up the family vocation just two months before he passed away.

It's a bicoastal bunch in the galleries: There's California politico John Burton, whose sister-in-law Sala Burton decided on her deathbed that she wanted Pelosi to fill her congressional seat. His brother Phil was one of the most powerful men ever to stride these aisles. Pelosi calls him, simply, a "lion." A broad, towering bear of a man, Phil Burton achieved more in Congress than most presidents achieve in the Oval Office. He honed Pelosi's political skills in California, bequeathing her a bit of the piss and vinegar she brings to her quests for social justice.

This is in large part a California affair, so the stars are out. Among Pelosi's family members in the visitor's gallery are Carole King, Tony Bennett, and Richard Gere. Gavin Newsom, the mayor of San Francisco and friend of the family, is there as well, as is Antonio Villaraigosa, the mayor of Los Angeles. Newsom's decreed "Nancy Pelosi Day" back in his hometown.

The entire Class of '62 from Pelosi's alma mater in Washington, Trinity College, has returned for the inaugural festivities, and some of them are in the Capitol as well. The current students and faculty of Trinity are gathered around a radio listening to the proceedings in the campus's stately old Main Hall. It's the same hall where Nancy used to sing up the staircases to her sister students at the all-girl's school. Trinity women can't watch history being made because the old building doesn't have cable television, and the major networks, in their infinite wisdom, didn't think the nation's first woman Speaker, warranted live coverage.

Several of the women in the House that day provided the shoulders Pelosi said she stood on to get where she is. Barbara Mikulski, who has well earned her nickname "the Mouth," was the first Democratic woman elected to the Senate. That was only 21 years ago—just a few months before Pelosi entered Congress herself—and Mikulski's still making laws. She and Pelosi went to the same all-girls Catholic high school in Baltimore. Funny how so many of the pioneering women in Congress went to all-girls schools, where all the role models were women. Mikulski came over from the North Wing to pay tribute to Pelosi this evening and give her a hug. Pat Schroeder, who was told she couldn't use the parking lot and elevator when she first arrived in Congress in 1972 because they were reserved for "members only," gives Pelosi an exuberant wave. Anna Eshoo, one of Pelosi's closest allies in the

House, has been in Congress longer than Pelosi, 25 years. It's not quite so lonely now. Little girls at schools she visits back home in Silicon Valley have come up to her lately and told her that Nancy's "in the Constitution." "This is my 25th year. I've never heard little girls spontaneously talk about the Constitution," Eshoo said. There are many, many other women in the chamber who helped push Pelosi toward the prize with their votes and encouragement and demands for a voice. Grace Napalatino, Rosa Delauro, Louise Slaughter, Marcy Kaptur, Maxine Waters. The list goes on until it reaches 74. "We wanted more," Pelosi said.

Pelosi has always been able to work effectively with men in politics, too, a legacy, perhaps, of growing up with five brothers. Two of the chamber's old bulls, John Murtha and George Miller, are two of her closest allies. Theirs is an unexpected but powerful alliance, forged around a passion for getting things done. Murtha, a decorated Marine from the coal country of Pennsylvania, and Pelosi, the tailored socialite from San Francisco, seem at first glance a strange pair. But the gruff old pol clearly connects with the Baltimore in her background. Representative James Clyburn sits in the audience front and center, Pelosi's third in command. The Reverend Clyburn, aides like to call him. He tends Pelosi's Faith Working Group, and Pelosi, a devout Catholic, has charged him with recementing the bonds between church and Democrat.

Rahm Emanuel likes to give Pelosi high-fives, and he's had cause for many lately. The representative from Chicago is the dynamic, potty-mouthed engine that drove the Democrats over the finish line in the 2006 elections. His raw energy echoes Pelosi's: Neither of them sleeps much more than four hours a night. Today he has the honor of nominating his boss for Speaker. Forgot decorum: He gives her another high-five as he stands up to give his introduction.

"As a father of three young children," Emanuel says up on the dais, "I am particularly thrilled to be a part of this moment, thrilled that a generation of young girls and boys across America are about to witness another historic step in our nation's march toward equality of opportunity."

Down on the floor with her grandkids, Pelosi is giddy and righteous on this day—her day. After the 233 to 202 vote, she causes the blue-gray sea to part—and applaud—as she walks to the podium to accept the gavel.

"Today marks an occasion I think the Founding Fathers would view favorably," says Republican leader John Boehner as he hands the hammer to Pelosi.

Surrounded by children, Pelosi takes the oath. She and the grandkids create an indelible visual that in one swoop redefines the trappings of political power. It is an image that will appear on newspapers and flat screens in every country in the world.

Ellen Malcolm, president of EMILY'S List, put it this way: "When she was sworn in there was such excitement about electing the first woman Speaker, and I think the combination of her holding the gavel of power yet surrounded by children on the podium told a tale to a lot of people that is a different day in America when you can give a woman such a high position."

This is what power looks like in Congress for the moment. This is the person who is most responsible for those record-breaking gains for women, not so much because of her example and inspiration this time (that will come next time around) but from her tireless, cross-country campaigning and fundraising. It may be that Pelosi has forever inoculated the country against its allergy to women in high office. But, then again, America may still have a long way to go. As Pelosi makes her way slowly to the podium, it's hard not to notice that blue gray still predominates, as do the country club walls and marbled earnestness of the room, which still give the place the look and feel of a Phi Delta House.

Congress is an institution that was designed 200 years ago by men who thought husbands could best represent their wives' interests in the political sphere. It continued to operate under that assumption for the next 133 years, until 1920, when American women finally earned the right to vote after much wheedling, cajoling, protesting, organizing, and storming of the Capitol. Despite all its recent gender upgrades, today Congress is still an institution mostly of, by, and for men. But forget about the furniture and the past for a moment. Today is for the ages. Today a woman is going to take charge of the frathouse. What, one wonders, will a remake of *Animal House* look like with Nancy Pelosi in the starring role?

"For our daughters and granddaughters, today we have broken the marble ceiling," Pelosi announces up on the dais to raucous, roaring cheers. "For our daughters and granddaughters today, the sky is the limit."

We're still struggling, after 200 years, to live up to that idea of Thomas Jefferson's that all men—and women—are created equal. This is still one of the unfinished battles of the American Revolution. Certainly our founders *meant* on some level to include women in their revolution, didn't they? If only John Adams had heeded his wife, Abigail, a bit more closely. In March of 1776 she wrote him a letter: "John: I desire you would Remember the Ladies, and be more generous and favorable to them than your ancestors. Do not put such unlimited power into the hands of the Husbands. Remember all Men would be tyrants if they could." Busy John forgot, of course, to remember the ladies when it comes to voting, although the Constitution he helped piece together a few years later makes no mention of gender when it describes the necessary qualifications for federal office. That meant a woman could run for office even if she couldn't vote, which is exactly what happened in 1916, when Montana sent the first woman to Congress four years before the Nineteenth Amendment was signed into law.

To pursue the implication of the simple idea that everyone is equal to everyone else, however, we'd have to be able, as a country, to promise each American when he or she is born that they will have access to the same *opportunities* as every other person, regardless of their gender, race, or income. This is where Pelosi's ascent gets interesting to a lot more people than the 51 percent of the population who are women. In fact, Pelosi said some of the strongest, most positive reaction she's gotten to her Speakership comes from the fathers of daughters, who can now tell their future presidents with some degree of honesty that anything is possible, the sky's the limit.

It's a damn high ideal, equality of opportunity, and it took 200 years to redeem its implied promise that women are just as equal as men when it comes to job opportunities in our most-representative political body, the House. No matter whether a person subscribes to Nancy Pelosi's politics or not, likes or dislikes her personally, approves or disapproves of the way she's handled the office thus far, it's hard not to give her this: She's helped the country fulfill one of its founding promises. She's an American first. "Now she belongs to history," said her brother.

Larry J. Sabato, founder and director of the University of Virginia's Center for Politics, tells an anecdote that has stayed with him from the years he lived in Great Britain as a young man. It's an anecdote about the power of role models. Margaret Thatcher was stepping down after serving as prime minister for 12 years. During her tenure, the constitutional monarch was also a woman, Queen Elizabeth II. When Thatcher retired and John Major succeeded her, a young girl was interviewed about the changing of the guard, and she seemed startled, saying "I thought that only women could serve as the leader here."

Such is the impact one person, one woman, can have in the highest offices in the land. As a result, Republicans and Democrats are fairly bipartisan in their applause for Pelosi the Role Model and Pelosi the Trailblazer. But what about Pelosi the Speaker? Pelosi the Partisan Politician? Pelosi the

Reformer? Pelosi the War Ender? Pelosi the banner carrier of the Democratic Party? Has she lived up to the hopes—or fears—so many people projected on to her in her first year in office? Has she risen above the partisan fray enough to act the stateswoman and heal divisions in the country, and begin to heal Congress itself? Has she fundamentally changed the way politics is practiced in Washington, or is she Newt Gingrich in a St. John's knit? Or worse, is she plunging the country back in time, to a kind of retro-liberal past that doesn't work anymore and might be dangerous to the country? Or has she let her liberal base down by moving too far to the middle?

Many of those answers—but not all—depend on which side of the aisle the observer is on. There are still two Pelosis battling it out in the public consciousness. Depending on their political affiliations and their media filters of choice, most Americans have experienced one of two carefully constructed Pelosis during her first year in office. One is the Pelosi created by a Republican message machine: the monied überliberal from the Left Coast's looniest quarter, San Francisco. A gal who talks a good game about reforming Congress but isn't much different from the lifer politicians she pilloried so successfully on her climb into high office. Republican strategists and spinmeisters have been borrowing a page from the Who: Meet the New Boss, Same as the Old Boss.

The other Pelosi on the national stage, created by Pelosi's own message machine, is Pelosi the American Everywoman from blue-collar Baltimore, the supermom who's come in to clean up the country. This Pelosi is the Listener and the Healer, leading her party on a steady course back to the center, bringing with her the return of civility and manners to Washington. This Pelosi is Alpha Mom come to tell Alpha Dad to stop the minivan and ask for directions. This Pelosi is the grandparent in chief.

Democrats in Congress are almost universal in their praise of Pelosi's management of the caucus so far. Republicans are almost universally disgusted. The two competing Pelosis beg the question: Who is she really? Is the real Nancy Pelosi to be found in her fixed smile and perfect grooming, or is it in the ruthless and formidable pragmatist who once said "If people are ripping your face off, you have to rip their face off"? Which image better corresponds with the actual person? Is she more cannoli and Chianti, or brie and Chablis? What's her unfiltered backstory? What are the cornerstones of her character? Is she where she is because of her own skill and hard work, or have the winds of history blown her onto stage? In other words, why Pelosi, and why now?

This book attempts to answer all those questions, taking a stab at objectively defining Nancy Pelosi, coloring in the outlines that have been presented to us by media consultants. This is an effort to chronicle the authentic values, scars, and drives of the country's most powerful woman, shining a light on the nuts and bolts, guts and glory that make up this person who is two heartbeats away from the presidency.

The best answer I've found to which of the two Pelosis is the real one is: a bit of both. Representative Edward Markey of Massachusetts put it best: "Nancy is San Francisco on the outside and Baltimore on the inside." She's a paradox in many ways: a political liberal and conservative Catholic. A San Francisco sophisticate with blue-collar Baltimore roots. A gracious grande dame who can back-room barter with the best of 'em. She's both a westerner and an easterner, both an advocate of radical reform to get money out of politics and one of the best political fundraisers in the history of the game. Does she contradict herself? She is complicated; she contains multitudes.

As prone as she is to attracting lightning, some pundits argue that she's the most important political figure toward the end of George W. Bush's administration, given the president's low approval ratings. Recent polls put her approval higher than the president or Congress itself. Not only has Pelosi somehow won the confidence of the long-entrenched boys' club of the House of Representatives and returned her party to majority status after 12 years of Republican rule, she's in the midst of passing significant legislation that had languished for years. She can already claim a string of accomplishments in her first year: a law to implement the 9/11 Commission recommendations; an energy bill that includes new taxes on oil companies while giving tax breaks for renewable fuels and conservation; an increase in the minimum wage and major ethics reform for Congress. She's also taken on global warming and made several trips overseas to meet with foreign leaders, including controversial ones, such as Syria's Bashar al-Assad, in an effort to restore America's image.

Pelosi is also leading the vocal opposition to the Iraq War, this generation's defining event. She pushed through the first resolution ever approved by Congress condemning the conduct of the war and pressured the president into accepting benchmarks for progress in Iraq. Though many of her liberal supporters are frustrated that Democrats haven't done more to end the war, Pelosi is still going head to head with President Bush over the question of when to pull troops out and end the war there once and for all, but she and her Senate counterpart, Harry Reid, are the ones who changed the debate in Washington to the question of when rather than if. Pelosi has been an opponent of the war from the very start, never wavering in her view that it is an illegitimate use of American power.

And as head of her party, Pelosi also is likely to be one of the kingmakers—or queenmakers—of the next Democratic nominee for president. Already in Washington politicos talk about the so-called Pelosi Primary.

Pelosi hasn't endorsed anyone yet, but candidates are competing hard for her support and behind-the-scenes help in opening wallets and influencing interest groups. Whoever wins her favor will have a national network of Pelosi loyalists to tap.

In order to paint a full and accurate picture of Nancy Pelosi, this will be the story of her life from stem to stern so far, focusing on her formative years, the crucible of motherhood, her rise to power, and her first year in the Speaker's office. It's also a story with broader themes concerning Washington's entrenched culture of gender politics that Pelosi had to fight her way through on her climb up Capitol Hill. This is also necessarily a story about the differences in the way men and women lead and the difficult balance women in politics wrestle with between family and work. Another kind of balance, between a reinvigorated Congress and a powerful presidency, is also a larger piece of the Pelosi tale. The book also examines a new kind of California-style venture politics that Pelosi represents, and the changes wrought in Congress by its fundraising imperative. This is also a peek inside the makeover of the Democratic Party in 2006 and its prospects in 2008. And last, because of Pelosi's complicated relationship with the Catholic Church, this is a also story about the mixing of religion and politics.

This account is based on more than 100 interviews with friends, enemies, family members, and acquaintances of Pelosi and other members of Congress, congressional staffers, and experts on Congress. The *Congressional Record*, the Library of Congress, and the Congressional Research Service have provided countless documents and transcripts I have used in telling Pelosi's story. Since this is a recent and still-unfolding tale, I've made use of blogs and other Web-reported material, including Pelosi's own blog, "The Gavel" (www.speaker.gov/blog) Many members of Nancy Pelosi's staff took time off from running Congress to sit down for extended interviews, as did the Speaker herself.

Here then is the story of Nancy Pelosi's improbable rise. Strip away all the facts and figures, ignore the spin of the Democrats and Republicans, and it's a Cinderella story really, but a Cinderella story with a twist. At the end of this fairy tale, Cinderella is in charge of the big white castle on the hill.

CHAPTER 1

THE FAMILY VOCATION

There are two lasting bequests we can give our children: One is roots, the other is wings.

—Hodding Carter, Jr., journalist and author, 1907–1972

We were all born and raised in politics.

—Nancy Pelosi, January 5, 2007

The neighborhood—all of it—starts gathering late on a Sunday morning outside the door of St. Leo's. Chatter and shouts ring out in both Italian and English, accompanied by backslapping and belly laughs, as Exeter Street fills with Italian Americans. It's June in late 1940s Baltimore, the days of Baltimore Catechisms and Forty Hours' devotions, when the teachers at parochial schools were actually nuns and the nuns all wore starched black-and-white habits. The party is already two days old, and spirits are high. Longtime resident Tommy D'Alesandro, the brand-new mayor of Baltimore, is there to join the procession with his wife, Annunciata, five boys and his seven-year-old, wide-eyed daughter, Nancy. Neighbors can hardly contain their excitement—one of Little Italy's own is lord and mayor of the whole town. But Tommy's month-old victory is punctuation for the festival, not its reason for being. His win only ratchets up an already exuberant *giorno di festivo*. As noon draws near, some residents start dancing in the streets to the strains of "The Glory of Italy" as the marching band tunes up. The smell of oregano perfumes the air; a dozen varieties of pasta, fried dough, and Italian sausage are loaded into stands for sale along Exeter and Stiles. Church ladies are selling holy pictures and buttons of St. Anthony to the swelling crowd. The streets of Little Italy are arched with lights. The light poles themselves are draped with bunting and festoons. Red, white, and green flags fly from second-story windows, from wires hanging over the streets, from everywhere. Every door in the neighborhood stands open. Everyone is welcome.

Little Italy is Baltimore, only more so. And Baltimore is the East Coast's Detroit, a gritty, blue-collar, by-the-bootstraps kind of place. The Sage of Baltimore, writer H. L. Mencken, called his beloved city in 1926 an "ancient, solid town" with the "impalpable, indefinable, irresistible quality of charm." Escaping from New York, where Mencken worked, back to Baltimore, where he lived, was like "coming out of a football crowd into quiet communion with a fair one who is also amiable, and has the gift of consolation for hard-beset and despairing men."

Little Italy's corner of the consoling city is 12 square blocks of narrow streets and cramped row houses hard against the inner harbor. The neighborhood isn't big, but its soul is. Since the Great Fire of 1904, it's been considered somewhat sacred ground by its residents. As flames were chewing up most of Baltimore City that Sunday in February, the Italian immigrants gathered in St. Leo's and began praying furiously to St. Anthony. "We thought the end of the world had come," wrote Marie O'Dea in the Baltimore *Evening Sun*. The flames were steadily moving east during the afternoon, drawing a bead on the blue-collar enclave. Tommy D'Alesandro III, Nancy Pelosi's big brother, remembers a story he was told about that day concerning the city's frustrated, exhausted firemen making a last stand on Jones Falls, the western edge of the neighborhood. Italians standing and kneeling along the eastern bank prayed through the night that the fire might spare their homes.

By three in the morning, most of Baltimore City had fallen to flames. Harold Williams, author of "Baltimore Afire," remembers seeing towers of fire growing taller and taller; "it seemed like they would crash into the church." Embers, bits of paper, even long boards sailed through the air from the burning east bank and fell like torches in Little Italy. But a brigade of residents armed with buckets of water doused every last missile. Over on the fire line, the hoses of the firemen weren't filling properly. They hadn't all night. The canvas tubes were overtaxed and leaking, and the flames were winning.

Suddenly, sometime during the middle of the night, the hoses all filled with tremendous force, for reasons never explained, and the battle was joined. At 6 A.M. the wind shifted, lessened in intensity, and turned south. The fire never made the jump over Jones Falls. Little Italy remained standing, the only neighborhood in the city spared. A miracle, many believed, crediting St. Anthony.

A grand celebration of the Feast of St. Anthony was promised on the spot and has been held every year since. It's the reason the crowds have gathered on this June 13 in 1947.

St. Leo's pastor, in the gold vestments reserved for special occasions, emerges from the church with his cross bearer and altar boys. They head the crowd up Exeter to President Street, and the procession is on. Behind him come the silk banners and proud representatives of 25 to 30 Italian societies—religious, fraternal, civic, political—all in suit and tie. A life-size statue of St. Anthony himself is next, borne through the streets on a flower-covered platform that rests on the shoulders of the six guards of honor. Six little flower girls, white-robed and gold-winged, drop blossoms in its path. White silk ribbons stream out from the statue at all angles. Spectators offer up dollar bills along the way, which the guardsmen pin to the ribbons until the strands are encrusted with greenbacks.

The procession is nearly a block long now as the Knights of Columbus, resplendent in red and blue capes and white-plumed Napoleon hats, join the line. Musicians and choirboys are at their heels, playing Italian folk songs. The people of Little Italy sit on their stoops, stand on curbs, lean out windows, and walk along with the parade as it winds down around every crooked corner and past every narrow street in the neighborhood, never going beyond. It is a parade that begins in the neighborhood and ends in the neighborhood, made up of neighbors, in honor of neighbors. Gilbert Sandler, author of a book on Little Italy simply entitled *The Neighborhood*, said, "Those robes on that statue were the ties that bound them all together."

Little Italy's thousand residents—its D'Alesandros and Apicellas and Bonomolos and Girolamos and Bugliottas and Pollogrinis and Maccioccas and Virgilios—have marched together on St. Anthony's Feast Day for a hundred years. They still do.

"Nancy saw all that, she was a part of it. It was the water she drank," her brother Tommy said. He thinks she developed in Little Italy a sense of compassion and community that was uncommon in other places even in those days. Being Catholic in the 1950s and 1960s meant a strong emphasis on neighborhood solidarity and family. Back then it meant putting obedience above autonomy, the community above the individual. That cohesion, that sense of belonging to one another, could not but help inform Pelosi's beliefs, Sandler believes. It may also be the root of her fierce, sometimes blind loyalty to people that has occasionally tripped her up in a city not quite so forgiving as Baltimore.

"You know how the battle of Waterloo was won on the playing fields of Eton?" Sandler asks. "Well, the battles she's winning right now were won on the streets of Little Italy." It's an intriguing theory: Congress as neighborhood. Pelosi's talent at keeping the Democratic Party in lockstep, at bringing cohesion to a caucus that is known for its lack of it, may come directly from the lessons she learned growing up on the streets of Little Italy. "Drink that up and it becomes part of your blood and sinew and tissue," Sandler said.

"Italians down here are like one big family," said Vince Culotta, whose restaurant, Sabatino's, has been a fixture in Little Italy for decades. The neighborhood has a deeply embedded culture of taking care of its own. When Nancy was growing up in the 1940s and '50s, no one from the neighborhood ever went to a nursing home. Three or four generations often lived together in the same small row house, as did her family, and neighbors and restaurants took care of the sick and old who were living alone. Little Italy had that Catholic communal heritage so many cul-de-sac dwellers long for today.

"Where she came and how she grew up is the key to figuring her out," said Marie Wilson, a friend of Pelosi's and head of the White House Project, an effort to recruit more women to run for office. "It's kind of like a family systems therapist: We ought to have a gene-a-gram on all these people. All that stuff makes you who you are and it helps you understand why you do what you do."

Italian families first began alighting in Little Italy from Sicily and Abruzzi in the mid-1800s—drawn by jobs at the nearby shipyard—and then stayed for generations.

"When Italians came over, they unloaded boatloads of them," Culotta recounts. They mostly came for a better quality of life at a time when quotas for immigrants were much larger than they are today. Some were sailors, some political refugees, others gold hunters. They arrived by boat in the harbor or by train from New York, settling right on the waterfront or close by the President Street station. "When immigrants get off the boat, they usually don't go too far," said Culotta. Originally, only men came over. After they saved some money, they went home to find a bride and bring her back. Culotta said the abundance of *trattoria* in Little Italy—23 restaurants are crammed into the space of a few blocks—can be traced back to those first male immigrants. "They all lived by themselves in tiny rooms in rooming houses. They had to eat somewhere."

Nancy's grandfather and grandmother were both born in Italy, she in Campobasso near Naples, he in Abruzzi, a village in the mountains near Rome. After they first came to America, they shuttled back and forth between Italy and Little Italy for several years. Some of their children were born in Baltimore, some in Italy. Annunciata, Nancy's mother, was born in Italy and came to the United States when she was one year old.

"A lot of people came not knowing what was waiting for them," said Tommy the Younger, as he came to be known around Little Italy. When Tommy and Nancy's grandfather came over, he started a little grocery store that sold all kinds of macaroni, rigatoni, and other pasta. He made the pasta in a factory right behind his house.

Baltimore was below the Mason-Dixon Line, so the city was a segregated one, a patchwork of Jewish neighborhoods, black neighborhoods, Polish, Irish, and Italian. By 1900, every home in Little Italy was owned by an Italian family. Houses almost never went up for sale; they were just passed along from one generation to the next. During the riots that raged through Baltimore after Martin Luther King's assassination, Little Italy's able-bodied men took to the roofs with guns to ward off trouble. Again the neighborhood was spared. When seemingly everyone in Baltimore City moved to the sub-urbs in the 1970s, the families of Little Italy stayed put. They loved their neighborhood fiercely. The residents "have an enormous staying power, which I don't think even they understand," said Sandler. "Here, the people have a mystical commitment to their own streets." And like the immigrants of Boston, New York, and Chicago, as their numbers grew, so did their political influence. Thanks in large part to Nancy's family, Little Italy's civic muscle in Baltimore in the 1940s was far beyond its weight class.

Though a bit frayed around the edges today, the neighborhood still proudly wears its heritage on its sleeve. Its fire hydrants are striped green, white, and red like Italian flags, bocce tournaments are held on the neighbor-hood court year-round, and the aroma of oregano and tomato sauce still sweetens the air on Sundays. An outdoor film festival draws thousands every summer to watch Italian movies projected onto the side of a building. *Cinema Paradiso* always closes the festival. "Living here is kinda like being in a movie," one resident told Sandler. People who come to eat in one of the many restau-rants are soon caught up in the ethnic spirit of the place. Sandler calls it an Italian village transplanted. And now Little Italy's row houses are becoming fashionable again as the surrounding area gentrifies. "Grandchildren are moving back into the houses their grandparents lived in," Culotta said. And every June, of course, hundreds of former Little Italians come back as residents-for-a-day during the St. Anthony festival.

In the 1940s, the D'Alesandro family was the beat of Little Italy's heart. Nancy spent a good chunk of her childhood playing on the polished white steps of nearby stoops—both sets of grandparents lived just down the block, Aunt Jessie was in the next block on Albermarle, and Aunt Mary lived around the corner. Everyone knew everyone in Little Italy in the 1940s, and their lives all orbited St. Leo's. The red-brick church was right around the corner from the D'Alesandro family's three-story row house, and the family was a fixture in church every Sunday. Their house served as a kind of community adjunct of the parish, neighbors say.

Perpetually wide-eyed Nancy, her abundant brown hair usually in pigtails, would race to church each Sunday at St. Leo's. Her brothers remember her as a bit reserved during the grade-school years but always kind, always considerate, always beautifully dressed. "Nancy was the apple of my mother and father's eye," said Tommy. There was no question in any of her brothers' minds that Nancy was the favorite. In fact, the devout Annunciata D'Alesandro—known to all as Big Nancy—thought her eager daughter had been hand-picked by God for a special purpose. She had already decided when Nancy was in grade school that her daughter was destined to become a nun. Little Nancy thought she wanted to help people, too, but she decidedly didn't want to become a nun.

"I'm going to be a priest when I grow up," she told her mother repeatedly. For most of her single-digit years, she said the same thing to anyone on the streets of Little Italy who would listen.

"I thought I might want to be a priest because there seemed to be a little more power there, a little more discretion over what was going on in the parish," she said in a recent interview. When Little Nancy was nine or ten, Big Nancy finally decided to break down and tell her daughter she was out of luck, that girls couldn't be priests in the Catholic Church, Pelosi had a reply at the ready.

"Well, then, I'll go into politics instead."

So began a lifelong interest in the arithmetic of power in a man's world. When she first set her sights on a political life, the upper chambers of the country's political bodies weren't much more open to a woman than the church's were. In 1947, no woman had ever served as mayor of Baltimore or governor of Maryland, and only one had ever represented Maryland in Congress. Only 7 of the 435 members of the House at the time and none of the senators were women. Only 40 women had ever served in the House when Pelosi was daydreaming, and only 5 in the Senate. Of the more than 13,000 Americans who have served in Congress to this day, only 249 have been women.

But even in 1947, politics for Nancy was not the foreign country it was for most women. She was raised in a political dynasty. When she was growing up, all things in Little Italy revolved around a holy trinity of faith, family, and the Democratic Party.

"We were all knee-deep in Democrats," said brother Tommy.

It was hard, at times, to distinguish between party and parish in Little Italy. If you were a candidate looking for a crowd, church was often the best place to find one.

"The large events in communities were usually church-sponsored or Democratic Club-sponsored," Maryland's attorney general Joseph Curran told a reporter. "If you went to a bull roast or an oyster roast or a crab feast it had to be at the church or at the Democratic Club . . . . Nobody had money for television [advertising]; you just had money to buy a $10 ticket to the bull roast so you could see 1,000 people."

The festivals in Little Italy were half-political, half-religious events, and the D'Alesandro family was always in the thick of them.

Pelosi's political style, and the keys to a substantial part of her later success, can be traced directly back to those Little Italy streets. Critics have tried to paint Pelosi as a dyed-in-the-wool Left Coaster from the most liberal city in the country, San Francisco, but her particular strain of liberalism is probably rooted more deeply in the East Coast ward-boss politics her father practiced for more than 22 uninterrupted years on the streets of Little Italy.

"Our whole lives were politics," Pelosi said. "If you entered the house, it was always campaign time, and if you went into the living room, it was always constituent time."

When she was born on March 26, 1940, her father was already a first-term member of the House of Representatives. She visited his office in the Capitol for the first time when she was four, and by her seventh birthday, Big Tommy had been elected mayor of Baltimore. Wearing a white dress and white gloves, Nancy held the Bible when he was sworn in for the first of three four-year terms. The photograph is displayed proudly in her office in the Capitol today. Her first speech: "Dear Daddy, I hope this holy book will guide you to be a good man."

Tommy the Elder, as he became known, served 22 consecutive terms in public office, from state delegate to city councilman to U.S. congressman to mayor, followed by a low-level appointment from President John F. Kennedy to the Federal Renegotiation Board. Another prized family photograph in Pelosi's office shows Nancy, Tommy, and Kennedy in the Oval Office after Tommy's appointment.

Tommy D'Alesandro III served on the Baltimore City Council and became the city's mayor in 1967. Two other brothers, Hector and Joey, worked for years in the courthouse as public servants.

"My parents taught us that public service was a noble calling and that we had a responsibility to help those in need. I viewed them as working on the side of angels," Pelosi has said.

The D'Alesandro family politics was the politics of FDR's New Deal, a politics born of the Depression and dedicated to lifting up the downtrodden. One of Pelosi's brothers is named after the thirty-second president: Franklin Delano Roosevelt D'Alesandro (Roosie for short).

Tommy taught his Nancy early on that elections were about taking care of people, that pragmatism trumped ideology, and that service came before ego. You scratch my back, I'll scratch yours, but be sure to keep track of each and every scratch.

In those days, all politics was not only local, it was personal, said Matthew Green, a politics professor at Catholic University and an expert on the history of the Speaker of the House. "City politics, particularly during that time period, depended a lot on personal relations and personal loyalties, particularly in one-party cities and areas, where the differences come down to who you're a closer friend with, who you've worked with, as opposed to ideology," Green said.

"It was retail politics in those days," Pelosi said. Shaking hands and kissing babies. "It was grassroots organizing, built around issues."

More than a civic duty, politics during Big Tommy's day was about survival for the sons and daughters of Italian immigrants who often could depend only on themselves. It was also about making deals and forming alliances, among the Italians, the Irish, the Jews, and the Poles of the still-segregated city, neighborhood by neighborhood, block by block.

"We need 100,000 votes," Pelosi remembers her father telling his political lieutenants as he worked backward to break down the numbers for a mayoral election. "'We need this many from this neighborhood. This many from this neighborhood. How do we get them?'" Pelosi went on to emulate that painstaking approach to vote-getting in her own campaigns and legislative battles. More than anything, friends and foes say, Nancy Pelosi knows how to count votes.

Mostly, however, politics in Tommy's day was about jobs. Jobs were tough to come by during Tommy's early years in office in the 1930s. The Depression bore down especially hard on blue-collar Baltimore. Family members remember when wood scavenged from demolished buildings was piled up in front of the D'Alesandro house for the poor to take home and burn for heat.

"The ward was where you got jobs. They would get you jobs," Sandler said. "Whole political machines were born out of these jobs. A job driving a car for city hall. A job picking up trash. Jobs were everything."

And Big Tommy "was the king of it."

Tommy the Elder was born in 1903 in a crowded row house on Baltimore's President Street, the fourth of Maria Antoinette Foppiano's 13 children. To support them, Tommy's father labored in a city rock quarry for 25 cents an hour, but his son had bigger plans. While still at night high school, he hung around the Third Ward Democratic headquarters and rang doorbells and passed out handbills at election time, learning his politics under Baltimore's Democratic boss, Willie Curran. He never finished school.

By the 1920s, gregarious Tommy was an insurance salesman by day and a ballroom dancer by night.

"My father was a dapper man, a very attractive, handsome man," said the younger Tommy. "He was a great ballroom-style dancer. Won some tournaments. In those days there were very few people in Little Italy who traveled out of Little Italy. With the dancing and the insurance business, he was an attractive character."

His dancing acquaintances and insurance clients both came in handy when he decided he wanted to run for the state legislature at the age of 23. The zest Tommy showed working church carnivals attracted the eye of the local sheriff, who saw him as a potential politico. In early 1926, the sheriff took him up to the Renner Hotel, headquarters of all the big pols of the day, to introduce him to Curran, the Democratic boss for that section of the city.

Curran was playing cards with his cronies at the time. The sheriff said he thought Tommy would make a good member of the House of Delegates, but Curran and the other bosses of the WASP-y city weren't sure they were ready for an Italian Catholic kid to join their ranks. Without looking up from his game, Curran told Tommy to go out and get 5,000 signatures and then they would talk.

So D'Alesandro did just that, collecting all the signatures on his own and qualifying for the ballot. When he came back to Curran, however, the old pol told him that if he had 5,000 signatures, he didn't need them. Besides, he said to Tommy, we already have our candidate. So Tommy ran without party support, against Curran's candidate. And won. It was the first of 22 consecutive elections he ran in and won.

When he entered the Maryland House of Delegates in 1926, he wore patent-leather shoes and spats, an Oxford gray suit, a polka-dot bow tie, and a derby. That first day in the House of Delegates, he said he thought he would encounter men of the stature of Thomas Jefferson, Patrick Henry, and the like, and was greatly disappointed when they were just ordinary people, recounts his former press secretary, Tom J. O'Donnell.

Throughout his political career he always dressed to the hilt— three-piece suits and a pinky ring—and the polka-dot bow tie would be his lucky charm.

"Sometimes at night, we'd be sleeping and would hear him call, 'Tommy, Nicky . . . Joey . . .' He'd call all of us up to his bedroom," remembers the younger Tommy. "We had to take all of his suits from his bedroom down three stories to the cedar closet in the basement, then we had to take all the suits in the cedar closet up to his bedroom. That took about three hours. And then when everything was through, and we'd go back to sleep, he'd holler, 'Where's my brown tie?'

"And we'd have to find the brown tie."

Friends say they think Nancy gets her penchant for Armani suits from her father rather than her mother.

After two terms in the state legislature, Tommy wangled an appointment in the Internal Revenue Bureau's New York office. Soon back in his beloved hometown of Baltimore, Tommy won a term on the city council, then ran for Congress, again taking on the Democratic machine-backed incumbent, Vincent Palmisano, who also happened to live just up the block from Tommy in Little Italy.

"I was a battler," the elder Tommy once told Sandler. "I went house to house; wherever I found a Palmisano sign in one window, I put a D'Alesandro sign in the other. The vote was close. I won by 48. They had a recount and I picked up 11 in the recount. It was wild."

In 1947, after eight years in Congress, Tommy decided to go back home and run for mayor of Baltimore. The mayor's office: that was where the true power was in the eyes of the people he cared about most. The city's top job had always been his goal line. The mayor could fix streets, build schools, create jobs. He would bring honor and glory to his neighborhood, and the neighborhood was always his measuring stick. Bucking the Curran machine again, Tommy won hands down.

"From first grade to college, he was mayor," Pelosi said, "so that was the only life I ever knew. He had a love affair with the city of Baltimore. He loved the city and he loved being mayor."

After his victory, neighbors expected him to move his wife and their six kids from Little Italy, which was and always had been poor, to a better neighborhood. But the D'Alesandros stayed put. "People always commented on that," said Senator Barbara Mikulski, who also hails from Baltimore. "No matter how big and famous they got, her father and mother never forgot where they came from and kept their roots in their community. I think that is a very big thing in Nancy's life."

"I'm a paisano," Tommy explained. "These are my people. This is where I belong."

The new mayor built 87 new schools, firehouses, and other facilities and 1,400 miles of new streets, and installed 21,947 new streetlights. He finished a new airport, Friendship International, luring President Harry Truman to opening day ceremonies. He won a second term and a third term. He brought major-league baseball back to Baltimore and became a Democratic National Committeeman. He kept winning by keeping his home on Albermarle open to constituents morning, noon, and night. When someone would stop by for a favor, Tommy would ask simply, "What's your story?"

His son tells the tale of a visit Tommy made to a funeral parlor. Five or six different bodies would be laid out in different sections of the parlor. "My father would go there to visit one, but since he knew everybody he would visit them all, and by the time he got through, he turned the funeral parlor into a rally." How? Magnetism, said Tommy. "He was unbelievable. Unbelievable. Unbelievable. An unbelievable guy."

Every time he found someone a job, or fixed a pothole, or simply fed a hungry family a cannelloni dinner, Tommy would write it down on a yellow sheet of paper. He'd collect the sheets, and have them stacked and stapled together at the end of each week. This was "the favor file."

"It was people who needed jobs, people who needed medical help or housing, or needed to get out of jail. That's where you really saw human nature in the raw," said Tommy. Then, at election time, Tommy recounts, they'd collect the favors. They'd borrow cars to get out the vote, ask neighbors to organize coffees, lick stamps, stuff envelopes.

"He recognized that you had to keep your word. They held a public trust. He took that seriously. So does she," Sandler said of Nancy. It was governing by give-and-take. "If you're gonna win in the give-and-take, you've got to keep your word. You're no good if you don't. That was the culture. That's how it was done on the streets."

The favor file in Tommy's day was all about respect, coming and going. Still, you didn't last long in big-city machine politics if you folded at the first sign of a fight. When Tommy Jr. once threatened to fire striking garbage workers, legendary union organizer Jimmy Hoffa sent an emissary to tell the mayor he wasn't happy. As O'Donnell tells it, "The mayor spoke up and said, 'You go back and tell Mr. Jimmy I'm very unhappy with the garbage piling up on the streets of Baltimore, and I'm not going to stand for it.'" The D'Alesandro house was pelted with orange peels and rotting vegetables, but by the following Monday most of the garbage men were back at work. Though Tommy was usually the man fighting corruption and standing up to the machine, he didn't entirely dodge scandal during his long career, however.

In 1955, his 21-year-old son Roosie and 15 other youngsters were arrested on a charge of taking two girls, ages 13 and 11, on an all-night joy ride and keeping them in a furnished apartment for a week. Roosie was acquitted of a rape charge in the incident but indicted for perjury during testimony, according to court records. Tommy brushed off the charges as ludicrous and announced his candidacy for governor while the case was still pending.

Shortly after, a longtime friend of Tommy's, Dominic Piracci, was convicted of fraud, conspiracy, and conspiracy to obstruct justice for shady dealings in his garage-building business. Piracci's daughter, Margie, was married to Tommy's son, Tommy III, who went on to become mayor later. This was a scandal Tommy couldn't ignore. Piracci had erased some names from his ledgers, one of them being Tommy's wife, Big Nancy. On the witness stand in Piracci's trial, Pelosi's mother admitted getting six checks totaling $11,130.78 from Piracci, but she swore that $1,500 of it was a gift to their newlywed children. The rest, she claimed, Piracci had lent her to pay off debts she'd incurred in her feed business and another venture with a skin softener called Velvex.

The scandal forced Tommy out of the governor's race and triggered a nervous collapse. He shed some 60 pounds because of the breakdown, which kept him from savoring the realization of one of his biggest triumphs, the return of major-league baseball to Baltimore after more than half a century. The new Baltimore Orioles were paraded through the streets amid 32 floats and the blare of 20 bands as D'Alesandro lay in Bon Secours Hospital.

He recuperated soon enough to run for mayor again. And win. His campaign posters simply listed the Orioles' home-game schedule and the claim: "50 Years of Progress in Eight Years."

Roosie was acquitted of all charges, and Tommy the Elder eventually shrugged off the scandals. "No one," he said to the press, "is infallible. I haven't done everything right." History has shrugged off the chapter as well: D'Alesandro and his three storied terms remain legendary in Baltimore. The scandals didn't even warrant a mention in the Baltimore media when Nancy ascended to office.

The family never got wealthy from politics, though D'Alesandro had a car and driver when he was mayor. Nancy, the baby of the family, was chauffeured to school at the Institute of Notre Dame a mile away, but she insisted on walking the last block to spare herself embarrassment. Though the family's means were modest, that didn't mean Nancy didn't have the nicest clothes to wear. Because she was the only girl, she got the best of everything, her brother said. She often made the rounds of public appearances with her dad, helping him campaign from his convertible with a bullhorn, or standing demurely at his side in a white dress and gloves during his speeches. "When she walked the boardwalk at Ocean City after a full day at the beach there wasn't a hair out of place," Tommy said. "She was always prim and proper."

Tommy's charmed life lasted just long enough for him to see Nancy take the mantle of the family vocation. After she married in 1963, Nancy moved with her husband, Paul, to San Francisco, where she rose up through the ranks of the Democratic Party for 20 years before running for Congress in 1987. Big Tommy dispatched his son Tommy out to San Francisco during her campaign in the spring of 1987 to make sure it was up to snuff, but Tommy reported back that her organization was better than theirs had ever been. "She used the same structure we used in Baltimore." Nancy, who spent more than $1 million on her campaign, won election to the House with 62 percent of the vote on June 2 in a special election to fill Sala Burton's seat after she died of cancer. Pelosi said Big Tommy came to the House floor on her first day, making a point of reminding her that he didn't need a ticket since he was once a member as well. Newspaper accounts say he wept up in the galleries. A little over two months later, on August 23, 1987, Big Tommy's heart gave out for good. He was 84.

His body was laid out in St. Leo's for two days, day and night. "There was no interruption in the flow of people who came by to pay tribute," said Tommy III. "They were looking at my father and they were seeing their father, their parents, all the struggles they went through. That's what he personified."

On the way to the cemetery, Big Tommy's hearse passed by many of Baltimore's public buildings, such as the fire department and the police department. Most all of the fireman and policeman in those buildings came out and saluted the casket as it rolled by.

Pelosi is the first to say that Big Tommy's ward-heeler politics directly and indelibly shaped hers. "What I got from them was about economic fairness," Pelosi said. "That was the difference between Republicans and Democrats all those years ago. It was always about the progressive economic agenda for a fair economy, where many Americans, all Americans, could participate in the economic success of our country." But the political instincts that have served her most in her rise Pelosi learned not from her father but from the women who caucused in the basement of the house on Albermarle. "Oh, my, those women," brother Tommy said. "Formidable, strong women. That's where the power was, down in that cellar."

"Women in this neighborhood," Pelosi agreed, "were very strong."

Although the women had been raised to marry and run households, World War II changed things, giving them a taste of power and wage earning while their men were away at war. The ladies who gathered in the D'Alesandro basement began to change politics as well, according to Michael Olesker, author of three books on Baltimore and a resident since the age of four. All those Little Italy ladies were the bedrock of Pelosi's path to becoming a breakthrough politician.

Tommy didn't marry the girl next door; he married the girl across the street. "My mother lived at 204 Albermarle Street. My father lived at 235 Albermarle Street. And when they got married they moved to 245 Albermarle Street, where they died," said Tommy the Younger. "My parents lived their whole lives on two blocks of Albermarle Street."

Stately Annunciata Lombardi didn't even know Tommy when he first came calling. But the dapper young politician was considered one of the most eligible bachelors in the city when he proposed to his neighbor.

Their wedding on Sunday, September 30, 1928, began at dawn and lasted well past midnight. The neighborhood turned into a carnival, according to one newspaper report, "a singing, dancing, eating marathon." Five thousand people reportedly jammed the streets. Big Nancy never went on her honeymoon. Tommy got sick eating too much.

Big Nancy was soon swept up into Tommy's political whirlwind. She studied law books for a while at night, but found the pressures of family and life as a politician's spouse allowed no time for law school. Not long after their wedding she became a leader at the local Democratic Women's Club operating out of her basement. She headed small armies of women who met regularly at the house, working the political precincts and organizing the rallies and fundraising affairs, according to Olesker. Pelosi's mother juggled six children with serving as precinct captain, strategist, and all-around enforcer in her husband's Democratic machine. When asked if Nancy's mother was as much a politician as her father, Tommy answers instantly: "More so."

Pelosi agrees. "She was the one. She's the star. Absolutely. If she lived in another era, God knows what she would have done . . . in anything— business, politics, the academic world, whatever. She was really a very dynamic women. Very intelligent, very lovely. And when the door closed after all the politics, she was mom."

"My mother knew everybody," Tommy adds. "My father had his traits and . . . and had his victories, and was a recognized personality, but my mother was the basis of his organization. She did all the favors. She knew all the people."

And people knew not to tangle with her. "Cross [my mother]? You're dead in the water. She'd get you," said Tommy. "With my mother, there was no forgiving."

"She was a wheeler-dealer, she knew where all the bones were buried," said Culotta, owner of Sabatino's restaurant.

"Once, when my father was mayor, some guy got in trouble," recalls Tommy. "My father was going to fire him. The guy said, you can't fire me. And my dad said, why can't I fire you?' Because I'm gonna tell Nancy if you do, that's why." Local lore has it that Pelosi's mother was so tough she once decked a precinct worker who got too pushy with her. It's a trait that sounds familiar to Pelosi's colleagues on Capitol Hill. "Nancy was a carbon copy of my mother," according to another brother Nick D'Alesandro, who still lives in the upper floor of the family home on Albermarle. "My mother tutored her, and they were confidantes and close friends."

Pelosi also may have inherited her fierce partisanship from her mother. Once, when Ronald Reagan was running for reelection, he came to Baltimore to dedicate a monument, and his aides called the house to see if Tommy wanted to tag along. Big Nancy is the one who answered the phone.

"After what he has done to poor people, he should not come near our house," she barked.

Everyone pitched in on matters of politics in the D'Alesandro home.

Pelosi's aunts would help cook big pots of spaghetti sauce for constituents who showed up hungry at dinnertime. "You could just open their door and walk in and socialize," 74-year-old Angie Guerriero told the *Baltimore Sun*. Guerriero grew up several blocks from the D'Alesandro home and still lives in Little Italy.

"Or they were at our house. We shared jokes. In those days, there wasn't much else to do. They were just fine people." Little Nancy was a 'stuffer and sealer'—filling envelopes with campaign literature, circulating ballots, mailing meet-and-greet invitations—as her five children would be for her. "We all worked on that. We had a desk in the front room of the house that was open to the public all day. We'd sit and help people," Pelosi recalls. This is where she first learned the fine art of constituency building. You had a yellow sheet, and you wrote down people's names and addresses and their problems, and you had to follow through. "We never thought it was a chore," her brother adds. "Just something we had to do for Daddy. We'd fill in those yellow sheets of paper from eight or nine in the morning until eight or nine at night."

When Nancy was 13, she took charge of the desk. She said she used to practice her penmanship by logging entries into the book. "I knew how to tell people who to call to go on welfare, to get a bed in a hospital, to get a place in a housing project," Pelosi recalls.

"And it didn't stop then," Tommy said. "At nighttime, people in those days were looking for food. And we had a big table." Call it big-table politics: The door was literally always open. "Politics was daily bread," said Tommy. "We didn't know who was sitting around that table. That's how we were born and raised. That's where we come from."

The skills Pelosi learned were things like how to organize a campaign from the street level up, how to count votes, how to build relationships, forge coalitions, and cash in favors.

Longtime ally George Miller, who represents the district across the bay from Pelosi in San Francisco, seconds the notion that what sets Pelosi apart is what she learned in Baltimore: tactical smarts, discipline and plain old hard work. "People are constantly astonished by her work ethic," Miller said. Because of the "Baltimore Effect," as colleagues like to call it, Pelosi is at ease with the old bulls of the Democratic Party, including Miller and Pennsylvania's John Murtha. "They're behind a personality that can deliver," her brother said.

She also has morphed her father's "favor file" concept into a formidable fundraising machine of her own. Her staff keeps a list of 29,432 loyal donors in a database at the headquarters of the Democratic Congressional Campaign Committee (the campaign arm of House Democrats). Pelosi's staff estimated that her peripatetic travels and phone calls on behalf of the committee, individual candidates, and her personal political action committee, PAC to the Future, generated about $100 million for candidates in the 2006 election, more than anyone else raised, and more than had ever been raised before.

The campaign cash helped bind members of the Democratic caucus tightly to her, ensuring her election as Speaker far before any votes were cast.

Marie Wilson said what Pelosi learned in Baltimore was "sewers and drains politics. If you are in city politics you're in the sewers and drains issues of the world." And when you do sewers and drains, you never forget, no matter how high-falutin' the office or world-weighty the issue, that all politics boils down to *necessity:* the essentials, the basics, the things people absolutely, really need.

In her first 100 hours as Speaker, that's exactly the kind of bread-and-butter agenda Pelosi made a priority: extended unemployment compensation, a tax rebate for "working families," and billions for transportation. The Pelosi package was long on the promise of jobs and roads. In fact, it was exactly the kind of plan that Tommy D'Alesandro supported when he represented Baltimore in the House his daughter now heads.

Walking up the steep stone steps under the entry arch and into the heart of the grand old Institute of Notre Dame on Aisquith Street, students find their feet fitting reassuringly into the footfalls spooned out by generations of past graduates. Sure, the pocketed slate could be replaced or refilled, smoothed out and made level again, but then today's girls wouldn't enjoy the same toe-to-toe contact with history's sisters.

The Institute of Notre Dame has a stubborn steak. When most prep schools of its ilk moved to the suburbs to attract a wealthier class of students in the 1960s, it stayed put just blocks from downtown, a red-brick neoclassical island in a sea of 1970s housing projects. When parochial schools started to consolidate and go coeducational as a survival strategy in the late 1970s and early 1980s as demand for their traditional brand of education began to wane, the Institute obstinately remained all girls. Though its stately 150-year-old, five-story-high main building is antiquated and creaky now, school leaders have opted to add onto it over the years—seven additions to date—rather than tear down and build something new. The Institute, as it is known in Baltimore, is an anomaly, a beacon and helping hand that has for 159 continuous years refused to budge from what is now one of Baltimore's poorest neighborhoods.

That stubbornness naturally rubs off on its grads, especially Pelosi. Little Italy's loyalty to its past and its community is telescoped tenfold by the nearby school Nancy attended from first grade to twelfth. Tradition is what mattered then, and what still matters now.

"It's a generational school," said Principal Ann Seeley, who attended the school—with Pelosi—in the 1950s. "Great-grandmothers went here and now their great granddaughters attend." In fact, Pelosi's grandniece was a member of the class of '07. "What's unique is its history," said Seeley. As a result, its hallowed halls and worn steps give its students a sense of both permanence and obligation.

The Institute has remained steadfast over the years in its central mission: educating young women "to make a difference." In the 1950s that was still a somewhat radical organizing principle. Barbara Mikulski (D-Md.), class of '54, credits her success in part to the education she got there.

"It was there we received not only a good education, but an emphasis on leadership for women and the lessons of putting values into action," Mikulski said in an interview. "We were taught by nuns, many of whom had graduate degrees, who were important role models. They taught us that we could be smart, effective and womanly."

President Sister Mary Fitzgerald puts it this way: "What we tried to inculcate in the students is the sense that each of them has some definite gifts, and the responsible use of those gifts has always to be in service to the betterment of the world in some way, shape or form. We hope they're making a difference with what they're doing."

Their location is a tangible expression of that philosophy. "We're committed to the city of Baltimore especially because this is an area which directly is able to help the poor," Fitzgerald said. She said the school goes out of its way to try to find financial aid and scholarships for neighborhood girls.

A dedication to helping women, youth, and the poor is woven into the school's DNA. Its founder, Mother Teresa Gerhardinger, was literally a saint, beatified by the church for her work in education as one of the School Sisters of Notre Dame. The Institute was the first school the order established in America shortly after its first sisters came to the country from Germany in 1847. Students have always been required to reach out to the neighborhood around them and do good works, now so more than ever.

Pelosi remembers words tacked on to a bulletin board that she saw every day when she went to school there. "The words were the first things you saw when you came into the building back then," she told 1989 grads of the Institute. "I still remember them: 'School is not a prison. School is not a playground. It is a time and opportunity.'" When she attended, Pelosi often went out with "mission groups" to do good deeds around the city. Girls were required to volunteer on Saturdays for Little Sisters of the Poor, serving meals, doing chores, generally tending the needs of the less fortunate nearby. The Institute encouraged community service as a way to build character before the term "community service" had been coined.

At times, Seeley said, she and Pelosi felt a little like nuns-in-training. The two were good friends and had religion classes every day for four years. They would go on retreats for three days at a time, be required to observe periods of silence, say daily prayers in the chapel, and often eat lunch in silence as well.

"It was really like the novitiate," said Seeley.

Nobody can ever remember a stitch out of place on the always impeccable Nancy. Those who knew her in high school describe her as always poised and always gracious, very nice to be around, very considerate, kind and devoted to her studies.

She had a wide circle of friends, and though she was the mayor's daughter, no one remembers her as being aloof or holier-than-thou. She loved to tell stories about her experiences in the rough-and-tumble world of politics, but never in a snobbish way. Her classmates remember when she brought in glossy eight-by-ten black-and-white photos of John F. Kennedy to show everybody after she sat next to the future president at a United Nations

Association dinner. They all reacted to the photos like schoolgirls with crushes, Seeley said. After Senator Kennedy wrote *Profiles in Courage*, Nancy took some friends with her to Baltimore's old Emerson Hotel, where he was being honored for the book. "We were high school students and John F. Kennedy sat at the table with us and we talked about his book and it was just astounding. We were mesmerized," recalled childhood friend Sally German. Nancy's reaction stands out in German's memory. "She was very composed. She wasn't star struck, but she admired him a lot."

"She was very open to people, no matter who they were," Seeley said. "She just was not the cliquey mentality. I guess that's the best way to describe her." She always knew she had a place in the world, but never lorded it over anyone.

Their mother was "absolutely beautiful," said Tommy, and Nancy was no different. Her brothers looked out for her and sheltered her, five footmen to a princess.

"[Nancy] didn't have very many dates because of her five older brothers [who] were very protective," neighbor Mary Anne Campanella told the *Baltimore Sun*. "When a fellow asked her out, the five older brothers had to chaperon." Nancy said they never let a single bad thing happen to her.

"I was pampered in the fact that I had five older brothers, which I highly recommend to anyone," she told Leslie Stahl during a *60 Minutes* interview. Her male posse also gave her an enduring comfort level and confidence around men from an early age, which came in handy when she first got to the Boy's Club of Congress. Observers say she has a way of disarming men with her charm.

D'Alesandro said that in high school, his sister never went through an awkward, ugly duckling phase, struggling with various hairstyles or the latest fashion trends. The school uniforms saw to that. She was just regular, said Tommy. A typical high school girl. Except when it came to debate team.

"She was very tenacious. What a surprise!" said Seeley. Friends and family members recall her as an excellent debater, a natural. "She didn't take crap from anyone," said Tommy. "Her rebuttals were very good," said Seeley. "She would demonstrate her tenacity for sticking to the point. She was forceful, never inclined to give up. But there was also a diplomacy there. She always made a point of acknowledging the other side's arguments, even if she knew in her heart they were dead wrong."

Pelosi was on the debate team all four years of high school, participating in interscholastic, competitive meets with other Catholic schools around Baltimore. By the time she was a senior, she had developed a small following of students. A group of loyal friends would go to all her debates and cheer her on. Sometimes, during debates, her face would flush if she got angry about a debating point, but she always regained her composure and she always ended her speeches on a positive note. Some of her public speaking mannerisms developed during those debates are still in evidence today. Seeley, who watches Pelosi work the House on C-Span sometimes, said even back then she continued to smile no matter how difficult the issue was or the confrontation became. "She could really keep her composure."

She also had a great sense of humor during debates, always self-deprecating. "She could be really funny," Seeley said. "She would often make fun of herself. She didn't take herself too seriously."

It was during this time that her brothers began to notice a growing streak of independence in their baby sister, a trait that colleagues say has carried forward to this day. Part of that independence came from bridling against her strict parents and their many rules.

"I wanted to be independent," Pelosi said. "And they were always, you know, 'Oh, you can't do this, you can't do that.' Telling me all the things I couldn't do," Pelosi remembers. Pelosi admits she sometimes snuck out at night in high school, the only real rebellion she recalls during the battened-down 1950s. She was beginning to develop her own way in the world, a path different from the rest of the family's. Part of that independence came from the school. Her brothers all attended St. Leo's for grade school, right in the neighborhood, but Pelosi's mother made a point of sending Nancy to the Institute so that she wouldn't be quite so tied to Little Italy.

One of the lasting benefits of the all-girl student body at the Institute for Pelosi was a lifelong "sense of sisterhood," especially important to a young girl with no biological sisters of her own. Pelosi said she is a walking advertisement for the strengths of a single-sex education. In an all-girl world, it quickly becomes clear that girls can and do ably run that world.

"When you're in an all-female environment, all the leaders have to be girls," said the president, Sister Fitzgerald. "It gives young women who might not have had the opportunity to be leaders a chance to rise to the surface as leaders, and they really do," she insists. The lack of boys is actually liberating, she adds. "An all-girls school frees a young woman to become all that she can be, to assume leadership, to develop all of her talents and skills, without any of the self-consciousness that typically accompanies a young woman during those delicate adolescent years when she's trying to figure out who she is and how she stands vis-à-vis the world and what people perceive of her." In the coed schools she has taught in, Fitzgerald said, she found that the girls—though they would never admit it—would hold back in class and let the boys answer the questions. "A lot of it was hinging on the fact that they didn't want to look terribly smart because then they wouldn't get the dates with the jocks," she said. In an all-girl format, girls don't have to perform to attract attention. They can focus on their schoolwork.

When local television stations visited the school at the time Pelosi was elected, the girls who were interviewed said things like: "When we see women accomplishing things like this, we know we can do it too." They all talked about this 'I Can' attitude, said Fitzgerald. "Truly, if you believe you can you probably will. So it really is like a catalyst to them in their development and it certainly is an incentive if nothing else."

That's in 2007. In the 1950s, most of the students in Pelosi's class went to nursing school, soon got married, or went to in-state colleges nearby. Very few went out of state. But Pelosi's mother had different plans for her only daughter.

"It was a different bring up" than the boys got, said Tommy. "My mother wanted to give her wings." Sending Nancy out of the neighborhood, to the Institute, was just the first step. The boys all stayed close to home after St. Leo's, going to Loyola High School and Loyola College in Baltimore and returning home after graduation. Tommy the patriarch had remained in Little Italy all his life and expected his family to continue the tradition. But Nancy's mother remembered the days when she was studying law books at night and finally just plum ran out of time to do anymore because of the needs of her children and her husband's large extended family: his constituents. Big Nancy wanted to make sure Little Nancy got the opportunity she didn't get.

So Big Nancy and Little Nancy conspired to find a college out of state, where Nancy might find some independence and see some of the world, much to Dad's chagrin. Out of state, in this case, meant 35 miles away, a tiny Catholic women's college in Washington, D.C., called Trinity College.

"I remember her brother telling a story at her mother's funeral," said Gene Raynor, a family friend and former Maryland election board administrator. "He said, 'My mother said to my father, "Nancy's going to Trinity College," and my father said, "Over my dead body."' So Nancy said to her husband, 'That could be arranged.'"

Trinity in the 1940s was the hallowed halls for Catholic girls on the East Coast. The world of Catholicism was a lot smaller than the rest of the world, and Trinity was right up there at the top of that world. Most of the students at Trinity in Nancy's day were from wealthy backgrounds, and many from political families as well. Its graduates include Kathleen Sebelius, governor of

Kansas, and former Representative Barbara Kennelly of Connecticut. When Kennelly was in office, Trinity was the only school in the country that could boast two female alums in Congress. At Trinity, Nancy's mother hoped her daughter would meet people from all walks of life. While Pelosi was at Trinity she would meet a husband-to-be who would take her 3,000 miles away from Little Italy, making her the first of her family to venture outside Baltimore. And after Pelosi left Little Italy for Trinity, she never returned as a full-time resident.

"That parochialism was broken," said Tommy. "Mom must have known that it would be."

Neighbors still remember the polite, reticent little girl who rode in the open-top convertibles in city parades and ran the family favors desk. She was raised right, neighbors say, and she's giving it back. Her name is permanently etched into the streets of her native neighborhood now. During a triumphant homecoming trip in January 2007, to celebrate her election as Speaker of the House, Baltimore renamed the 200 block of Albemarle Street Via Nancy D'Alesandro Pelosi.

"Every step that I took to the Speakership began in this neighborhood," Pelosi told the crowd of old neighbors, family, and friends gathered for the event. "I wanted to come back here to say 'thank you' to all of you for the spirit of community that has always strengthened and inspired my life that started here . . . . Italian immigrants built America. They were told: 'The streets were paved in gold.' And when they got here, they found out that they were going to be paving the streets . . . ."

Anna Eshoo was by her friend's side for the ceremony, and couldn't keep the tears from coming. "You look at her family and you see the story of America," she said.

The Select Choir from Pelosi's high school sang at the event. When Mikulski, who gave one of the speeches, looked over and saw the familiar uniforms, she flashed her Institute of Notre Dame ring at the girls, and they all went crazy, hands in the air waving their rings back. Mikulski and Pelosi came over after the ceremony, shook hands, and spoke to each girl. As they piled onto the bus for the ride back to school, Sister Mary Fitzgerald asked: "Do you realize how privileged you are? Do you realize what a moment in history you just experienced?" And they were all star-gazed, Fitzgerald said. "It was something they will remember forever."

Nancy's mother, in the end, had been wrong about Pelosi becoming a nun but right about her helping people. Pelosi didn't get to law school; she ended up making laws instead. There still may be a third act ahead for Pelosi too. She mentioned recently that she still firmly believes the Catholic Church ought to let women be priests. Married ones.

CHAPTER 2

THE SOCIAL GOSPEL

Preach the gospel always. When necessary use words.

—St. Francis of Assisi, 1181–1226

*My parents did not raise me to be speaker of the House. They raised me to be holy.
They raised me to do the right thing.*

—Nancy Pelosi January 2, 2007

In the autumn of 1958, for the first time in her life, Nancy wasn't tied to the cadence of her father's elections. As she left for her first day of college in Washington, D.C., Tommy D'Alesandro was winding down his third term as mayor and would never win another election. Yet eighteen-year-old Pelosi arrived at the white stone halls of Trinity College in 1958 on the eve of two elections that probably influenced her as lastingly and profoundly as any of her father's. Pope John XXIII was elected two months into her freshman year, and John F. Kennedy was elected the first Catholic president three months into her junior year. The pope's election led two years later to Vatican II, the great gathering of church leaders that voted in a host of reforms and liberalized rules, bringing a wisp of openness to a hermetically sealed Catholic Church. And the election of Kennedy, whose campaign Pelosi volunteered for while she was a sophomore, gave her a political role model and touchstone she drew on for the rest of her life.

"It was a start of a very important time for Catholics in this country," she told the students of Trinity when she returned there to receive an honorary Doctor of Law degree in 2003. "It was a time of optimism and hope. Inspired by President Kennedy, young, idealistic Americans joined the Peace Corps. Courageous African Americans became Freedom Riders, challenging the evil of segregation and leading to the greatest demonstration for justice in American history—the Reverend Dr. Martin Luther King Jr.'s 1963 March on Washington."

A call to service sounded by a dynamic, progressive Catholic president, mixed with the call for reform from a forward-looking pope, and reinforced by a college dedicated to both upholding Catholic tradition and realizing the full potential of its women students, made it seem like a time of opening doors and infinite possibilities for a Catholic undergrad in Washington. Trinity president Pat McGuire said Pelosi and her generation were right on the cusp between an age of tradition and modernity. They were pioneers, McGuire said.

Trinity is a city on a hill overlooking a neighborhood in need. It was founded in 1897 on the premise of helping women in a society that placed them at a disadvantage. For years it served as a sister school to Georgetown, which didn't admit women when Pelosi enrolled in 1958. (Georgetown didn't become fully coed until 1971.) The similarities between Pelosi's high school in Baltimore and her chosen college in Washington, D.C., are fairly striking. In the late 1950s, both were Catholic, all-girls' schools dedicated to public service as much as education—"learning for larger purposes" as Trinity's president said. The Institute of Notre Dame, Pelosi's high school, was founded by the School Sisters of Notre Dame; Trinity by the Sisters of Notre Dame de Namur. And both schools obstinately refused to leave their neighborhoods as those neighborhoods grew increasingly poor. It's as if the schools wouldn't be what they are if there weren't a glaring need for their community service ethic right out the front door. "Look all around you," the schools seem to shout. "The world needs us more now than ever."

What Trinity had that Pelosi's high school didn't was a much better vantage from which to view the wider political world. Trinity sits less than three miles from the White House, the Capitol, and the Mall. While attending school there, it's impossible not to become involved in the city's debates and gossip, its enthusiasm for the great issues and ideas of the day, its embassies and think tanks, its grandiose but well-intentioned desire to make the world a better place. Sister Margaret Clayton, president of the school when Pelosi was there, wanted the women of Trinity to be involved in the great social movements of the time. And "involved" is the single word that probably best describes what Pelosi's college days were like. The energetic undergrad majored in political science, joined the Political Affairs Club, the International Relations Club, the Dramatic Society, and the French Club. Her work for the Young Democrats during Kennedy's candidacy continued her education in the nuts and bolts of running a campaign, this time on a national stage. Pelosi was there to hear Kennedy call a generation to public service in his inaugural address.

"Our professors encouraged fresh thinking and gave us confidence," Pelosi told Trinity students in 2003. "Trinity challenged us to expand our horizons. We had living laboratories—whether it was the U.S. Capitol or Embassy Row—to learn about our own government and those of other countries. We had all of that at our doorsteps."

Forty-five years later, however, when Pelosi hoped to return to campus for a celebration Mass on the eve of her election as Speaker, the church and school that helped fling open so many doors for her in 1960 was under pressure to close them on her, to keep her from attending the celebration at her alma mater's chapel. Some Catholic activists and several alumnae thought it hypocritical of Trinity to open *its* chapel doors to a strong proponent of abortion rights and gay rights, stances that collide with the church's official views.

"Nancy of course is a lighting rod in Catholic circles," said George Wesolek, director of the San Francisco archdiocese's Public Policy and Social Concerns Office. "The people on the right are extremely upset with her because of the fact that she does a real good job on a whole series of issues that come from Catholic social theology. But when you come to the life issues, which are based on those same principles, she does a terrible job."

The Trinity predicament was an uncomfortable but familiar one for Pelosi. She has said she never knows when her church back in San Francisco, St. Vincent De Paul, might refuse her Communion because of her views. "I never knew if this was the day it would be withheld. And that's a hard way to go to church," she said in an interview in 2003. The conflict for Pelosi probably isn't going away any time soon. During a visit to Brazil in May 2007, Pope Benedict XVI said that political leaders have a "grave and clear" obligation to oppose abortion rights. Asked by Brazilian reporters whether legislators who legalized abortion in Mexico City should rightfully be considered excommunicated, Benedict replied "Yes." Benedict's spokesman, the Reverend Federico Lombardi, quickly issued a clarifying statement saying

Benedict was not setting a new policy and that he did not intend to formally excommunicate anyone—a rare process under church law that severs all ties between the person and the church. But Lombardi added that politicians who vote in favor of abortion had already "excluded *themselves*" from receiving Holy Communion.

For a time, Pelosi took to shuttling among different churches when she attended on Sunday so she wouldn't be subject to a preemptive ban. "I'm in a different church every week. I'm a moving target," she said in 2003. The archdiocese of San Francisco, which once denounced her political support for abortion, has on occasion told nuns at its schools that Pelosi couldn't speak at an event. "And that's hurtful because we have so much in common," Pelosi said. "But it's the decision the church has made."

Pelosi has always defined her Catholicism with "shoulds" rather than "should nots," with "ands" rather than "either/ors." She calls herself a "conservative Catholic" *and* pro-choice; she goes to church every Sunday *and* also believes firmly that women ought to be priests someday. She considers all people children of God, her fellow Catholics *and* her gay constituents in San Francisco. She's a Catholic who works from within for change. She was raised in a strict Catholic family, which saw to it that she attended Catholic schools for 16 years, but those schools taught her a more progressive brand of Catholicism than people associate with the church today. Her daughter, Alexandra Pelosi, puts it this way: "In my family, we have a hundred years of Catholic school experience, and none of us ever heard that homosexuality was a sin. At my school, the nuns taught us about evolution." (Pelosi has called science "a gift from God.")

Wesolek, who has worked with Pelosi in San Francisco for 21 years, makes the point that the church Pelosi spent her formative years in was a culturally different church from what it is now. "I grew up in a church that started out with the civil rights movement," said Wesolek, as did Pelosi. "I was taught by priests who were in the march at Selma, and that's where I got my first kind of introduction to social justice. And I worked with César Chávez, and I know others who did, in the farm worker movement. We worked against the Vietnam War at that time. There was a very strong commitment within the church to labor, and to labor unions and the right to organize. And all of that was very much a part of our history."

In an interview with Joe Feuerherd of the *National Catholic Reporter*, Pelosi explained how she reconciles her liberal political views with her allegiance to the Catholic Church. "I was raised . . . in a very strict upbringing in a Catholic home where we respected people, were observant, [and where] the fundamental belief was that God gave us all a free will and we were accountable for that, each of us," she said. "I believe that my position on choice is one that is consistent with my Catholic upbringing, which said that every person has a free will and has the responsibility to live their own lives in a way that they would have to account for in the end." In a different interview, she added: "If you don't want an abortion, you don't believe in it, [then] don't have one. But don't tell somebody else what they can do in terms of honoring their responsibilities."

The Catholic Church calls this the *primacy of conscience* argument. The Second Vatican Council said a person's conscience is "divine law written in the human heart," and following your conscience is as important as following church rules. The doctrine insists that a person can't go against what her conscience tells her to do. Judging the sinfulness of any particular act or stand is a matter between God and the individual, according to instructions released after Vatican II. The Church has since backed away from that interpretation some, but not Pelosi. The divine voice known as conscience, for Pelosi, trumps the church's demand that all Catholics, and Catholic politicians, adhere to every order from the church if they want to call themselves Catholics. (Some critics call this "cafeteria Catholicism"—members picking and choosing which church teachings they decide to follow.) Pelosi believes her private view on abortion in no way should prevent her from having a deep relationship with God and her church. In her view, God is bigger than that— his kingdom contains multitudes—and the church's tent should be big enough to include them, too, controversial views, sins, warts and all. The word "catholic," after all, means universal, all-inclusive.

Church officials say the *primacy of conscience* argument rests on the idea that a person forms her or his conscience correctly, however. In other words, it doesn't mean you just believe whatever you want. The Catholic Church has never said that. Catholics believe in the authority of scripture and conscience, but they also believe in the authority of "tradition": the hierarchy of the church, the pope, and the bishops, according to church officials. A Catholic conscience that doesn't heed the church's teachings is an improperly formed conscience. One church official who asked to remain anonymous said that no one in Catholic circles would feel at all upset if Nancy Pelosi said "'You know, I don't really feel this particular thing in my conscience and therefore I don't want to call myself a Catholic anymore.' That's the way you solve that problem. And that's why so many people are so angry with her, because she insists that she is Catholic in terms of her identity and uses that in a political way, and at the same time is so totally adverse to the teaching of the church on these very foundational issues."

The gray area in the whole argument is how bad a person thinks abortion is. If it's murder, as the church teaches, then it's not enough for individuals to hold themselves accountable; society must hold individuals accountable because it's a crime against society. Pelosi does not, however, see it as murder. Her party and her Supreme Court agree with her; her church does not.

Pelosi has consistently voted to support abortion rights while in Congress. She voted against a law that prohibits third-trimester abortions, also known as partial birth abortions. She voted in favor of allowing the use of district money to promote abortion-related activities. She has also voted in favor of using federal funds to perform abortions in overseas military facilities, against parental notification when a minor is transported across state lines for an abortion, and in favor of providing funding for organizations working overseas that perform abortions or promote abortion-related activities.

On February 28, 2006, a majority of Catholic Democrats in the House issued a statement of principles that backed up Pelosi's approach to the conflict between being pro-choice and Catholic. Fifty members signed the statement, including Pelosi. The key passage that supported Pelosi's tack:

> In all these issues, we seek the Church's guidance and assistance but believe also in *the primacy of conscience*. In recognizing the Church's role in providing moral leadership, we acknowledge and accept the tension that comes with being in disagreement with the Church in some areas. Yet we believe we can speak to the fundamental issues that unite us as Catholics and lend our voices to changing the political debate—a debate that often fails to reflect and encompass the depth and complexity of these issues.

Interestingly, the statement also contained a ringing condemnation of abortion itself, a condemnation that Pelosi signed on to:

> We envision a world in which every child belongs to a loving family and agree with the Catholic Church about the value of human life and the undesirability of abortion—*we do not celebrate its practice*. Each of us is committed to reducing the number of unwanted pregnancies and creating an environment with policies that encourage pregnancies to be carried to term. We believe this includes promoting alternatives to abortion, such as adoption, and improving access to children's healthcare and child care, as well as policies that encourage paternal and maternal responsibility.

The language is careful to remark on "the undesirability of abortion" without committing to any sort of opposition to the Democratic platform's pro-choice plank. Certainly you can not like abortion even if you fight for it to be legal.

Pelosi has argued that keeping the right to safe abortion legal is different from approving of abortion itself. She's careful to say she's for choice, not abortion. But her endorsement of the statement did suggest publicly, for the first time, that she has more reservations about abortion than her votes suggest. And Kristen Day, the executive director of Democrats for Life America, applauded Pelosi for helping recruit and support six new anti-abortion Democrats who won seats in the House in 2006: Heath Shuler of North Carolina, Joe Donnelly of Indiana, Brad Ellsworth of Indiana, Charlie Wilson of Ohio, and Chris Carney and Jason Altmire, both of Pennsylvania.

"We've said for years that when we expand the big tent of the Democratic Party, Democrats win," Day said. "We look forward to working with Congresswomen Nancy Pelosi and the new leaders of the House to promote an agenda that will dramatically reduce the abortion rate in America. We applaud Congresswoman Pelosi understanding that Democrats need to govern from the center."

It may be that Pelosi is simply moving a bit toward the middle as a practical, tactical move as Speaker and her personal views remain unchanged. Or Pelosi may harbor some unspoken ambivalence about abortion. It's hard not to read her emphasis on individual accountability in the end as meaning that she's aware her position on abortion conflicts with the church's. But she's willing to take a gamble that God doesn't see it the way the church sees it right now, the church will eventually change, or God will let the whole matter slide, when all is said and done, because of all the good on the other side of her ledger. In her family, she said, "each person had that accountability, so it wasn't for us to make judgments about how people saw their responsibility and that it wasn't for politicians to make decisions about how people led their personal lives; certainly, to a high moral standard, but when it got into decisions about privacy and all the rest, then that was something that individuals had to answer to God for, and not to politicians." Politicians ought to keep their noses out of people's private spiritual lives, in other words.

For many colleagues, Pelosi's ability to stick to her pro-choice views even in the face of criticism from the hierarchy of her own church is a plus, a show of strength and individuality. Thanks in large part, ironically, to her upbringing in the church, she's a woman of principles, they say, ready and willing to defend those principles against attacks from multiple fronts, even the altar. In other words, the Catholic Church informs her views on issues, sustains her values, but doesn't control them.

But others say she can't have it both ways: pitch herself as a "conservative Catholic" to win Catholic voters back to the Democratic fold and simultaneously earn an almost perfect rating from liberal organizations such as the National Abortion Rights League that keep tabs on voting records. Former representative Robert Dornan, a fellow Californian, lashed out at "Nancy Pelosi's faith in the culture of death," in the March–April 2007 issue of *Celebrate Life* magazine, which is published by the conservative American Life League. Dornan called Pelosi a "propaganda maven who branded herself as a devout Catholic grandmother" even though she "favors diabolical partial-birth abortion." He went on to label her as "maybe the most dangerous leader in the long campaign by anti-Catholics within the Church who mislead Americans."

Other critics say she's now trying to camouflage her true colors, steeped in the ultraliberal mores of her hometown of San Francisco, by emphasizing the retro-Catholic politics of her upbringing in Baltimore. But Representative James Clyburn (D-S.C.), a close ally of Pelosi's who now serves as majority whip, said that's hogwash. "Nancy Pelosi was born in a strict Catholic environment, educated in a strict Catholic environment." Pelosi started a Faith Working Group in Congress and put Clyburn in charge of it.

He said that her San Francisco "values" were once criticized during a meeting of the group when she wasn't there. Clyburn defended her to everyone by reminding them that she went with her husband to his home in San Francisco when she was nearly 30. Her years in Baltimore, in a strict Catholic household, were her formative ones. He also reminded the group of a proverb: *Train up the child in the way he should go, and when he is older, he will not depart from it.* "Now tell me something," he asked them. "Which [city] would have the most influence on her, if you believe in a strict interpretation of the Bible?"

Representative Anna Eshoo, a 30-year friend of Pelosi's as well as a fellow Catholic and Californian, said that, for Pelosi and her family, "there was a fierceness about" their faith and its calling, a sense of high moral purpose. "This is who they are, what they are. So you ask, who has influenced us the most? It's the people who brought us into this world." When Pelosi calls herself a "conservative Catholic," she is not using the word "conservative" to describe her stands on issues, she's talking about her family and its values. "Conservative" to her means strict, devout, and engaged. "In the family I was raised in, love of country, deep love of the Catholic Church and love of family were the values," Pelosi said.

In the family in which she grew up, however, Pelosi was the only one who was pro-choice. She has said that she and her brothers and mother and father used to avoid arguments on the issue by patiently observing the respect they were taught to have for each other's views and God-given individuality. "Having said that, I think there are occasions where they would like me to be less visible [on the abortion issue], that they don't like to see any disagreement between the church and any of us," Pelosi said.

If, as she likes to say, her family taught her almost everything she knows about politics, but didn't teach her the pro-choice, feminist, and gay rights values that she has been such a champion of, where did they come from? She herself said her liberal stances spring from "deep in my soul." Certainly San Francisco influenced and deepened her liberalism, especially when it comes to gay rights. And she's always closely adhered to the Democratic Party line. But it was really Trinity, or more precisely Trinity at the onset of the 1960s, that marked the beginning of Pelosi's progressive interpretation of what it means to be a Catholic.

To explain how important her time at Trinity was to her, Pelosi always emphasizes the president and the pope. She said that while she was an undergrad, Pope John XXIII "reinvigorated the church with a new openness while remaining true to the unshakable foundations of our faith, and he intensified our faith in God and in each other."

The Catholic Church and churches in general were key players in many of the social movements and social programs born at that time, including the War on Poverty and the civil rights movement. In 1960, Pelosi saw the church as an evolving, progressive force for good in the world, and that view stuck. Pope John XXIII, when asked why the Vatican Council was needed, reportedly opened a window and said, "I want to throw open the windows of the church so that we can see out and the people can see in."

The church invited Protestant and Eastern Orthodox clergy to attend, a radical reaching out to other denominations in those days. It declared the Blessed Virgin Mary as Mother of the church, greatly elevating her prominence as a role model for Catholics. Vatican II in fact marked a great divide between the old church and the modern church. The reforms gave laypeople a much greater role in services and encouraged diversity in the language of those services and the rites practiced. Before Vatican II, all Masses were said in Latin, with the priest facing the back of the church. Afterward, Masses were said in a hundred different languages and the priest faced the congregation. The social upheaval in the United States only amplified the council's importance and impact. Times they were a-changin'.

Vatican II also opened the doors to discussion of many topics once considered improper, including feminism, the oppression of women, and even women and the priesthood. Before the council, which was convened by the world's bishops to bring the church into the twentieth century by addressing the challenges posed by all the political, social, economic, and technological changes, church teachings insisted that salvation for women came from a denial of individuality for the greater good. The church itself, under Pope John XXIII, opened the discussion about redefining the role of women in church, the downside of which was that many nuns left the faith after Vatican II, looking for fulfillment elsewhere. It's hard to imagine today's Catholic Church ever holding such discussions without relentless prodding from outside the leadership hierarchy, but it was the leaders who initiated the conversation in the early 1960s.

After Vatican II, Catholic women began to question the teachings of the church that insisted on defining women in light of their procreative role in society. Mary Daly, a professor of theology at Boston College, wrote an influential book, *The Church and the Second Sex*, that heralded the coming of radical Catholic feminism. Inspired by Vatican II, Catholic women founded major international social groups, Catholic publishing houses, and spoke on street corners. Social action became the outlet by which many Catholic women began to satisfy their need to serve a larger purpose, to live their lives for a greater good that was no longer defined around their roles as wives and mothers.

Catholic women coming of age at the dawn of the 1960s were beginning to realize the limitations of being a woman in the Catholic church—recall Pelosi's line, "I want to be a priest when I grow up"—but that didn't keep them from answering their faith's call that they lead a Christian life in a secular world. They were women on a mission to bring truth, love, and life to a secular world. Getting and spending and the raising of children were not always enough to quench that spiritual thirst.

Pelosi's experience of the Catholic Church and its political activism was essentially an expansive, empowering one, in other words, rather than a limiting one. This was the church of *Godspell* and *Jesus Christ Superstar*, when religion was on the side of the rebels and counterculture. The campus activism that was just beginning to brew while Pelosi was at Trinity had religious underpinnings. She sees that activism-driven-by-conscience continuing.

"In my diocese years ago . . . our archbishop got a standing ovation for standing up on issues related to disarmament. And our churches in San

Francisco and across the country we have worked together on issues relating to sanctuary for people from El Salvador and to end the violence in Central America," she said recently. "All of these issues are not only important values that the church has taken the lead on, worked closely with its parishioners and [its] following on, [but has provided] moral leadership for the rest of the world."

"The Catholic Church's commitment to social justice is one of its best kept secrets," adds Wesolek. Nuns and other religious women leaders played a crucial part in the civil rights movement, for example. A PBS documentary, "The Sisters of Selma," commemorated their participation in the march on Selma in 1965. Several of the nuns who were there said the Second Vatican Council inspired them to become involved. They were responding to Pope John XXIII's plea to "go where the need is."

"All the people who'd been hurt that day, they were the body and blood of Christ," recalled Father Maurice Ouellet, a pastor of one of Selma's black parishes at the time. "They had walked the stations of the cross . . . and they had been crucified."

And it wasn't just the Catholic Church. Clyburn points out that, in the late 1950s and early '60s, all of the leaders of the civil rights movement were ministers, many of them Baptist ministers: the Reverend Dr. Martin Luther King. Andrew Young, Fred Shuttlesworth, Wyatt T. Walker, Joseph Lowery, Jesse Jackson, Ralph Abernathy, King's closest associate, Bernard Lee, a veteran demonstrator, and C.T. Vivian. The southern churches were the staging area for the first marches and protests, Clyburn said, mainly because they were the only independent group in the black community, the only place where African Americans weren't somehow subservient to white institutions. Black churches were informal courtrooms for settling community disputes, community bulletin boards, banks, support groups, and political headquarters all rolled into one. But the churches also rose to the call because morality was their business, and they saw civil rights as a moral issue. Ministers made good activists because their oratory was charismatic—they knew how to rally people to a cause. They used emotional, evocative language to explain that the fight for civil rights was a religious as well as an historical one, according to Clarence Taylor, professor of history at Baruch College. "Ministers at the time spoke of a holy crusade to push America to live up to its promise of equal rights for all."

Civil rights activism and the coming church reforms were two pieces of the backbeat to Pelosi's college years, and then there was Kennedy himself. He was Trinity's commencement speaker in 1958 when he was a senator. In his speeches and remarks, Kennedy frequently alluded to "the Almighty," cited scripture, and continued the long political tradition of framing America as a nation charged with projecting its liberties in order "to light the world." Pelosi echoed the phrase in one of her often-repeated quotes: "America must be a light to the world, not just a missile." In his inaugural address, which Pelosi heard in person, Kennedy contrasted America and the Soviet Union by saying that God, not man, was the author of freedom. And what is Kennedy's inaugural speech if not a call to public service, a speech that a handful of historians say drew on Kennedy's Catholic upbringing as well. "Ask not what your country can do for you," he urged, "Ask what you can do for your country."

"I certainly was inspired, as were other members of my generation, by President Kennedy, his candidacy and his election and by his beautiful words. . . . His death left a terrible mark on all of us," Pelosi said in a 2001 interview with C-Span. The assassination of President Kennedy affected her more than any other event in American history, she said, and she made a point of mentioning Kennedy's Catholicism in a speech at the National Hispanic Prayer breakfast in 2005.

"In 1960, when John F. Kennedy was running for president, his critics raised questions about whether his faith should disqualify him from the presidency. Then-Senator Kennedy went to a gathering of ministers in Houston, and said in his address—the issue is 'not what kind of church I believe in . . . but what kind of America I believe in.' "

"The America he believed in," she went on, "is the one we believe in today: one in which each person can practice his or her own faith in his or her own way." It is our faith, she said, that obligates us to do something about the issues of education, healthcare for the uninsured, poverty, jobs, diversity. "That is why so many of the policies we pursue should not be viewed as legislation, or regulations, or programs. They should be statements of our values." Preach the gospel through deeds, in other words.

In a sign of how differently Democratic politicians view their relationship to religion today compared to Kennedy's day, however, Pelosi didn't quote the very next sentence of Kennedy's speech, one of the most quoted passages:

> I believe in an America where the separation of church and state is absolute—where no Catholic prelate would tell the President (should he be Catholic) how to act, and no Protestant minister would tell his parishioners for whom to vote—where no church or church school is granted any public funds or political preference—and where no man is denied public office merely because his religion differs from the President who might appoint him or the people who might elect him.

Kennedy's speech to the Methodist ministers was, in fact, a ringing defense of the sanctity of the separation of church and state, the kind of defense that is not heard much these days as each party tries to cozy up to "values voters." Then Democrats were eager to distance themselves from the power of the church; today it's an all-out scramble to associate themselves with it.

Together, the progressive ideas of Kennedy and Pope John XXIII instilled in Pelosi the sense that her Catholic upbringing gave her a special responsibility to do good works in the world a long time before she translated that call into a run for office. It was an era during which political activism and religion were joined at the hips.

Throughout her public life, Pelosi has cited her faith as the root of her call to public service. "The gospel of Matthew is something that drives many of us in our public service," she said during a St. Patrick's Day speech on Darfur in 2006. More so than the other gospels, St. Matthew's emphasizes that a holy life requires good works, that without service to others, faith is unfilled. "By their deeds you shall know them," Matthew reads.

Eshoo says that, for Pelosi, "The Catholic faith and the Democratic Party were totally entwined with one another. There's not the dimmest light that could ever come between the two." Because of that convergence of faith and liberal politics in the early 1960s, Pelosi's own faith and her liberal politics are more linked than most people realize. Her majority leader, James Clyburn, has gone so far as to call her legislative program for Congress during the 2007 session a "faith-based agenda." When she was a spokeswoman for Pelosi, Jennifer Crider argued that on nearly every Democratic position, the party's agenda mirrors the values "the faith community lives by."

It's ironic to some that the Democrats are so willing to embrace a faith-based agenda after pounding Bush for years on his faith-based initiatives that linked government and religious organizations, trampling on the separation of church and state. But Jon Meachem, author of the book *American Gospel*, points out that faith has been at the center of the country's public life from the beginning.

"Our finest hours—the Revolutionary War, abolition, the expansion of the rights of women, fights against terror and tyranny, the battle against Jim Crow—can partly be traced to religious ideas about liberty, justice, and charity," Meacham wrote. "Yet theology and scripture have also been used to justify our worst hours—from enslaving black people to persecuting Native Americans to treating women as second-class citizens."

Meacham thinks Thomas Jefferson wisely staked out an American middle ground that allows religion to shape the life of the nation without strangling it. "Belief in God is central to the country's experience, yet for the broad center, faith is a matter of choice, not coercion, and the legacy of the Founding is that the sensible center holds. It does so because the Founders believed themselves at work in the service of both God and man, not just one or the other."

Professor Green of Catholic University sees the influence of religion on politics over time as generally a good thing. "Legislators' religious beliefs, and speakers' beliefs, can play a role in the policies they choose to follow," he said. "For example, [former Speaker of the House] Tip O'Neill became a strong opponent of Reagan administration policy in Nicaragua. That was partly a result of Tip O'Neill being a Catholic, and hearing from Catholic nuns in his district about human rights abuses against Catholics in Central America."

Pelosi has linked the issues she cares about and her faith in her speeches for years, but more so since the fall of 2004, when exit polls showed that values voters—voters who voted for the party they thought better matched their basic moral views—had been crucial to Republicans holding on to Congress and keeping Bush in the Oval Office.

In her inaugural address, Pelosi quoted Saint Francis of Assisi, as did Margaret Thatcher when she was elected. (Democratic representative David Obey and others have called Pelosi "our Maggie Thatcher. She's tough as hell—and has a very nice style to her.") "Lord, make me a channel of thy peace," Pelosi recited the day she took the Speaker's gavel. "Where there is darkness may we bring light, where there is hatred, may we bring love, and where there is despair, may we bring hope." Sifting back through recent speeches, it's remarkable how often Pelosi cites direct passages from the Bible as specific calls for action on a wide range of issues:

- *Pelosi on healthcare* at a Hispanic prayer breakfast: "In the Book of Hebrews it is written: 'Make level paths for your feet, so that the lame may not be disabled, but rather healed.' Today, creating those 'level paths' means providing health care access for all."

- *On the environment*, in September 2005, during a speech calling for a tougher Endangered Species Act: "In Isaiah in the Old Testament, we are told that to minister to the needs of God's creation—and that includes our beautiful environment—is an act of worship."

- *On Hurricane Katrina* in a speech at the National Press Club: "It says in the Bible, 'when there is injustice in the world, the poorest people, those with the least power, are injured the most.' That was certainly true for the people of Hurricane Katrina."

- *On immigration* at a Hispanic prayer breakfast: "In Leviticus, the Israelites are told by God: 'When a newcomer lives with you in your land, do not mistreat him. The newcomer living with you must be treated as one of your native-born. Love him as yourself, for you were newcomers in Egypt."

In addition to a faith-based agenda, Pelosi seems to be assembling a faith-based kitchen cabinet. Clyburn can quote the Bible like the son of a fundamentalist minister he is and the minister he almost became. Pelosi told him she wanted him to head the faith group because many of his writings and speeches had a faith component to them. When he subsequently rose to the number-three spot in the Democratic hierarchy in the House after Pelosi became Speaker, many observers thought it was because of the importance Pelosi attached to the faith initiative.

Many other members of her House posse share the faith, specifically her Catholic faith. Catholics dominant the ranks of her closest advisers and top appointees: Anna Eshoo; Representative George Miller, head of the committee that sets policy for her; Representative John Murtha, the on-floor commander of her Iraq strategy; Dave Obey, architect of Pelosi's spending priorities; Charlie Rangell, head of the powerful Ways and Means Committee; Rosa DeLauro, head of the Democratic Steering Committee; and close confidants Dennis Cardoz, Jim Costa, Diane Watson, and Grace Napolitano, all representatives from California. Confidantes Barbara Mikulski and Barbara Boxer also attended all-girls Catholic schools when they were growing up.

Former presidential candidate Howard Dean, now head of the Democratic National Committee, launched a Faith in Action Initiative shortly before the 2006 elections to strengthen and build relationships with members of the faith communities through national and state outreach programs. According to him, reaching out to communities of faith, including evangelicals, is a high priority of the 2008 elections.

The 2006 statement of principles by Catholics in the House probably best articulates the connection Pelosi and other representatives feel between their faith and their public service:

> We are committed to making real the basic principles that are at the heart of Catholic social teaching: helping the poor and disadvantaged, protecting the

most vulnerable among us, and ensuring that all Americans of every faith are given meaningful opportunities to share in the blessings of this great country. That commitment is fulfilled in different ways by legislators but includes: reducing the rising rates of poverty; increasing access to education for all; pressing for increased access to health care; and taking seriously the decision to go to war. Each of these issues challenges our obligations as Catholics to community and helping those in need.

The president of the University of San Francisco, the Reverend Stephen Privett, delivered one of two invocations at Pelosi's inauguration, making the connection between the House's work and God's work.

"God of compassion and mercy, we pray that the new leadership of this Congress and all of its members will write into law the story of a country that measures its success by God's standard of how well it cares for the weakest and most vulnerable among us," he said.

Pelosi has strongly encouraged other Democrats in the House to speak up about their faith, as well, although an aide said she has cautioned against invocations of faith from those who aren't truly faithful. Authenticity is what she's looking for.

Clyburn, an African Methodist Episcopalian from South Carolina, said this isn't anything new, just forgotten. It's his charge to repair the ties between faith groups and Democrats that have been "ruptured" over the years, not create something new. But just when did things start to go south, religiously speaking, for the Democrats? When did the GOP become God's Only Party?

Wesolek, Clyburn, and others think it dates back to the late 1970s, a time when a "born-again" Jimmy Carter actually lost churchgoing voters to Ronald Reagan. Bill Clinton won the Catholic vote in 1992 and spoke comfortably about faith, but the God Gap continued to widen even then. Four years later, George W. Bush brought regular churchgoers firmly into the Republican camp. Clyburn thinks much of the shift was originally driven by Pat Robertson and his Christian Coalition and the recently deceased Jerry Falwell and his collection of political action committees known as the Moral Majority. At one point the Moral Majority counted a million members, making it one of the largest conservative lobbying groups in the United States. Capitalizing on the patriotic sentiment on display in the country for the Bicentennial in 1976, Falwell, a fundamentalist minister, seized the moment to portray America as a Christian nation that had lost its way after 200 years.

"Somehow I thought the separation doctrine existed to keep the church out of politics," Falwell told his audiences. "I was wrong. In fact, to our nation's forefathers . . . the separation of church and state had been designed to keep the government from interfering with the church. Never during the founding years of this great democracy had our forefathers meant to distance the government from the truths of the Christian faith or to prohibit Christians from applying Biblical principles in their influence on the state."

Just as King used black churches for political purposes in the 1950s and 1960s, Falwell launched his campaigns from white evangelical churches in the 1970s. Tapping the talents of 70 performers from his own Liberty Baptist College, Falwell put on a musical called *I Love America* in 141 cities.

"Pat Robertson, Jerry Falwell, all of them were very political," said Clyburn. "Pat Robertson ran for president. Then here comes the Moral Majority, saying We are Moral, and They are Immoral. And that was the whole thrust." Conservatives had begun the successful effort to paint liberals as godless. By 2004, conservative politicians had joined the culture wars in droves, successfully rupturing the relationship between Democrats and faith groups. "They had defined us in such a way that people were saying, you can't be a Democrat and a Christian," said Clyburn.

In 1960, according to the Gallup Organization, 70 percent of Catholics identified themselves as Democratic or leaning Democratic. By 2004, that number was down to 44 percent. Between 1960 and 2004, the Pew Research Center for the People and the Press reported that white evangelicals went from favoring Democrats by a 2-to-1 ratio to favoring Republicans by about the same ratio. In 2004, 78 percent of white evangelicals supported President Bush.

Nancy Pelosi saw all of this come to a head in Ohio, in 2004. "We lost Ohio, and therefore the president, because of faith voters rejecting us out of hand," said Clyburn. She initiated the Faith Working Group shortly afterward as a long-range effort to retie the bonds between the Democratic Party and faith groups. "We agreed that what we have to do is try to get our members more comfortable with what we knew to be their yearnings, their learnings and . . . leanings" Clyburn said. "If you look at the programs that we advocate, they're faith-based. And here's a political party (Republicans) trying to destroy all these programs. All of a sudden they become the God-fearing party? How do we make intolerance a faithful thing to be?"

The Reverend Jim Wallis, a liberal minister and author of the book *God's Politics: Why the Right Gets It Wrong and the Left Doesn't Get It,* was called in to help in 2005. He has since become the Democrats' chief theorist on faith. He was asked by Pelosi to coach Democrats in the House on talking about their faith more in public, and he regularly addresses the Faith Working Group, which meets about once a month in the Capitol.

Wallis said the Bible is filled with messages that align more closely to Democratic policies than GOP policies.

"As an evangelical Christian, I find 3,000 verses in the Bible about the poor," far outnumbering mentions of same-sex unions or low taxes, he told the *Washington Post*'s Dana Milbank.

Wallis believes there's a right way and a wrong way to mix religion and public life, and he thinks Pelosi has found the right way, appealing to a hunger out there for a fuller engagement of faith and politics. He thinks Abraham Lincoln best articulated the right way to mix the two: We should not invoke the name of God by claiming that he is on our side; rather we should pray and worry whether *we* are on *his* side. The first approach, claiming that God is on our side, leads to triumphalism, self-righteousness, and bad foreign policy, Wallis believes. The other way, Lincoln's way and Pelosi's way, leads to accountability, humility, reflection, even repentance. Wallis thinks we need much more of these types of values in politics and much less of the arrogance of the former. In his Democratic keynote speech in 2004, Barack Obama said: "We have an awesome God in the blue states."

Many pundits and bloggers have criticized the Democrats for suddenly getting religion after the 2004 vote. Religious conservative Gary Bauer wrote an e-mail to supporters mocking Pelosi. "They just don't get it!" he wrote. "The American people are tired of the radical left's assault upon all things religious . . . . For a party so dominated by Michael Moore's Hollywood, liberal academia and the ACLU, it's going to take a lot more than politicians quoting Scripture to win votes."

Yet many newspapers reported that the God Gap between Republicans and Democrats narrowed in 2006. For a variety of reasons—ethics accusations against Republicans, questions about the morality of the Iraq War, imbalances in the economy—exit polls clearly showed that Republicans' advantage among values voters diminished in the last election. White evangelicals and Catholics in particular increased their support for Democratic candidates.

Wallis said Democrats cut the GOP's advantage among regular churchgoers 12 percentage points last fall. Still, nobody thinks the Democrats are done yet. Pelosi, Clyburn, Dean, and others are trying hard to recement the links between religion and Democrats, even evangelicals and Democrats. There are signs of a larger tectonic shift. A Pew survey taken in the spring of 2007 found young evangelicals greatly concerned about the environment, a traditionally Democratic issue. One third of young evangelicals under 30 said they do not oppose the idea of same-sex marriage, compared to 10 percent of older evangelicals. Redeem the Vote, a group formed in 2004 to register young evangelicals to vote, is helping black churches in Alabama campaign for a cap on the interest charges on short-term "payday" loans, which can climb as high as 400 percent.

Aides to Pelosi say her emphasis on faith issues goes far beyond the political calculus of wooing back voters. "I think this has been a part of her for a long time," said Wesolek. "This is not something that just came up after the elections with her. I think she really does look to her faith as a source of energy for herself. However, I would add to that that I think there is a political, practical calculation after the election that she and other Democrats made about 'Hey, here's a place we're really missing here by a few percentage points. People think we're faithless people, that we're somewhat godless. We've got to beef up the language and rhetoric.' So I think there is that calculated move there. But in her personal case, I don't think it's like all of a sudden she's taken on religion."

"Seventeen centuries ago, St. Augustine said any government that is not formed to promote justice is a bunch of thieves," Pelosi said recently. "In order to do the job, you have to have a belief. It's what drives your engine, what you keep coming back to." What religion gives Pelosi is a kind of moral confidence to make the tough decisions she faces every day. Aides say she sees such a values-based approach to her job as transcending partisan politics. Spiritual values actually are an area where she and President Bush find common ground, aides say. "I think you can judge from somebody's actions a kind of a stability and sense of purpose perhaps created by strong religious roots. I mean, there's a certain patience, a certain discipline, I think, that religion helps you achieve." That's Bush talking, not Pelosi.

One day before her inauguration, however, Pelosi's religion and her politics were not mixing in a positive way. Shortly after her staff announced their plans to have the speaker attend a Mass for the children of Darfur and Katrina at Trinity's Notre Dame Chapel, protests ensued. The American Life League, a Roman Catholic group that supports anti-abortion activities, legislation, and magazines, implored Archbishop Donald Wuerl of Washington to intervene "in an effort to prevent her from using the Mass for political gain." Judie

Brown, director of the league, also wrote a letter to Trinity's president, Pat McGuire:

> We know that you are aware of the recent announcement from Congresswoman Pelosi's office that she will be "using" a Catholic Mass at Trinity to showcase her new image as "Roman Catholic mother and grandmother" as she prepares to be sworn in as Speaker of the House in January. We are sure that you are aware of Congresswoman Pelosi's unqualified support for abortion on demand. Therefore, we see no reason why a pro-abortion Catholic alumnus of Trinity should receive accolades when she is defying Catholic teaching because of her support for aborting preborn children. Ms. McGuire, Congresswoman Pelosi is exploiting the Mass as part of her personal agenda and we respectfully ask that you cancel the January 3 event.

McGuire also received e-mail pleas from alumnae like this:

> Nancy and I are both alumnae of Trinity, an institution which was when I attended, a respected Catholic college where women were prepared for life and for on-going learning, not only in academic subjects, but also with a solid grounding in the teachings of the Church. Ms. Pelosi has taken a decidedly anti-Catholic stand on many moral issues of the preset day (late term abortion, same sex "marriage," and embryonic stem-cell research, to name a few). As one of many alumnae who treasure and appreciate the lessons learned at Trinity, I cannot share your pride in one whose rise to political power has been based so largely upon her rejection of much of her Trinity education. I am ashamed of her, and of Trinity for honoring her.
>
> Margaret

In the days right before the event was scheduled to take place, during Pelosi's week of celebrations in Baltimore and Washington, some protesters held up signs that read "Pelosi Preys on Children" as the Speaker and her family drove past. Protestors showed up with signs outside Notre Dame Chapel on the day the Mass was scheduled as well.

Washington's archbishop called McGuire to inquire about the controversy. McGuire told him that whenever an alumna asks to have a Mass at Trinity, a Mass is held. "It's a long tradition," she said, arguing that she didn't think Pelosi should be treated any differently. McGuire said Archbishop Wuerl is generally very pastoral in his approach to controversies, which means he uses such moments to teach, persuade, and reinforce the principles of the church rather than making demands and issuing edicts. Wuerl and other bishops see much that is positive in what Pelosi brings to the national table and didn't think her views on abortion ought to cancel out all the good she does in other areas.

Susan Gibbs, spokeswoman for the Archdiocese of Washington and the archbishop, eventually responded to all the complaints in January by side-stepping the whole hornet's nest. Archbishop Weurl did not interfere because Trinity University was under the jurisdiction of a religious order, the Sisters of Notre Dame, not the archdiocese, Gibbs said. In a later interview, Wuerl said: "That was a matter between the university and Nancy. They were offering their location, and the Mass was celebrated by a priest with faculties, and there was no reason to make any comment about it."

And so, much to the relief of Pelosi and her family, Trinity and McGuire let the event proceed. The only adjustment McGuire made in response to the outcry was a decision to keep it private, to keep media away. Pelosi arrived via a back route, so the only pictures that appeared in the press that day were shots of protestors outside the gates of the school.

When it was all over, McGuire said she was approached by several people in the archdiocese concerned that a small number of very vocal Catholic groups were tarnishing the image of Catholicism overall. McGuire said Catholic institutions such as Trinity are "afflicted" by many blog-driven "third-party groups" that don't feel the bishops are strict enough on social matters. She said it was these groups who were driving the objections to Pelosi's Mass, not the bishops themselves.

The bishops themselves have decided "let's not draw the battle lines at the Communion rail, that's not the way to do this," said Wesolek. "Some of them are so concerned that this would cause such a public outcry and scandal that it would lose more people than they would keep in. They would prefer to persuade a Nancy Pelosi, to persuade a Rudy Giuliani, to persuade many others." They have said they look forward to working with Pelosi on other pieces of their social justice agenda, especially stopping the Iraq War.

Cardinal Theodore E. McCarrick, retired archbishop of Washington, has known Pelosi since she first came to Washington. He said he's always found her to be "a very thoughtful and committed defender of human rights."

"We don't always agree—on life and education issues especially—but my experience has been that you can always talk to her," McCarrick told a journalist in January, 2007. "You can't always change her mind, but you can always talk to her."

McCarrick is chairman of a bishops' task force on Catholic politicians. Pelosi and other Democrats in Congress have started a dialogue with McCarrick about the role of their religious beliefs and political responsibilities, and the talks are ongoing.

When Pelosi finally arrived on the Trinity campus on the morning of January 3, students and alumnae engulfed her, constantly surging forward to get her autograph, to talk to her, to be with her, students said. Pelosi is Trinity's Mick Jagger, after all. The students were still on Christmas break on that day in January, but many came back early. Much of the Class of '62 returned for the event as well. Pelosi almost always attends class reunions and remains close to all of her college friends. "They're still my best friends," she said. "I don't know anyone that has kept her friends better than Nancy has," said Eshoo.

A three-story banner was hung in the cavernous well of Main Hall congratulating Pelosi. One student was overheard saying: "I want my poster hanging there 20 years from now." Everyone was trying to get a moment with Pelosi, yet she remained completely composed, completely poised, recalls Aimee Olivo, class of '99. "She had this glow about her. You could tell that she was really happy." The controversy over the abortion protesters never came up.

Pelosi had requested that the Mass at Notre Dame Chapel be dedicated to the children of Darfur and Katrina. Her daughter Nancy Corinne Prowda had played a CD of the St. Camillus Choir over the phone to Pelosi, and Pelosi arranged for the choir to do the music, planning out every detail, as is her way. The multicultural choir gave the ceremony a raucous, almost evangelical feel, with African overtones. Pelosi and her five grandchildren sat in the front row, right beneath the domed mosaic above the main altar that depicts the Coronation of the Virgin. Her brother Tommy did a reading, and several grandchildren said the Prayers of the Faithful. Pelosi had asked Jesuit father Robert F. Drinan, the first Catholic priest to vote in Congress, to lead the Mass. "Today is a new epiphany for all of us, for our country and for the world," he said at the opening of his homily, which was dedicated to children. "This is a new and wonderful moment for all of us. The new Congress has 16 percent women and for the first time the Speaker is a mother."

Drinan was the perfect pick for the Mass if Pelosi wanted to herald her coming efforts to mesh spiritual priorities and political ones as Speaker. He was also a controversial one, and his presence may have fueled the flames for Catholic activists. Wearing his white collar and black frock, Father Drinan represented Massachusetts' Third District in the halls of Congress from 1971 to 1981. "Our father, who art in Congress" became his unofficial campaign slogan. Among his most historic moments was his introduction of the first formal resolution to impeach President Richard M. Nixon. During his decade as a congressman priest, he constantly pushed both Congress and America to assert their "moral authority" in the world. And Drinan, like Pelosi, sparked controversy for showing independence from the Catholic Church as well. He

supported federal funding of abortions and opposed constitutional amendments that would have banned abortion and allowed prayer in public schools.
As a result, in 1980, Pope John Paul II ordered him to either forgo reelection
or leave the priesthood. Drinan left Congress instead.

He used the moment at Trinity to once again press the need for America
to shine as a moral beacon. "Imagine what the world would think of the
United States if the health and welfare of children everywhere became the top
objective of America's foreign policy. *It could happen*—and it could happen
soon—if enough people cared."

Pelosi said in remarks afterward during a gathering at Social Hall that she
and the school would need to report back to Father Drinan in a year to tell
him what they had accomplished toward his challenge. Unfortunately,
Drinan's last public act was Pelosi's Mass at Trinity. He died 25 days later at
Sibley Hospital in Washington.

The only sign of the controversy that day was a cluster of protestors outside
the gate chanting "Speaker Pelosi, Catholics Don't Kill Children," a protest
Pelosi neither saw nor heard. Robert Dornan, the former congressman who is
now a vocal critic of Pelosi, snuck into the invitation-only service, coming out
afterward to tell reporters that Pelosi was "the most arrogant pro-abortion person in Congress." But during the service itself he stayed respectfully quiet.

McGuire acknowledges that the Mass crossed signals for some Catholics,
and said the school does not share or endorse Pelosi's—or Drinan's—views on
abortion. And she's careful not to let the college be used as a political soapbox.
Some students had wanted to bring the head of the National Organization of
Women to Trinity for a speech, but McGuire forbade it on the grounds that
NOW sought a platform to target the church. But when it comes to alums, she
thinks the college ought to maintain a climate of "hospitality and welcome." A
same-sex couple had worried about returning for alumnae events, and
McGuire told them that of course they were welcome, despite the church's
opposition to gay rights. McGuire said she thinks a college is the kind of place
that should serve as forum for opposing viewpoints, not as judge of them or
sanctuary from them. "Alma mater means the mother of us all," she said.

Mothering its students, intellectually and spiritually, is the same mission the
school has always had—when it was founded in 1897, and when Pelosi went
there from 1958 to 1962.

"You feel that spirit of our founders here," said Olivo. "Those cloistered nuns stood up to the priests at Catholic University, they wrote to the pope and got the school incorporated by Congress." They eventually persuaded the Church that Washington needed a college exclusively for women. In fact, a few of the nuns of the Notre Dame De Namur order still live on campus in the Main Hall, still serving as spiritual godmothers to the girls on campus and still pushing Trinity to live up to its high ideals of social justice and emancipating women. About 20 years ago, they pushed Trinity to redefine itself and open its doors to the women right in its backyard. In Pelosi's time, Trinity had been the elite destination of Catholic girls all along the eastern seaboard. But today, it is working-class and first-generation college students who benefit from Trinity's blend of service education and its nurturing of women leaders.

"The reason Trinity was founded was to reach out to young women seeking a higher education" at a time when the idea of a Catholic women's college was heresy, said Sister Margaret Claydon, who was president when Pelosi was there and still graces campus as professor emerita of English. "We're still reaching out to the needs of women. They're just not the same women."

McGuire said 95 percent of her students are now on student aid, and nearly half come from troubled high schools right in Washington. The shift in focus came in the early 1990s when the school was foundering because so many of its best recruits had been siphoned off by Georgetown and other Catholic men's schools when they went coed. Trinity thought about going coed, too, but decided its core mission was too tied up with improving women's lives. Instead, it opened a weekend college aimed at older working women who were trying to get or finish a BA. Under McGuire, the college leapt with both feet into the burgeoning continuing education market. Eventually, some of the daughters of those older women students started applying to the undergrad program, and Trinity reacted by seeking out more. Enrollments started going back up. Alumnae who initially resisted the change in philosophy came around and started donating more money. Now Trinity is thriving again.

"It proves the old adage, you *can* do well by doing good," said McGuire. "We do what we do because we want to do good, to make the world a better place."

Trinity, said Olivo, "is truer to its original mission now than it has ever been. Pelosi told us how proud she is of that when she was her for the Mass."

Leah Martin, a 2007 graduate who was president of the student government her senior year, said Pelosi's ascendance makes her think anything's possible for a woman. Leah, like the majority of Trinity students now, was the first of her family from "southern, southern, southern Hickville, Louisiana," to go to college. "I was supposed to cook for lots of people and make Italian babies," she said. Instead she went to Trinity and now is one of 10 students nationwide taking part in a Charles B. Rangel International Affairs Graduate Fellowship. The State Department program guarantees her a spot as a U.S. Foreign Service Officer after grad school.

Leah sounds a lot like a certain famous alumna when she talks about how Trinity shaped and deepened her commitment to social justice. "Because we are a superpower," Leah said in a recent interview, "we have a social responsibility, yet in many situations, that seems to be forgotten. Infusing ethics in foreign policy is where I feel I can have the greatest impact." Just days before graduation, she said: "It's now up to us to serve people. Not help people, serve people. To whom much is given, much is required."

Though black and Latino students from poor backgrounds make up a larger proportion of students at Trinity in the twenty-first century, they still hold singing contests in the dorms as Pelosi and her friends did, they still get their Trinity pins sophomore year when they declare their majors, they still wear an unusual garment called a "stock"—a sheer turtleneck that gives the students a kind of clerical look—under their graduation gowns.

And they still gather in the Main Hall's Hogswartsesque stairwell for the Well Sing after juniors get their class rings, just as Pelosi and her classmates did. It remains the most beloved tradition at Trinity: freshmen on the top floor, seniors on the ground—four stories of women lining the banisters and singing to each other across the well and across the years to all the sisters who came before.

CHAPTER 3

PELOSI'S FAMILY VALUES

To me, the center of my life will always be raising my family. It is the complete joy of my life. To me, working in Congress is a continuation of that.

—Nancy Pelosi, February 5, 2003

Georgetown University, an all-male-boys school at the time, and Trinity, an all-female school, were like brother and sister in the 1960s. Although the two colleges were separate academically, socially they were Washington's Harvard and Radcliffe, more or less one big Catholic family. Georgetown and Trinity often held joint dances, parties, mixers, even bridge tournaments. Trinity had afternoon teas that Georgetown boys were invited to, and it was not uncommon to see a Georgetown lad talking to all the gals in the smoker at Cuvilly Hall, though the nuns kept a careful watch on them. The visiting students had to sign in and out when they visited campus, and no boys were allowed overnight. "It was a strict environment," said a classmate of Pelosi's, Joan Clarke. "We had curfews every night. They were looking after us."

That didn't mean the girls didn't try to get around the rules a bit—all that authority made a little rebellion that much more irresistible. Pelosi was part of the "Green Class" of 1962—every incoming class was assigned its own signature color—and "being Green" obligated the girls to go over once a year to drink green beer at Georgetown behind the nuns' backs.

"We used to go down to the Library of Congress just to meet the Georgetown law students, because that's where they studied," said Clarke. "Plus, we used to have these touch football games with the Georgetown prefects.

We knew a lot of the boys at Georgetown." It was at Georgetown that Pelosi would meet her future husband.

Clarke describes Pelosi as very popular in college, a friend to everybody. "If you wanted to go talk to her about anything she was such an excellent listener," said Clarke. "She takes everything in and assimilates it. It's probably what makes her such a good politician." Clarke said Pelosi was very well respected even then and remembers her as always very happy, with a sunniness that was infectious. "Pleasant," "affable," and "reachable" are the three adjectives college friends use the most to describe her. (She and former Senator Al Simspon were once named the best dinner companions in Congress.) "I loved Trinity College," she told students there during a return visit. "It was an absolute joy to go there."

During the summer of 1961, she took a class on sub-Saharan African history at Georgetown, where she met a tall, thin Foreign Service student from out West, Paul Pelosi. Paul's family was active in Democratic politics in San Francisco, which gave the two something to bond over right away. Paul's brother Ron was a long-time member of the city's Board of Supervisors and a well-known personality on KQED, San Francisco's educational TV station. Like Nancy, Paul had attended Catholic schools growing up, including an all-boys prep school in Pennsylvania, Malvern. He was good with numbers and was planning a career in banking after college. Nancy describes him as a "lovely, calm person. He's a good sport. Magnificently cooperative." Her friend Anna Eshoo said "They just don't come any better. We've all adopted him because he's so fabulous." One other observer remarked that he's extraordinarily handsome as well.

Among prominent Catholic families of the day who sent their children to Washington for school, it was pretty much assumed that Trinity daughters would marry Georgetown sons. A year and three months after graduation, on September 7, 1963, Nancy and Paul did just that. A D'Alesandro cousin, the Reverend Felix Cardegna, performed the service in Baltimore's Cathedral of Mary Our Queen rather than St. Leo's in Little Italy, another small sign of Pelosi's independence from the family legend. Nancy, all of 23 years old, wore an embroidered lace mantilla for the ceremony and carried a bouquet of white glamellias, an invented flower handmade from gladiolus petals. "I went in relatively young by today's standards," Pelosi said.

Friends say Paul and Nancy have a great marriage, that Paul is easy to be around and extraordinarily proud of Nancy. In a Today Show interview in 2005, when Pelosi was minority leader, Paul was asked what it was like to be married to Nancy. He hesitated a bit before answering. "What's it like?" he asked back. "I'm interested in hearing this answer myself," Nancy interjected.

"It's an extremely demanding job, so it hasn't been a lot of laughs," answered Paul rather forthrightly. The grueling schedule of a congressional leader means a lot of time apart for the couple, but her powerful position doesn't rattle his male ego in the least, people close to them say. "When you're a man who has made $25 million, like Paul has, you're pretty secure in your self-esteem," said one friend.

Though she thought she would be headed to law school after Trinity, Pelosi's plans were set aside—as her mother's had been—when she gave birth to her first baby, Nancy Corinne , in 1964, less than a year after she and Paul were married. She then proceeded to spend the remainder of the 1960s pregnant. In six years and one week, she gave birth to four girls and one boy—the mirror image of her own family in Baltimore, which was four boys and one girl. Pelosi has "no amnesia about how much work it was." In addition to Nancy Corinne, she bore Christine, Jacqueline, and Paul Jr. in New York, where she and Paul moved when he took a job with First National City Bank (now Citicorp). After five years there, they moved the family to San Francisco, Paul's hometown, when he went to work for a company that was leasing computers to the businesses that were just starting to populate an area south of the city that came to be known as Silicon Valley. Paul familiarized himself with all aspects of the new economy on the way to amassing his fortune, mostly from property investments. Alexandra was the only child born in San Francisco.

For 25 years, family came before politics for Pelosi—in theory. When most politicians of her age were cutting their teeth in state legislatures or city councils, Pelosi was changing diapers—gladly and proudly. Ironing was God's work in her world; she refused to outsource any of the childrearing chores. She also turned down invitations to run for office until her youngest, Alexandra, was nearly finished with high school.

"I really was forged by my children," Pelosi recounted in an interview in the Speaker's office. "Having five children in six years and understanding the difference in personalities, from one to the next, is a real lesson, but also you become so disciplined in terms of schedule and use of time and respect for everyone's needs that I think I'm a much different person coming out of raising my kids that I was going in. I didn't realize I had as much energy as I did. Let's put it that way."

"She ran her household and raised her children in a very serious way," said Eshoo. "And she knew that it was serious work. And she did not have maids and servants. She insisted on doing it herself." Eshoo recounts a conversation they've had on the subject: "I raised five children," Pelosi told her.

" 'People think: Isn't that precious? Now, stop and think about it. You really have to know what you're doing to run a household.' "

Pelosi often cites her years as a mother of four girls and one boy as the best preparation anyone could have for Congress. What is Congress after all but eighth grade on steroids, a houseful of overgrown egomaniacal kids all jockeying for love and power?

"Having five children in six years is the best training in the world for Speaker of the House," Pelosi told the *AARP Bulletin*. "It made me the ultimate multitasker and the master of focus, routine and scheduling." She has said often in her speeches that the arts of negotiation, compromise, and relationship building that women practice at home are perfectly suited to lawmaking.

"She has a maternal style. She brings a discipline, an understanding, a kindness, a respect that is reflected in the focus that she brings to each member. It's authentic," said Eshoo.

Anyone who has been a mother knows a secret: Motherhood *is* power, said Berkeley professor Robin Lakoff, who writes about gender differences in language and leadership. "Anybody who has ever had a mother knows that one thing that a good mother does, is . . . when you need to crack down, you crack down. And no matter how you crack down, whether it's time-outs or whatever, you gotta be tough. And that's what the Democrats clearly needed. Somebody had to say 'Be nice to your brother.'" Prior Speakers and majority leaders such as Tom "the Hammer" Delay often governed by force and intimidation, sheer machismo, or threats and blustering: "the alpha male silverback strategy," Lakoff argues. While that does often produce the desired results, it can also lead to secret (or not-so-secret) resentments. And when someone who has run things by brute force finds himself in trouble, very often the others are only too happy to pull him down and drive him out. Pelosi takes a more consensual approach, just as a mother might. She's tough, but never lets her toughness damage her relationships with people over the long term.

There's some hard evidence to back up Pelosi's case for the advantages of a Motherhood School of Management. A recent study out of Wellesley College asked a large group of prominent women from around the world where they thought they gained their leadership skills. A majority of them said through mothering. The 60 participants in the study were leaders in education, nonprofits, communications, and finance. They spoke of mothering as "both a training ground for leadership and a metaphor for describing leadership behavior. . . . The majority of these leaders combined a strong focus on results with equal attention to the growth and development of the people surrounding them." In her best-selling book, *The Price of Motherhood*, Ann Crittenden, a former economics reporter for the *New York Times*, cites studies that estimate a market value of mothers' services to the economic well-being of communities as worth about $100,000 a year. And that was in 2001.

Columnist Ellen Goodman recently wrote that some well-known companies are now deliberately and directly recruiting from an older, female hiring pool. They see child-raising skills as qualities that are needed at the office. "Need someone for multitasking? Instant problem solving? Motivating and organizing people with, um, different personalities? Mom's the one," Goodman wrote. "Pelosi's a reminder to women that life is longer than you expect. She's a reminder to companies and the country that we have a lot to gain from welcoming parents into the second act."

Pat McGuire, president of Trinity, thinks Pelosi's unique balancing act of motherhood and career make her an interesting model. First of all, "She inspires middle-aged women, or women returning to the work force after having kids or raising kids, that there is a second act," said McGuire. And she also inspires a new generation of women who are looking for more balance between their careers and their home lives than the career "superwomen" of the 1980s and '90s.

"The supermom model is a relic," McGuire said. "For Generation X and Generation Y in the late 1990s, the having-it-all model generated a lot of cynicism and apathy. It just couldn't be done." Millennials—the generation that started entering the workforce right after the turn of the century—are a more pragmatic, more idealistic, more politically engaged lot, McGuire finds. They want good lifestyles, they want families, and they all expect to be treated the same as men coming out of college. They expect the businesses they work for to provide adequate benefits, flexibility and time off for them to be moms and still keep their jobs. Some of those expectations are thanks to the hard work of the superwomen who came before them, of course.

Often, said McGuire, these young women get smacked in the head by residual cultural prejudices they didn't even know existed, such as an employer telling a young woman during a job interview that he can't hire her because of a chance she may have children. "Mommy track barriers? You can't tell that to a 19-year-old or a 20-year-old," said McGuire. "They don't believe it until it happens to them."

In general, the millennials are much more inclined to believe that their professional identity is only half of who they are, McGuire said.

"They want a good lifestyle, but I hear them saying: 'We want a balanced life' above all. There is this yearning right now for balance, a yearning for [role] models to look at."

Pelosi has a strong professional identity, but her domestic identity is every bit as important to her—she said it's *more* important—and she's not afraid to announce it to the world. She told *USA Today:* "Nothing in my life will ever, ever compare to being a mom. Not being a member of Congress, not being Speaker of the House. I wish I could do it all over again, but my children won't give me my grandchildren."

This is what makes Pelosi so relevant as a model, McGuire believes: The most powerful career woman in America is proselytizing for the joys of motherhood. That kind of double prioritization of what's most important resonates right now with 19- and 20-year-old women. You can have it all, Pelosi is advising, but maybe just not all at the same time.

"Somebody like me, as Speaker of the House, has a responsibility to the younger generation of women to say: Don't think of this as a minus," Pelosi said. "This is a plus, being a mother, having an experience of raising a family."

Pelosi is especially a realist about "having it all" when she's advising women interested in going into politics. "Public service 'is the Lord's work,'" she explained recently. "I have always believed that, and it comes with tremendous rewards. But make no mistake, it is hard work. My advice to young women who are thinking about a commitment to public service: 'Have a life first.' Don't make public service your whole life first. Don't give in to being totally consumed by it, because you can be. Have a family. Nurture your family, and if you are single, develop friendships and relationships," she added. "Make sure your life in public service is not a total sacrifice of your whole life. Devote time to having a balanced life. Because the success of politics can overwhelm you. You cannot have your personal well-being depend on your political success. This is hard. There will be disappointments and you can't tie everything to it. You must have a sense of self beyond the politics."

With such straight talk, Pelosi is breaking ground culturally as a role model. Until now, women in Congress and in other powerful positions in the United States have mostly downplayed their maternal qualities, downplayed their family commitments, and even downplayed their femininity. Political analysts have long believed that the first woman to shatter the marble ceiling as Speaker or president would be a "Sister Mister," a woman with the body of a woman but the character traits of a man. Pelosi is no Sister Mister. Beginning in January 2007, when she brought a gaggle of children onto the Speaker's dais with her during her inauguration, she has *shown off* her mom creds rather than hidden them away. And for months since she took office she's taken every opportunity possible to remind people that she is not just a great fundraiser and crack political tactician, she's first and foremost a mom and grandmom. She's making a conscious effort to elevate the status of motherhood in the country, to bring it up onto the same plane as, say, national defense. In her speeches and though the agenda she's setting, Pelosi is making the case on a national stage that motherhood and children and families deserve as much attention from Washington as missile throwweights, homeland security and trade with China. Bush is guns; Pelosi is butter. It's a deliberate attempt to reset priorities, and she's in a position and has the popularity and clout to do it.

During her inauguration week, she mentioned so-called women's issues in all her speeches: better daycare, better flex time, better preschools. Pat Schroeder, the former Colorado congresswoman who enshrined the idea of parental leave for both men and women in the Family Leave Act, said she repeated it over and over: "We've got to deal with working family issues, we've got to deal with the working poor."

As a congresswoman, Pelosi won increased funding for breast cancer research, doubled the budget for the National Institutes of Health, and has long supported stem-cell research, much to the chagrin of the Catholic Church. In her first seven months as Speaker, she pushed through a hike in the minimum wage to help working moms, cut the interest rates on student loans, made some college tuition tax deductible, and passed legislation to continue and expand health insurance for children. There are promises—and demands—of more family-friendly legislation to come. She has labelled this "The Children's Congress."

"I have never heard anybody make those front and center, and now those are front and center," said Schroeder. "The American family, the real American family, is front and center."

Even before she was elected Speaker, Pelosi was promising that a new crop of female elected officials would have a "wholesome effect" on Washington. There is some evidence already of a snowball effect from the 2006 elections. Other women in Congress are following Pelosi's lead, asserting their agendas while they have a receptive leader. "Legislation that I work on will have a direct effect on the life of my children and even could save the lives of some of their peers," said Debbie Wasserman Schultz (D-Fla.), who introduced a pool safety bill this year. Wasserman Schultz is one of only four women in Congress in history who have had a child while in office.

"This is the first time in the history of our nation that a mother and grandmother is a Speaker. First time in the history of our nation that the Speaker bore children," said Eshoo. In other words, family may come first for

Pelosi, but "family" is more than nuclear to her. It's an agenda, a cause, a holy purpose—the gravitational center of her operating philosophy in politics. And it's not just in the last year that Pelosi has trumpeted this focus. In an interview with C-SPAN seven years ago, Pelosi said: "I always say that the three most important issues facing our Congress are our children, our children, our children." She called her work then, as minority whip, a seamless extension of caring for her own children. "There are some things you can't do for your kids at home," she said. "There are some things that are a matter of public policy. Like giving them clean air. That's the excitement of this for me. What are we doing for the next generation? What are we doing for the future?"

Eshoo said this isn't a campaign bromide, this is Pelosi to the core: "The more the American people see her and hear her, they understand that she's doing everything that she can with her power on behalf of their families."

Pelosi, truth be told, has always mixed politics and motherhood. It's never really been a question of one before the other. Daughter Alexandra Pelosi, a documentary filmmaker, can picture her mother with a phone in one hand and the iron in the other, managing both family and party.

"My mom says that my political activism began in the stroller," recalled Christine in an interview. "Every year, right before Halloween, we went door-to-door through our apartment building with election leaflets. Then a few days later we returned for trick-or-treating. To this day, my mom is not entirely sure whether the leaflets we handed out had any bearing on the kind of treats we received. Maybe all that excess chocolate from certain neighbors was a coincidence."

On weekends when Pelosi was volunteering for the party, the kids became the "stuffers and sealers."

"We five kids would have a little assembly line system," Christine told the *San Francisco Chronicle*. "One of us would stuff, one would seal, one would stamp and so on." Alexandra, the youngest, licked until her tongue was parched. Sometimes the children would sing "He's got the stuffers and the sealers in his hands" to the tune of "He's Got the Whole World in His Hands."

Pelosi often dressed up the kids in matching outfits and took them along to get-out-the-vote drives or campaign fundraisers. The outfits helped her keep track of them. Though Pelosi always says family came before politics, her children say their experience more closely resembles the political childhood Nancy had, where family life *was* politics. Though Pelosi didn't enter Congress until she was 47 and most of the children grown, her political apprenticeship began long before that, blurring the lines between the business of politics and the business of raising kids.

Right after her wedding in September of 1963, Pelosi went to work as an intern for Senator Daniel B. Brewster of Maryland, alongside the man who was to become her longtime leadership rival, Steny Hoyer. Pelosi, who like her father rarely forgot an injustice done to her, may have gotten off on the wrong foot right with Hoyer because of the institutional sexism of Congress. Her internship was her first taste of the double standard accorded men and women on the Hill: While Steny got a plum assignment working directly for Brewster on different projects right out of college, Pelosi, daughter of a political dynasty, was assigned secretarial work. Brewster called her "an excellent front person."

Asked if he and Pelosi were friends 40 years ago, Hoyer said the term "friends" would overstate it. "We didn't run in the same crowd. Nancy came from an extraordinarily prominent family," he explains. Hoyer was already married and working full-time for Brewster when Pelosi interned there. "I was there year-round. I worked for Brewster four years," he said. "But I do make the observation that if somebody had come in the office and seen a very bright, exciting, enthusiastic young woman sitting there as a receptionist, and seeing this skinny kid over there in the corner opening envelopes, and somebody told him that woman there is going to be Speaker and that young man there is going to be Majority Leader, I'd say you gotta be crazy. No way that's gonna happen. I mean it really is an irony."

Though Pelosi left the East Coast to follow Paul, she said she wasn't about to let her mind atrophy during the mom years. "One of the things I insisted on when I moved to California was that I would get the *New York Times* delivered every day," she said. "That was harder in those days. But I had to keep in touch. Do that daily crossword puzzle. It kept my brain going."

Once ensconced in San Francisco, Pelosi quickly began to replicate all the rituals and practices of the big Catholic family she had grown up in. Her girls all went to the Convent of the Sacred Heart school, and she began raising them with strict Catholic discipline. Even her three-story house in Pacific Heights looks like the three-story brick row house she grew up in Baltimore.

Or, more correctly, it looks like two of her childhood homes linked together by a courtyard.

"She modeled our house in San Francisco after the house where she grew up in Baltimore," according to Alexandra. "Our house was like a VFW hall. She'd be working the issues from there, stuffing mailers, having parties."

"When I asked your daughter Christine how you rule, she said you were motherly," Leslie Stahl told Pelosi on CBS's *60 Minutes*. "I guess it depends on your definition of motherly. If motherly means—we'll have order in the house, yes," Pelosi replied.

Christine said Mom was the disciplinarian in the family. "We were always expected to make sure our homework was done; and that we were prepared for what we did. She would always say, 'Proper preparation prevents poor performance.'"

Pelosi organized her house like it was a precinct headquarters. After clearing the dinner table each evening, the children would set it again for breakfast. A variety of lunchmeats, ten slices of whole-wheat bread, bags of pretzels, and apples were laid out along the kitchen counter in the morning, and the kids put together their own lunches as if they were working an assembly line again.

"She was a total mom," Alexandra, told the *Baltimore Sun*. "She was always the class mom baking cookies. She would go to all our games." Alexandra said Pelosi doted on them, even sewing Halloween costumes for all the children. "I was an angel one year with these elaborate wings that she made." Mom never hesitated to hand out philosophical advice to her girls. "Never marry a cheap man," she'd tell her daughters. "If he's cheap with money, he'll be cheap with love."

Alexandra told People magazine that she and her siblings were not an easy crew, however: "We were like the kids from *The Simpsons*—she couldn't get anyone to babysit." When Alexandra was breast-feeding, Pelosi's other children were two, three, four, and five respectively. Might as well have been quintuplets. Pelosi confirms the lack of babysitters, but puts a positive spin on it: "When you raise five children born six years apart, you do most of the work yourself. You can't attract a good deal of people to help out. It trains you to anticipate, to be organized, to be flexible."

Schroeder points out that all families are like that in reality, and all mothers have to deal with it. "People talk about how families are this little island of tranquility. Hell no. It's the Bermuda triangle. It's chaos. Let's face it, that's how the average American family lives, and how a single-parent family lives is beyond me."

Eshoo said one of Pelosi's secrets to survival was Paul Pelosi. "She has an exceptionally wonderful life with Paul," said Eshoo. "There isn't anything this man hasn't done for his family. They just don't come any better." Though he keeps his distance from the political world, he spends a week or so every month in Washington to be with her and is at her side during many fundraisers. He also will TiVO *The Daily Show With Jon Stewart* for her.

"My father is the best advertisement for my mom," Alexandra told Vogue. "He is the opposite of those buzzards in Washington. He's interested in art, loves singing, acts in plays like *The Music Man* for charity. You'd be amazed at how little politics gets talked about at their dinner table."

In the *60 Minutes* segment filmed in the fall of 2006, Paul admitted to Stahl that he buys Nancy's suits for her, mainly because she herself doesn't have the time or the inclination to shop. He also told Stahl that the notion of a political career for Nancy never came up when they were raising their kids. "It wasn't even on the table. It wasn't even part of the discussion," he said. "Nothing in her personality—it was never going to happen. Well, we end up in San Francisco. We raise our five children and when the children were in school all day, then she started doing volunteer stuff."

Alexandra thought her mom would become known for her Thanksgiving cranberry sauce, not politics. "My mom always said she would start selling it, and if you'd asked me fifteen years ago what was going to make her famous, I would have said it would be that sauce. Sort of like Mrs. Fields," she said to Vogue.

Christine said her mom's re-entry into politics came in baby steps. "It was unfathomable to us then that she would become Speaker of the House 40 years later. But politics isn't about the big leap to power; it's about the thousands of steps you take with your neighbors along the way."

Actually, Pelosi started volunteering shortly after her arrival in San Francisco—first by offering up her house in the elegant Presidio Terrace neighborhood for Democratic Party functions. Even with three children in diapers, Pelosi found time to host fundraising parties, coffees, and meet-and-greets for Democratic candidates. She learned the territory in those years, learned where the levers and valves of a complex political town were. She found that pretty, pastel San Francisco, so different in style and reputation from her down-and-dirty hometown of Baltimore, wasn't that different politically. Both cities are Democratic port towns with strong unions running the shipping industry and therefore deeply involved in each city's political life. Both cities are a gumbo of nationalities and political leanings. In 1940s Baltimore, when she was growing up, it was Italians, Poles, Jews,

African Americans, and Irish all trying to mix together as the city slowly desegregated. In San Francisco in the 1970s, it was Asian Americans, gays, hippies, whites, blacks, and the suits of one of the West Coast's most important financial districts all maneuvering for power.

"San Francisco has an extraordinarily strong pressure cooker," said Alex Clemens, a longtime political activist, organizer, and consultant in San Francisco. "And the people who hold public office who come out of San Francisco have built up several centimeters of new thick skin. They're able to talk about any topic under the sun with a great deal of authority and knowledge because we have so many cutting-edge issues that affect San Franciscans." Both San Francisco and Baltimore are roiling cauldrons of political interests, and both have a history of rough-and-tumble door-to-door political combat as a result. They're both towns that tend to produce politicians with a bit of piss and vinegar in them as a result, from Tommy D'Alesandro to Barbara Mikulski to Hiram Johnson to Phillip Burton to Dianne Feinstein.

Paul was interested and involved in Democratic politics as well. He attended St. Ignatius High School in San Francisco with Jerry Brown, who was elected governor of California in 1974. He and Paul had stayed friends, and Brown asked for his help when he decided to take on Jimmy Carter in the race for the Democratic presidential nomination in 1976. Carter had rolled up a number of wins in the earlier primaries before Brown jumped into the race. Most pundits had already ordained Carter as the nominee by April, 1976. But Brown thought he could stop the juggernaut. He decided that the Maryland primary, on May 18, 1976, was his best shot. Brown asked Pelosi to use her family's political muscle in Baltimore to help him. Always the overachiever, Pelosi instead volunteered to run the Maryland campaign for Brown herself. She was 36 at the time.

Pelosi accompanied Brown to Baltimore and the favor file kicked in. Governor George Mandel, whom Tommy D'Alesandro had helped win the chairmanship of the Democratic caucus in the state legislature, met Brown at the airport, repaying the favor Tommy had done for him by putting the Baltimore Democratic machine to work for Brown. Many of Baltimore's biggest political figures campaigned for and with Brown, helping him win the state 49 percent to 37 percent, Carter's first primary defeat.

Back in California, the four daughters fought over who got to serve bagels to singer Linda Ronstadt at fundraisers for Brown when the two were dating. But Brown couldn't hold his home state, and Carter went on to beat him in the race for the nomination. Pelosi, however, had proven her ability to deliver results thanks to the D'Alesandro machine, and from then on she was a player in California Democratic politics.

"That's the episode that took me out of the kitchen and put me into official party responsibilities," she told the *Los Angeles Times*.

She often tells interviewers that she got involved in politics almost by accident, but the personal ambition and commitment to the party she showed in those years while she was raising a family belie that particular piece of the Pelosi myth. As a young mom, she went door to door for various Democratic causes, often pushing a stroller in one hand and carrying another baby in the other. She said she didn't have time to wash her face when the kids were growing up, but she did find time to march against the Vietnam War when Alexandra was an infant. When she was campaigning for Brown on the other side of the country, her youngest child was 5 and her oldest was 11. Because of her success in that campaign, she was named northern chairwoman of the California Democratic Party. She served for three years, from 1977 to 1981. Her children at the time ranged in ages from 7 to 13, still in need of plenty of attention. But none of the children has ever complained about an absentee mom, because she took the kids with her. Jacqueline Pelosi Kennally, the third of Pelosi's children, remembers seeing her mother at a town meeting in San Francisco immersed in conversation with her "shocking" and "wild" constituency—the transgendered group in one corner, the homeless activists in another. Jacqueline remembers thinking "Oh my god, what's my mom doing here?"

"I raised my children outside of consulates and embassies, where we could protest repression in any country around the world," said Pelosi. "In San Francisco, we were regulars outside the Soviet Consulate. We picketed the civic dinner in honor of Ferdinand Marcos when he came to City Hall."

In 1981, thanks in large part to her networking abilities, which translated neatly into fundraising prowess, Pelosi was elected to a two-year term as chairwoman of the California Democratic Party. This is not a part-time job. By this time, Pelosi had her hands full on both the political and domestic fronts because she had an 11-year old and four teenagers on her hands. Friends say she coped by tapping her enormous reserves of energy, often sleeping only four hours a night.

In 1984, she chaired the host committee for the Democratic Party's national presidential convention in San Francisco, sharing the credit for bringing it to her adopted hometown. The convention was an inspiring one for Pelosi, planting the seeds about the possibilities ahead for women in politics. The convention was organized by a woman, Pelosi; chaired by another woman, Kentucky Governor Martha Layne Collins; and produced the first woman to be nominated by either party for the Presidency or Vice-Presidency, Geraldine Ferraro. In her book about the media and presidential elections, *Sneaking into the Flying Circus*, Alexandra mentioned that the 1984 convention was her favorite. "The first thing she [Pelosi] did when there was a glitch in the convention schedule was order more food and alcohol for reporters," Alexandra writes. "She said that as long as they are eating and drinking they won't be writing bad stories."

That was when Alexandra knew she wanted to be a journalist, she added.

The convention was a huge success logistically and Pelosi's career as a political operative really began to ramp up as a result, fueled in no small part by her own ambition. It was during this time that Leo McCarthy, the Democratic elder statesman of California politics, began to notice what an asset Pelosi was to the party and took her under his wing. McCarthy was "one of her great mentors," said Eshoo, who was a staffer for McCarthy before she became a congresswoman. "Leo McCarthy was a statesman, a great champion for justice, a dear friend and a purposeful mentor to me," Pelosi said after his death in early 2007. "I am proud to have called Leo friend for more than 30 years. He encouraged me to not only support candidates but to go into politics in my own right."

McCarthy and his high school friend, former state senator John Foran, formed the heart of one of San Francisco's two major political factions. The other was the Burton Machine, made up of Phil and John Burton, George Moscone, and Willie Brown. In the 1960s, the two political powerhouses and their protégés battled for political control of San Francisco. It's a testament to Pelosi's powers of conciliation that she can count both the Burtons and McCarthy as mentors.

McCarthy was Speaker of the Assembly from 1974 to 1980 and lieutenant governor of California from 1983 to 1995, all the while counting Pelosi as one of his closest allies. "Leo promoted a values-based agenda to educate our children, grow our economy, and protect our environment," Eshoo said, all things Pelosi would later stress in her time in Congress. "And he did so living up to the highest ethical standard." Pelosi has said McCarthy was the inspiration for her consistency in sticking to her principles, for following her conscience in politics. From him she learned a politics steeped in social justice. "Simply put for me, without Leo's guidance over the years, there would not be a woman Speaker of the House," Pelosi told graduates at the University of San Francisco.

McCarthy knew Pelosi inside and out, especially her long memory for insults and her myriad methods of payback. "When she meets someone who has done some conniving or tried to carve her up behind her back, she often will treat that person graciously, because she knows there are always an infinite number of ways you can retaliate," McCarthy once told the *Baltimore Sun*.

McCarthy and other party bigwigs, including Governor Mario Cuomo of New York, supported Pelosi later in 1984, when she ran for national party chairman against party treasurer Paul G. Kirk Jr., a former aide to Sen. Edward M. Kennedy. Pelosi thought Kirk was too liberal and would alienate southern voters, a criticism that would later be lodged frequently against her. "The Democratic Party must move to the center," she said in a letter during her campaign. "In America, there is only one center that counts—that is the economic center." She urged that Democrats become the "party of capitalism." She was also betting that California gave her the numbers to make her a viable candidate.

After a hard-fought campaign, Pelosi ended up withdrawing from the race on the day it was to be decided, saying it was clear that she didn't have the votes to win. It was the only significant loss she has ever endured in her political career, and she was bitter about it. "People tell me that I was the best-qualified candidate. But some of them tell me that it's too bad that I'm not a man," she said privately. "If I had known I would be judged as a woman, I wouldn't have entered it. . . ." At an impromptu news conference the next day, she told reporters that many delegates had said to her: "'How can you expect me to support a woman?' I really think it isn't the message the party needs right now."

Several Democratic Party officials admitted that her gender worked against her. Many Democrats at the time thought another Italian American woman, Ferraro, had hurt the presidential ticket in 1984 by prompting Democratic white males unhappy with her candidacy to vote Republican. So Ferraro's unsuccessful run actually hurt Pelosi's candidacy.

"This is a lousy time for Democratic women," said one Democrat from the West. A North Carolinian said the party didn't need another Italian American lady leading them. The gender gap was alive and well at that time, and men weren't ashamed to admit it. Pelosi said that during the campaign, a union official working for Kirk's campaign had labeled her an "airhead." When a union spokesman was asked if the allegation was true, he both denied it and repeated it. "He never called her an airhead, a female airhead or a Baltimore airhead." More than any other single incident, the loss and the reasons for it left her with a moral indignation that drove her up Capitol Hill for years and years after. Her own ambition could now be lashed to the greater, more selfless cause of helping emancipate politics. That sense of being an outsider, of not having a seat at the table, provided much of the rocket fuel that would propel her rise. After raising her family, she had a holy mission again: to smash the old boy's network in Washington once and for all.

Pelosi's aggressive campaign did land her a significant consolation prize: the job of finance chair for the Democratic Senatorial Campaign Committee. In that role, Pelosi was on the national stage for the first time, and she rose to the occasion by raising hundreds of thousands of dollars for Democratic Senate candidates, sharing in the credit when the Democrats retook control of the Senate in 1986.

Throughout her rise, Pelosi was asking social friends and Paul's investment banking acquaintances to donate to the Democratic Party, always making the argument that they could use their wealth to make a real difference in the world. Pelosi quickly found she had a knack for converting wealthy friends to the Democratic cause. "If you travel in upper-socioeconomic circles, it's always good to tap those people," Agar Jaicks, a San Francisco Democratic activist, told *the Chronicle*, "She became very good at it, and the better she got, the more in demand she was."

Once she got beyond her own circle of friends, Pelosi made new friends out of the donors she rounded up. She has a way of making contributors feel they are part of a small club with mighty purpose, when in reality that club has become enormous. She maintains a mind-boggling number of friendships, regularly touching base with as many as 2,000 people, sending them notes, remembering children's birthdays, calling the friends/supporters up seeking advice on policy. Her father was the same way, her brother said, never forgetting a constituent's vital stats. Friends say Pelosi has a prodigious memory for birthdays and details of the lives of her friends' families.

"She's made friends with people from all over the country over the years, not only in the roles she has played in Congress, but from the roles she played in her party before that," said Eshoo. "I don't know anyone [else] that has made a friend that has so kept her friends and her friendships for her entire life. You know how people have different chapters to their life? Not Nancy. She'll be the first one to call a college roommate to say I know today is the birthday of your grandchild."

John Burton said Pelosi has too many friends and supporters in San Francisco to name. "She doesn't have a close circle, she has an ever-widening circle," Burton told the *San Francisco Chronicle*.

It was a friendship with John Burton's sister-in-law, a friendship that outlasted Sala Burton's life, that put Nancy Pelosi into Congress for the first time.

CHAPTER 4

BACK IN THE GAME

I'm determined to make the universe a better place. Not the world, the universe.

—Phillip Burton, congressman from San Francisco, 1926–1983

It was a request made on a deathbed, a dying wish to which Pelosi couldn't say no. Congresswoman Sala Burton, the 61-year-old widow of one the giants of Capitol Hill, Phil Burton, knew Pelosi wouldn't be able to refuse. Pelosi was hosting a tea for the Convent of the Sacred Heart school, which all four of her daughters attended, when she got the call from Sala summoning her to Washington in January, 1987. Already many of the biggest names in California politics were jockeying to replace Burton as she lay dying, and she had made up her mind about who she wanted to fill her legacy.

Sala had won reelection in November but was losing a parallel battle with colon cancer that had taken a turn for the worse in early 1986. She disclosed the illness publicly before the vote and promised voters she would beat it, but her closest friends knew it was a long shot. She'd had surgery in August and had never really recovered; she'd been too ill to attend her own swearing in and instead had taken the oath of office in her bed at George Washington University Hospital.

As she lay there confronted with the undeniable fact of her own mortality, Sala summoned her family and closest friends for some final instructions and good-byes. In the room with her were her daughter Joy, her brother-in-law John Burton, who had represented an adjoining congressional district in San Francisco, Representative Don Edwards, pioneering congresswoman Mary Rose Oakar of Ohio, longtime friend Agar Jaicks, several other aides and relatives, and Nancy Pelosi.

Sala had called John to her hospital room earlier to tell him that she wanted "Nancy" to succeed her in Congress. For a moment, Burton wasn't sure who this Nancy she was talking about was—at the time Pelosi was a *former* state Democratic Party chairperson. She didn't hold any official title in the party in 1987 except "volunteer." But Sala soon made it clear that the Nancy she was talking about was Pelosi. She wanted to make sure the seat she held, the so-called Burton Seat because it was the same seat her late husband, Phil, had dominated for 20 years before she took it over when he died, would be kept in safe hands. She believed Pelosi was the person who would best represent the people who the Burtons had served for 30 years.

John Burton, a former state senate president as well as a former congressman, said Sala saw something in Pelosi way back then. "She saw it all, she saw it all, everything that Nancy is now," Burton recalled. "You know how Al Davis would say, the greatness that is the Oakland Raiders? Well, Sala saw the greatness that is Nancy Pelosi."

On the floor of the House after Pelosi's election as Speaker, George Miller, one of Pelosi's closest allies, said: "Sala made a decision that changed the history of the House of Representatives and our country forever."

Pelosi had been asked five years earlier by Phil Burton to consider running for John's congressional seat after John had decided not to run again. But Pelosi's five children weren't all out of the house yet, and she said she was not ready to start a congressional career. This time around, however, her youngest, Alexandra, was in high school, and Sala thought she might be ready. Pelosi had guessed what was coming and talked to her family about it, asking for their approval, but she herself was not certain she was ready. Alexandra answered her mother's doubts and worries succinctly: "Mom, get a life!"

"When Sala called everybody back to Washington when she was dying, I truly thought she was going to say 'Nancy's been my friend, she's Phillip's friend, she's our friend, and we ought to support her,'" said Burton. "None of that even got into it. It was all about her commitment to progressive Democratic principles and the fact that she's very smart, she's very hardworking, she's very diligent."

On her sickbed that night, Sala grilled Pelosi to see if she was truly interested in the job. Was Pelosi fully committed? Was she ready for long and grueling hours? Could she stand to be 3,000 miles away from Paul and her five children most of the week? She told Pelosi she would love it in Washington. She said: "You must promise me that you will run for my seat."

Pelosi looked Sala in the eyes and said: "I expect you to get well. If you do not, I would be honored to succeed you."

Marie Wilson, author of *Closing the Leadership Gap: Why Women Can and Must Help Run the World*, said Pelosi's entrance into politics mirrors the route taken by women who came into political life because they made a promise to their dying husbands. Early congresswomen were mostly a collection of widows who inherited their dead husbands' seats. "She has one of those histories that has not to do with political ambition. She has one of those stories that isn't about herself. It isn't about her," said Wilson.

Sala died on February 1, a month after she was sworn in. Sixty-three members of Congress attended the memorial for her in San Francisco City Hall. House Speaker Jim Wright of Texas described her in his eulogy as a "sort of den mother" for Congress. She served there for 10 years, but she had partnered with her legendary husband to dominate California Democratic politics for dozens of years before that. She was the human link between two of the most important public officials to come out of California: Nancy Pelosi and Phillip Burton.

Senator Gaylor Nelson of Wisconsin once said: "I spent thirty-two years in elective office, and I only met one absolute political genius. That was Phil Burton." Harold Meyerson of the *Washington Post* called Burton the single most important member of the House of Representatives in the 1960s and '70s. When Newt Gingrich and his Republican Revolution swept to power in 1994, *Almanac of American Politics* author Michael Barone called it "the collapse of the House that Phil Burton built." The late John Jacobs, in his extraordinary political biography of Burton, *A Rage for Justice*, said that to most people who encountered him, Phillip Burton was "the most compelling personality they ever met, a man whose relentless day and night politicking, strategic brilliance, and zest for combat distilled the raw essence of their profession."

"He was quite a figure," Pelosi said. "He was a lion, really a lion."

His brother, John Burton, said: "There's nobody smarter politically than Phillip."

One acquaintance called Burton a "one-man spectacle." Another, a "force of nature" and "politically superhuman." He was a towering eminence in the halls of Congress, with piercing brown eyes that bored into his targets and a "rasping voice he could magnify like a howitzer," Jacobs wrote. "He towered over his fellow politicians in hallway encounters, thumping his finger on their chests, spitting saliva as he shouted, consuming, as one witness put it, 'their very oxygen.' "

No one worked harder for liberal causes in California than Phil Burton. And if those around him didn't match his commitment and passion, they were subjected to the man's legendary rage. It was Sala who "cleaned up his messes," Jacobs wrote, "soothing and placating those he insulted or abused. She alone could intervene in a conversation to shut him up." With her as his sounding board, costrategist and edge-smoother, his achievements were legion.

He campaigned for civil rights at a time when the labor unions that supported him were doing everything they could to keep blacks out. In the 1960s, he pushed the Democratic Party to embrace the antiwar movement. In the 1970s, he forged a coalition between environmentalists and labor unions. In the last campaign of his life, according to Jacobs, he brought together police officers and gay rights activists. In his 19 years as a congressman, he brokered a landmark deal that created black-lung compensation for coal miners; pushed through legislation that established Supplemental Security Income for the aged, blind, and disabled; made strikers eligible for food stamps; pushed through the biggest expansion of the national parks ever; and abolished the House Un-American Activities Committee. He was one of the first members of Congress to introduce an AIDS bill. He also reformed Congress by subjecting committee chairmanships to secret ballot elections, breaking the power of the old Dixiecrat barons in deciding who led those committees.

"Phil Burton was an extraordinary politician," said Matthew Green. "Very aggressive, incredibly smart. And very arrogant. Burton loved the game. Issues were less important to him then getting things through." He also cared more about getting things done than getting the credit, and if by letting others claim credit to an accomplishment, he could guarantee a vote on a future piece of legislation, so much the better.

"I like people whose balls roar when they see justice . . ." Burton told Rian Malan in the November 1981 edition of *California* magazine. He saw the whole country as his jurisdiction, not just California. In a rare interview with a conservation magazine, Burton said that as far as he was concerned, poor people, workers, and racial minorities needed all the help they could get. The rest, especially corporate lobbyists who manipulate legislation for clients, were his enemies. "You have to learn how to terrorize the bastards," he told the interviewer.

Almost everyone who ever worked behind the scenes with Burton acknowledges his brilliance and effectiveness, but when he ran against Jim Wright for Democratic majority leader under Tip O'Neill, he lost by one heartbreaking vote. His arrogant style, his dominating personality, often amplified by alcohol, certainly got things done in his 19 years in the House but also rubbed his colleagues raw. His friend and colleague Abner Mikava said Phil "had a way of coalescing his enemies."

John Burton, who shares his brother's salty expressiveness, put it this way: "Phillip was liked and he was admired and he was feared, but I don't think love is the right word to describe what people felt with Phil. I mean they loved what he did, but they didn't love him. . . . Tip O'Neill once said, If Phillip had my bullshit, he wouldn't have been just the majority leader, he could have been the president."

Green believes the main ingredients of Pelosi's leadership style are the D'Alesandro family, Leo McCarthy, and Phil Burton.

"I think what she got from [Buron] was a machine," Green said. Burton "helped recruit candidates for office and even went so far as single-handedly redrawing the districts in California in the 1980 census to help certain people get elected and to screw the Republicans and favor the Democrats."

Corey Cook, who teaches politics at the University of San Francisco and keeps a close eye on California state politics, thinks San Francisco is more of a fabulous political support group than a get-out-the-vote-and-bust-some-kneecaps kind of political machine like the one invented by legendary Chicago mayor Richard J. Daly. "I think it's a misnomer to call it a machine, because it's not a machine in the sense of it actually being a real political machine . . . but it's clearly a network of folks who are developing leaders behind them as well. It's a nurturing environment for political leaders." Burton used to call Pelosi every Sunday morning, her former chief of staff, Judy Lemons, said. He points out that Pelosi and John Burton have known each other for 30 years, and San Francisco Mayor Gavin Newsom and Pelosi have known each other for 20. "These folks are very much invested in her career. I think that's the case with a lot of San Francisco politicians," said Cook. "Those sort of long-term connections in a small politically engaged town with high political stakes produces these statewide and national leaders."

Pelosi and Phil Burton started working together shortly after the Pelosis arrived in San Francisco from New York. "You have a big house" is the first thing Pelosi remembers Phil telling her. "We'll be using it for Democratic Party events."

But John Burton said Phil didn't necessarily take Pelosi under his wing, mentor to mentee. "I mean, Christ, this is a woman who was brought up in Baltimore politics. He wasn't working with some neophyte that all of a sudden he had to explain 'Well, here's how it works.' They got along because even though she was an 'amateur' at that time, she was still a pro. And Phil was clearly a pro." Burton said Pelosi got her sense of service from her father. His brother then helped her "hone her skills."

Asked how Burton added to the political education her family gave her, Pelosi said: "Actually, my family really prepared me more for Phil Burton. One of the reasons I got along with Phil is because I wasn't afraid of him. I knew a lot of people like him."

Pelosi worked on Phil's congressional campaigns as a volunteer and was state Democratic Party chair when he ran for Speaker of the House in California. "She and Phil were very close," John said. George Miller, another of Burton's protégés, said Phil and Pelosi had the same value system about why they were in the business of politics. "There's a lot of Phil in her in terms of shared principles of government. Why people come to public service. Why people should be in elective office. What you're supposed to do if you get the privilege to have one of these seats in the Congress."

Miller said Pelosi was able to observe Burton's style of governing closely. "He was a person who thought three moves ahead, or down the road in terms of the Congress. Sometimes Phillip would talk to you in January, and the clarity of the conversation wasn't apparent until May or June." A lot of that is in Pelosi, Miller believes. She has a great field of vision. "She sees the end of the road, where she wants to be. It's about what has to be done to get there and what's the sequencing of that. The caucus has now come to appreciate that vision, that sort of horizon that she has."

"Phil saw in her the drive, the good instinct, and the leadership that she could bring, and he saw how she could organize. And so he had great respect for her skills in that way and the success that she'd already brought to Democrats in the state," said Lemons.

"Phil knew that a seed had been planted, and that he intended to nurture Nancy as much as he could. And of course Sala picked up that mantel and loved Nancy with all of her heart and chose her and wanted her to succeed her," Lemons added.

What Phillip—and later Sala—saw in Pelosi boils down to one word, Miller said. "Operational. Flat-out operational. He saw this smart person that understood politics and policy and was operational in getting things done. That's all he was about. At the end of the day he would ask you, what did you do to pay the rent today? He'd call me up and ask 'What'd you *do*? What'd you *do*? What'd you *do*?' He was about using this office to get things *done*."

John Burton was the same way. Anna Eshoo calls John one of Pelosi's most important mentors. He shared his brother's brilliance, Eshoo said, and although he "rubs people like sandpaper he knows how to win, how to get things done."

It wasn't love at first sight between John and Pelosi, however. Pelosi recalled that when she met John at a 1972 McGovern for President rally, he would not talk to her because "I had not earned my stripes." Burton said that was more because, at the time, she was part of a different wing of the Democratic Party, the Leo McCarthy wing as opposed to the Burton wing. "Her brother-in-law, Ronald, was part of Leo's group, and that's how they got her active in politics. And she became active when Leo was speaker."

Pelosi was getting political advice from Leo McCarthy until the day before he died.

Although Leo, Philip, and John were huge influences, Pelosi isn't a carbon copy of any of them. "Oh my god, she has all these actual human qualities" that Phil Burton didn't possess in the least, said Miller.

"My approach was quite different from Phil's. His would not be described as diplomatic or listening, or any of that. But we are both results-oriented," Pelosi said. And both shared a deep-rooted passion for righting social wrongs. "Oh my God, yes," Pelosi agreed, "liberty and justice For All."

"She was kind of a combination of Phillip and Sala," John Burton said. "Sala was very charming, she could just charm people out of their socks. Nancy is like that. Nancy is tougher than nails, but she's a gentle person. Phillip was just hard-ass and hard charging. He could be charming some times but I can't quite remember when."

Is she as brilliant a politician as Phil? "I think she's a nicer politician," said John Burton. "It was different times. I mean in the old days, except for some of the Dixiecrats, everybody was just Democrats. It was just all just Democrats. These days you've got the Blue Dog, the Yellow Dog, the White Dog, the Red Dog, the Out of Iraq, the Into Iraq, you've got all these caucuses, and she's kept them together on every issue."

Miller thinks Pelosi's ability to keep the caucus together is an echo of Phil's talent at assembling diverse and improbable coalitions of adversaries. Burton's imprint is also apparent in the way she separates friend from enemy, cosseting her allies and ostracizing the disloyal.

"She talks to everybody. She reads people," said Burton. And, like Phil Burton, she's not afraid to make decisions—and enemies—to get results.

She is a lot more transparent in her day-to-day dealings than the secretive Burton was, however, and her father taught her to "never lose the nice in her voice," said Eshoo. But make no mistake, friends say: Pelosi's ambition is to resurrect the House that Phil Burton built. She's a Burtonista through and through. Her election as Speaker was in one sense sweet revenge for Phil Burton's loss to Jim Wright all those years ago, bringing the Speakership back to his home district.

"I came to work for Phil Burton in the spring of '75, and he wanted to be Speaker then," said Lemons, who was also Sala Burton's chief of staff before she helped Pelosi set up shop. "He's the member of Congress from San Francisco who wanted to be Speaker. And when the votes were counted, he'd lost by one. So it was interesting for me to have these bookends of greatness surrounding my career. There was Phil on the one hand, who aspired to be Speaker and didn't make it, and then 30 years later, there's Nancy winning it."

John Burton honored Sala's deathbed request of him, as well, becoming Pelosi's campaign manager and closest adviser for the 1987 special election to fill Sala's seat. "I was with her damn near every day and night," Burton said. He chauffeured Pelosi to countless public events, working to build support for her within the Burton family network. "I think what I brought to Nancy, as much as a comfort level, was an absolute connection to Phil and Sala," said Burton. His presence in her campaign cemented the idea of Pelosi as their political heir in voters' minds.

Officials set the special election for April, giving Pelosi and 13 other candidates who entered the free-for-all less than 60 days to campaign.

Pelosi threw herself into the election D'Alesandro style, going door to door all over the Eighth District, which includes Golden Gate Park, Fisherman's Wharf, Chinatown, Haight-Asbury, and the Castro. Pelosi and Burton together drafted 4,000 volunteers. The people for whom she had hosted parties, coffees, and meet-and-greets during her years as a campaign operative began hosting parties, coffees, and meet-and-greets for her. The favor file was active for a new generation. She attended more than 100 parties over the span of those 60 days. Her husband and Leo McCathy formed the other two sides of her campaign leadership triangle. Paul moved the family from their Presidio Terrace home into a rented house in Pacific Heights so that Pelosi was firmly inside the congressional district she was campaigning to represent.

John Burton was impressed with how Pelosi connected with people of all sorts of income levels and ethnic groups. "She's at home with the people in Pacific Heights. And she's at home with the people out in the Mission," he said.

Her father was on the phone with her every day with advice. He dispatched Tommy III out to check on the campaign, and Tommy found that she was organizing just like they had organized in Baltimore, only better. "She's a great organizer," Tommy said at the time. "That's her forte. She doesn't leave a stone unturned." She had a ward executive for each ward, a precinct executive for each precinct, and a block executive for each block in the district.

Although the campaign structure was inspired by her dad's model, "raising money was something she perfected herself," Tommy said. Pelosi raised and spent nearly $1 million in less than two months. About $250,000 was borrowed from her husband, but the rest it she raised on her own from the huge network of contacts she'd amassed in her years of volunteer work for the Democratic Party. Pelosi had begun to show a knack for raising money back on the Brown campaign in Maryland. It was a skill that Phil Burton had excelled at as well. She essentially buried her opponents in money.

Her leading opponent was San Francisco City supervisor Harry Britt, political heir to Harvey Milk, the gay city supervisor who had been assassinated a few years earlier. (The Board of Supervisors is essentially the city council, governing both the city and county of San Francisco.) Britt hired a private detective to look into the Pelosi family and its business dealings, the *San Francisco Chronicle* reported at the time. While the investigation apparently failed to turn up "any heavy scandals," Britt did publicize a rent dispute Paul Pelosi had with residents of a Lake Street apartment he owned. Rather than let the issue somehow taint Nancy's run, Pelosi sold the apartment building and limited his investments to less controversial commercial property. It was a strategy the Pelosis would use whenever the hint of impropriety came up concerning Paul's holdings. Rather than stoke rumors, the Pelosis usually just sell a property if any question arises. "I've made a conscious effort to not be involved or give the appearance of being involved in her political career," Paul told *The Chronicle* in 2004. "People should realize that she's the one."

Campaign signs up and down San Francisco's steep hills asked voters whether they wanted "the legislator . . . or the dilettante?" A televised debate among all 14 candidates turned into a San Francisco-style circus. A Republican candidate in a fedora called for bombing Nicaraguan president

Daniel Ortega, and another candidate calling himself a communist and Trotskyite was led away by a security guard after denouncing the absence of debate over impeaching President Reagan.

When she ran for the post, Pelosi was better known in national Democratic circles than she was in San Francisco. She argued that she could give the city some clout through those national political connections. Her campaign tried to tout her as the more mainstream, more moderate, more conservative choice, which is ironic given the "ultraliberal" label she was slapped with during the 2006 campaign. Her TV ads for the special election could be seen as trying to tap into "traditional values" voters by using Handel's Hallelujah chorus as background music. The ads closed with the tagline: Nancy Pelosi: A Voice That Will Be Heard.

Pelosi campaign manager Clinton Reilly said at the time that his strategy was simple: Concede most of the gay vote and win with older Democrats, Republicans, and especially younger women.

Britt, a leader in the gay community, conducted an aggressive get-out-the vote drive aimed at galvanizing gays, who accounted for about 15 percent of San Francisco's population at the time. "All of us know that the meaning of our lives is what we do about AIDS," he said. "If I go to Congress, it is to work on AIDS. If I lose, my life will still be measured by whether I was responsive to this horrible, horrible epidemic."

Many observers of the election thought that Britt indeed did mobilize the city's gay population to vote in high numbers, but there was evidence that many did not vote for him. James C. Hormel, a longtime activist in the gay community back then, supported Pelosi. "Nancy is in much better position to attract attention to [the fight against AIDS] and get congressional support for it. I like Harry personally . . . [but] I also feel frankly that, if we are promoting a congressional candidacy as our Jackie Robinson, that person ought to be a .300 hitter and not a .150 hitter." A survey commissioned by the *San Francisco Examiner* showed that 21 percent of gays voted for Pelosi, while Britt won the votes of 23 percent of those voters who said they were gay. In the final results, Pelosi beat Britt by only 4,000 votes, her closest election in her 20 years in Congress. Because she didn't win 50 percent of the vote outright, she faced a Republican candidate, Harriet Ross, in a June runoff, which Pelosi won handily given the fact that 64 percent of the population in San Francisco's Fifth District is registered Democratic.

The night she won the election, it was Burton who introduced Pelosi to cheering supporters. Her victory was reported around the country as a vote of continuity for the Burton legend. Tommy III, who had come out to campaign during the last week, was ecstatic: "She fought like a tiger. She fought all the way. They came right after her and she did not buckle. They brought the fight to her and she stood there toe to toe and slugged it out."

"If you can survive San Francisco politics, you can survive anything," John Burton said later. "It's like surviving god-damn Tammany Hall 50 years ago. It's fucking brutal."

A congressional aide had saved the massive chair Phil Burton had used during his two decades in Congress for Pelosi to use when she arrived. But the diminutive Pelosi felt like Goldilocks sitting in Papa Bear's chair. Rather than return the chair to a government warehouse, Pelosi and aide Lemons came up with an idea. Sala Burton had been like a mother to Pelosi's loyal ally George Miller. In many ways, she was his political mom. The day Miller was installed as chairman of the House Interior Committee, Pelosi threw a party for him. When everyone had arrived, she wheeled in the chair, which was wrapped in a big red bow. "George, this was Phil Burton's. You're in your mother's armchair."

Nearly 20 years later, when Pelosi took the oath of office as Speaker, John Burton was watching over her from the gallery like a guardian angel. Friends of Pelosi's say John is still probably her most trusted adviser back in California, a characterization Burton himself scoffs at. "We talk a lot but trust me, it would have to be a weird issue that I would have to give her advice on. She gets it, she's the best. She's beyond belief."

On the day of her inauguration, "I was just very happy for her, happy for me, and happy for the country," he said. He had told a reporter beforehand, however, that even though he was in the House gallery that day, his thoughts would probably be elsewhere.

"Phil, Sala," he said.

CHAPTER 5

A VOICE THAT WILL BE HEARD

They say that women talk too much. If you have worked in Congress you know that the filibuster was invented by men.

—Clare Booth Luce, congresswoman, journalist, playwright, diplomat, 1903–1987

It was Tuesday, June 9, 1987, Pelosi's first day in office, and she was getting plenty of advice from other members of Congress. She was one of 22 women among 413 men, and much of the counsel was about the proper way to do things if she wanted to be taken seriously. "Typically, you're not supposed to speak, and everybody said, 'Nancy, whatever you do, don't talk,'" remembered Judy Lemons. Congress, it should be mentioned, has always been preoccupied with its arcane rules and protocol. There's a proper way of doing things, even when it's hardly doing anything at all.

"I get sworn in and they say to me, whatever you do, don't say a word when you go to the floor," Pelosi recalled. "Just raise your hand, say 'Yes, I do . . . I will' . . . whatever. The usual. But don't say another word!"

Pelosi saw an irony in this. Because she already knew more than 200 members of Congress through her work with the national Democratic Party, the state party, and various "campaigns, causes, issues and all the rest," she ran for office using the slogan "A Voice That Will Be Heard."

"How can I not say a word if I'm the Voice That Will Be Heard?!" laughed Pelosi when recounting the tale.

"She's *totally* driven by speaking out," remarked Lemons.

Less than a week after her election, and she already was on a collision course with the tradition-bound Congress. Pelosi found her way to her wing-back leather seat and dutifully promised she would recite the "I do," "I will," et cetera of her oath. And then Speaker Jim Wright piped up from the rostrum: "Does the gentlelady from California wish to be recognized?"

This caused the freshman lawmaker some confusion.

"I thought, 'Oh my god,' they told me I wasn't saying anything," recalled Pelosi. But like a seasoned pro, she rose to deliver an impromptu floor speech. "I thanked the Speaker for the recognition, and said how glad I was that my family was there," remembers Pelosi. Her father was in the galleries to see her first floor speech, as were her mother and several other D'Alesandros. "The day Nancy was sworn in was one of the happiest days of my mother's life," brother Tommy III told the *Baltimore Sun*. "She was the reincarnation of my mother's ambition." Her father reportedly wept during the swearing in.

Pelosi went on to pay tribute to the Burtons, too: "I told the people of the Fifth Congressional District who sent me here that when I got here I would tell you all that I would change the circumstances under which I came if I could but I cannot. I wish Phillip were here, I wish Sala were here, but they are not and I cannot do anything about that except to follow in their tradition of excellence, of commitment and of making Government work for people.

"I told the people of the Fifth Congressional District when I got here I will tell you, 'Sala Burton sent me.'"

And then Pelosi couldn't resist saying: "We are very proud of the Fifth Congressional District and its leadership for peace, for environmental protection, for equal rights, for rights of individual freedom and now we must take the leadership, of course, in the crisis of AIDS. And I look forward to working with you on that."

After her floor speech, she was asked: "Why do you want that to be how you are known? As the person who mentioned AIDS on her first day in office?" "And I said, 'Well, it's the reason I came,'" recounts Pelosi. "I came here to fight against AIDS because it has affected our district so much." There was just the faintest twinkle of pride in Pelosi's retelling of the story, a certain satisfaction that she stood up to the status quo right off the bat. She would have many more run-ins with the status quo in the next 20 years. "So when I first came as the Voice That Will Be Heard, I was told don't say a word. And then when I got up it was like, Sit Right Down," summed up Pelosi. She adds some punctuation to the tale: "Well, now I am the Speaker."

It was quite a while before Pelosi got another opportunity to speak on the House floor, but she went to work immediately on issues near and dear to her constituents. In her very first year in office, Pelosi kept her vow to become a leading force in the fight against HIV/AIDS.

"The thing she came here to do was to fight the AIDS epidemic," said Lemons. "That was the thing that came out from Day 1 for her, from her speech before the House."

The year she arrived, 1987, was really the year Washington finally began to take AIDS seriously. The first cases had been identified in 1981 in gay men in New York, but the disease hadn't been given a name until late in 1982. New York and San Francisco quickly became its twin epicenters. By 1984, all the gay bathhouses and private sex clubs in San Francisco had been closed as a public health precaution, and by 1985, 13,000 people had died of the disease in the United States. AIDS was ravaging San Francisco and the gay population across the country, but Washington, and President Reagan, had been slow to recognize the seriousness of the scourge and even slower to take action. Reagan didn't use the word publicly until 1985, more than four years after the first cases appeared. Pelosi, on her very first day in office, was announcing that Washington had to do better.

Truth be told, the California House delegation had already been pushing the Reagan administration hard to increase money for AIDS research and education before Pelosi arrived. Barbara Boxer, who also represented portions of San Francisco, had led the way in getting the House to double the federal commitment to AIDS, to $970 million, 82 percent more what had been sought by the Reagan administration. Congress, thanks to the clout of a 45-person-strong caucus from California—where the disease was hitting hardest—was leading the way in Washington on the national emergency. But activists and health officials say Pelosi took the attention AIDS got nationally to a new level altogether.

"In 1987, people were dying," said Alex Clemens, campaign strategist and community organizer in San Francisco. Nobody was doing much about it in Washington, said Clemens, and some religious leaders were calling the "gay plague" God's way of punishing an immoral lifestyle. "Many leading members of our community are still HIV positive and still searching for a cure," Clemens adds. Pelosi said the same thing at a recent party marking her twentieth year in Congress. "I went to Congress to fight AIDS and we're still fighting," she said.

What Pelosi did when she arrived in Washington was immediately increase public awareness of AIDS. She became an outspoken advocate for gay rights, antidiscrimination legislation, needle exchanges, and better healthcare for AIDS patients. Just four months after taking office, she joined comedian Whoopi Goldberg, actor Robert Blake, Broadway producer Joseph Papp, and Massachusetts Democratic representatives Gerry Studds and Barney Frank in reading the names of the 25,000 victims of AIDS who were listed on giant quilt unfurled on the Mall. She attended numerous funerals and memorial services for gay friends and supporters back in her district during her first years in office, staking out a very public profile as a champion of AIDS victims. By 1988, President Reagan was already changing his tune. He issued a directive banning discrimination against AIDS patients, and his administration mailed out 107 million copies of a booklet, "Understanding AIDS," written by Surgeon General C. Everett Koop.

But Pelosi quickly saw that she would need to get on the powerful appropriations committee if she wanted to get real funding to fight the epidemic. That was easier said than done in the seniority-minded Congress. What most people outside Washington don't realize is that politicians have to mount political campaigns for seats on committees. That was something Pelosi had learned from Phil Burton. As a politician, you're always campaigning for something or someone. At any given time, there are dozens of campaigns going on within the halls of Congress for various leadership posts and plum assignments, so Pelosi's experience as a party operative was called into action from the get-go.

Here's how aides sum up the Pelosi How-to Plan for her first mini-campaign in the House:

Step 1. Maintain constant contact. Send letters out to all the relevant members of the Appropriations Committee. Tell them you're running and why, and tell them you want their support.

Step 2. Solidify support. Ask to go before the next caucus meeting of the various caucuses that might help you plead your case, such as the California delegation, the women's caucus, the moderate "Blue Dog" Democrats, the Hispanic caucus, and so on, and talk to them personally, answer their questions. Target the senior members of each caucus, lobbying for their support. Go to all the caucus meetings you can, making sure the different pieces all fit together. Always know where you stand in terms of number of votes.

Step 3. Lobby members of the party's steering committee, because they are the ones who actually make the committee selections for the party. Get your delegation of supporters together and ask them to contact steering committee members. Try to figure out how each person can help you. It's complicated. And sometimes it takes a while, but "failure is not an option."

Pelosi didn't get on Appropriations the first time she tried in the early 1990s. But the next time around, when there was an opening, she was prepared. She'd laid all the groundwork. The campaign was there, all she had to do was reactivate it. This time, the support was there.

She continued working publicly to raise awareness of AIDS, but she was finally able to push behind the scenes for increased federal funding of research, better care, hospitals, and clinics. It was a double-barreled pattern of fighting for her causes that Pelosi would continue for the next 20 years. Although many of the issues that she championed were new, such as AIDS, the way in which she helped push through legislation was good-old-fashioned arm-twisting. "I don't accept that there is a clash between traditional Democratic values and new ideas," said Pelosi.

"You have two sides of a personality," said a senior Democratic staff member. "She has a very mechanistic, organizational way of looking at politics with an incredibly empathetic way of looking at policy. She is the most complete mix of political calculation and legislative strategist that I know exists in the Congress."

That two-pronged approach led to her very first major legislative victory in Congress: the creation of a program to provide federal housing assistance to AIDS victims and their families. When she sponsored the bill, in 1990, the National Coalition for the Homeless was reporting that there were no shelters in Chicago that allowed homeless AIDS patients, only 3 beds available in the Virginias, and only 5 shelters out of 42 in Los Angeles that would accept people with HIV or AIDS. Today, more than 60,000 people receive help with the rent from the program.

On Appropriations, Pelosi was also able to add millions to federal budgets for research into an AIDS vaccine, money that was crucial to the development of the first cocktail of drugs to help control the symptoms of AIDS. She also sponsored legislation extending Medicaid funding to AIDS sufferers and voted to allow gay couples to adopt children for the first time in Washington, D.C. She opposed a constitutional ban on gay marriage and eventually came out in support of San Francisco mayor Gavin Newsom's decision to license gay marriages in San Francisco in 2004, a decision later overruled by the state.

Soon the *Advocate*, a gay rights magazine, was hailing Pelosi as "one of the House's staunchest supporters of gay rights and a leader on AIDS issues since she arrived on Capitol Hill."

"By all counts, she's done a tremendous job, not just helping the San Francisco Bay area ensure that we would do appropriate research into HIV and AIDS, but that it remains a national priority," said Clemens.

San Franciscans have complained of late that Pelosi has shied away from her liberal, pro-gay rights past now that she's in the high-profile position of Speaker. And she certainly has emphasized her Baltimore roots more in speeches and events since she was inaugurated, especially during her inauguration week, than she has her 37 years in San Francisco. In May 2007, though, she publicly demanded an explanation from the Bush administration for a $8.6 million cut in AIDS-related federal funds for the San Francisco Bay area. "The drastic nature of this cut will have a devastating impact on services that keep people living with HIV/AIDS in the Bay Area healthy," Pelosi wrote in a letter to the secretary of Health and Human Services. Pelosi has recently fought Republican efforts to curtail or redirect funds for the Ryan White program, which is named for an Indiana boy who died of the disease in 1990. The program was started in Pelosi's third year in Congress to improve the care given to people with HIV/AIDS.

Pelosi told the *Advocate* in January 2007 that she is willing to take up new gay rights issues as Speaker—when the political climate bodes well for success. "There are quite a few issues that are significant to the gay community that I believe present opportunities for consensus among House Democrats and can attract moderate Republican support," she said. "Legislation like the Employment Non-Discrimination Act and a federal hate-crimes bill have earned this type of wide-ranging support."

Gay advocates have privately admitted that they are not looking for big legislative victories while Pelosi is Speaker. Still, they say the fact that such a strong advocate of gay rights is in a position of real power is good for the gay rights movement for many reasons. For one thing, activists won't have to defend their funding from a hostile Congress trying to siphon it away to other needs and cities other than San Francisco. "What we get out of this is a champion on our issues, someone who speaks up for our health and our dignity and our first-class citizenship," said California assemblyman Mark Leno, who is gay. "That has symbolic benefits as well as legislative ones."

Though ads targeting Pelosi for her "San Francisco Values" were legion during the 2006 elections, the effort to paint her as an ultraliberal out of touch with the country's mainstream didn't stick. The day of her election, Pelosi told the *Washington Post* that she thought people probably found the ads offensive because of the implicit gay-bashing. "When people say 'San Francisco liberal,' are they talking about protecting the environment, educating the American children, building economic success?" she asked. "No, they are talking about gay people. Well, I was brought up to believe that all people are God's children. And the last time I checked, that included gay people."

Pelosi has a statue made of coal to thank for a good chunk of her early success in rising through the ranks of Congress.

"When I first took office, my father gave me a couple things, like his desk set, and he gave me this carving of a coal miner made out of coal that he had had in his office when he was a member of Congress," Pelosi said in an interview in her office. Tommy D'Alesandro represented urban Baltimore in the 1940s, but he also worked hard on behalf of the miners in the western parts of Maryland, and the statue was given to him as a token of appreciation.

Pelosi and burly Congressman Jack Murtha had been working on a project to convert the famed Presidio army base in San Francisco into a national park early in Pelosi's tenure. Murtha also happens to represent Pennsylvania's coal country. "One day Jack was walking past my office and he came in and saw that carving," said Pelosi. They formed a bond then and there, a bond that has lasted 20 years and counting. Murtha would eventually manage both her minority whip and minority leader races and himself make an ultimately unsuccessful and controversial bid for majority leader with Pelosi's backing.

"One key to her rise was building an alliance with more powerful senior legislators, in particular Jack Murtha," said Matthew Green. "That alliance was absolutely essential because Murtha had a lot of connections, he was well respected among Democrats, was able to help her build relationships with members who might be suspicious otherwise."

It was Pelosi who first approached Murtha about working together, but it was the ex-Marine who saw the spark of great potential in Pelosi. "I would suspect that Murtha saw in Pelosi the potential to become Speaker, saw that leadership potential in her, saw that she had the ability necessary to achieve power," said Green. "I think to make that kind of decision to support a more junior member of the caucus over a long term means that you see something in that person and you want to take them under your wing and help them achieve their potential."

Anna Eshoo said the bond between Murtha and Pelosi is about respect. "He respects her hard-core knowledge. He understands how capable she is. He understands how she could put something together and be effective, i.e., she knows how to win. And anyone who is in politics respects that. That's the ultimate: win. Win your election. Win the votes. Win the legislation. Win the day. Win for the country."

The partnership began in earnest with the work on the Presidio, which was once perhaps the country's most scenic military base. It sits at the foot of the Golden Gate Bridge with sweeping views of city and sea. When Congress created the Golden Gate Recreation area in 1972, Pelosi's predecessor, the wily Phil Burton, factored in a clause that said if the military ever relinquished control of the Presidio, it would become part of the recreation area. In the late 1980s, with the cold war coming to an end, the army did decide to close the base after

200 uninterrupted years of service, but Congress balked at the Burton park plan. By the time Pelosi inherited the issue, Murtha was the chairman of the Defense Appropriations Committee, so she had to make her case for a park to him.

The Presidio was a unique problem. It was a little bit army base and a little bit wild land, all in a prime urban setting. It had nearly 800 buildings that Pelosi and others thought should remain part of the base's heritage, as well as a 6,599-yard golf course, a huge urban forest, and an environmentally sensitive waterfront. Because of the infrastructure, paying for the Presidio's conversion and continued operation and care was going to cost a lot more than traditional parks, Pelosi realized. Together, she and Murtha devised the Presidio Trust, a unique management and funding model among national parks that required it to become self-sufficient by 2012. The trust manages the area of the park that includes most of the buildings, and the National Park Service manages the coastal areas.

"It was a very entrepreneurial idea," said Pelosi. "A public-private partnership, with nonprofits as well. It required a transition from army post to park and all that that implied in terms of appropriations to do it and the cleanup involved. I worked closely with Mr. Murtha on that, and that was a long time ago."

"I think she is so perceptive that when she first came she recognized I was in a position where things that she was trying to get done, I could help her," said Murtha. "And she listened. She convinced me that there was a lot of work that had to be done before we turned it over. The Parks Department wanted it right away. Well, I knew they didn't have the money to do it so we put a lot of military money into it initially, and then the Interior [Department] came along and put money in."

What Pelosi did that impressed Murtha was to bring together San Francisco community decision makers with congressional decision makers. She'd fly people from San Francisco in to talk to Murtha and the chairman of the Interior Committee to convince them that the public-private trust was the right way to go.

"Most people in San Francisco were anxious to get that turned over," Murtha recalls. "She recognized right away if we didn't spend some money on that version it wasn't going to come out right." Murtha eventually approved $100 million for the Presidio makeover. "She was patient," he remembers. "She convinced them [San Franciscans] that this was going to require time and money, and then they convinced the Congress. Even though she was involved, they were the ones that brought the plan forward, they were the ones that brought the vision forward, talked to the committee." She steered the project to shore from the rear of the boat, in other words.

Surprisingly, the toughest resistance to the plan came from her own side of the aisle. Democrats, worried that the expensive project was going to suck the National Parks budget dry, had effectively tabled it when Newt Gingrich and his Republican Revolution took over Congress in 1994. Many people associated with the project back then thought that was the death knell, but patience is one of Pelosi's most prized leadership traits. She showed the caucus a talent for bipartisan dealmaking by getting the trust approved during a Republican Congress. It may have been that the Republican leadership liked the public-private partnership deal better than the Democrats ever had. She was assisted greatly in the effort by a Republican congressman from Ohio, Ralph Regula. At one point Regula took his entire subcommittee out to San Francisco to look over the project. With his support, Pelosi's plan for the Presidio was finally adopted in 1996, 18 years after she first started working on it and 24 years after Phil Burton first launched the conversion process. Her painstaking pursuit of the endgame on the Presidio may shed some light on her resolve and willingness to take the long view on getting the country out of Iraq. "She sees all the dots and she knows how to connect them," even if it takes years, said one aide.

On the road to self-sufficiency, the trust has rented out 23 acres of the Presidio to the Letterman Digital Arts Center, new home to *Star Wars* director George Lucas's Industrial Light and Magic, LucasArts and several divisions of Lucasfilm. Some liberals in San Francisco balked that Lucas and other private interests got a piece of the precious land, complaining that Pelosi had sold out the prime Bay area real estate to checkbook politics. It's a complaint that has been aired repeatedly during her 20 years in Congress. In general, Pelosi has endured the hardest hits from the left in her home district. Several area activists say she is too cozy with the local business and political elites, and not representative enough of the city's progressives.

The Presidio deal was one in a string of environmental projects she focused on over the years, the most recent being the formation of an independent commission within the House to hammer out a policy on global warming. One of Pelosi's earliest environmental accomplishments, predating the Presidio preservation, came while she was on the Banking Committee in her first three years in Congress. She authored what has become known as the Pelosi Amendment to the International Development and Finance Act of 1989. The provision requires the World Bank and other development banks to review and make public all the potential environmental impacts of development projects they fund. A report six years after the Pelosi Amendment took effect said all major development banks had put new environmental procedures into practice, thanks in large part to Pelosi. Ironically, though the amendment prodded the banks to report to Congress on their projects, Congress rarely makes those reports public. Still, the reports are available for the asking, and the amendment is considered a significant early accomplishment for a junior member of Congress. It's something Pelosi looks back to proudly.

Pelosi keeps another statue in her office: a small replica of the 30-foot-tall papier-mâché and Styrofoam Goddess of Democracy erected by art students in China's Tiananmen Square during the student uprising there in the spring of 1989. The replica, which bears a striking resemblance to America's Statue of Liberty, commemorates Pelosi's own protest in the square two years later, a demonstration she staged as an act of solidarity with the dissidents who were killed by the hundreds and arrested by the thousands during the government's crackdown. Pelosi was nearly caught up in a small crackdown herself after she and two colleagues from Congress slipped away from their government handlers and unfurled a banner in Tiananmen that read: "To those who died for democracy in China." Turns out they hadn't really gotten permission, and were immediately surrounded by police and "tourists" who happened to have walkie-talkies in their backpacks. "I started running," Pelosi told a reporter, "and my colleagues, some of them, got a little roughed up. The press got treated worse because they had cameras, and they were detained." Chinese officials denounced the demonstration as a "deliberate anti-China incident" and a "premeditated farce." Somehow, a photo of the incident made it back home with the delegation, and Pelosi always waved it on the floor of the House during her frequent speeches condemning human rights abuses in China.

Just a few years into her tenure as a congresswomen, Pelosi was already showing a willingness for bold, imaginative, sometimes controversial gambits to draw attention to her issues. In her early years, Pelosi was more an advocate than a conciliator. Great moral quests are what animated her, whether it was AIDS, human rights in China, or, later, stopping a war. She was headstrong in her championing of the issues she believed in, not much interested in looking for the middle road. When one of her fellow members of Congress told her he would have to agree to disagree on the subject of China trade, Pelosi shot back: "Well, I hope you can live with your conscience."

Though some critics have complained that Pelosi seized on human rights in China as one of her core issues to raise her profile in Congress for a later bid for leadership, it's more likely the choice was constituent-driven. As with the Presidio and the AIDS crisis, the needs and nature of Pelosi's constituents are what shaped her first few years in Congress. In the late 1980s, 150,000 Chinese Americans lived in Pelosi's home district, and most were outraged by the events at Tiananmen Square. In fact, more Asian Americans reside in the Eighth District than in any other outside Hawaii. And keeping constituents happy is the first lesson Pelosi learned at her father's knee.

"She understands grassroots and her constituents," said Senator Barbara Mikulski. "She knows that no matter who you are, you've got to always remember where you came from. I think she carries that in her heart and in her legislative agenda." With one eye on that Asian American base, Pelosi went on to choreograph dozens of anti-China incidents during her early years in Congress.

"Nancy was so horrified by what happened at Tiananmen Square," said Lemons. "And she said 'I've got to do something because there are so many pro-democracy students here in America who will face an uncertain future if they have to go home.'" Pelosi sponsored a bill to extend visas to Chinese students in the United States—there were 40,000 of them at the time—so they could remain. President George H. W. Bush vetoed the bill, but after much loud and public complaining by Pelosi, he eventually signed an executive order that did much the same thing.

In 1996, she refused to attend a reception in honor of General Chi Haotian, chief of staff of China's army. In 1997, she joined a protest outside of Blair House in Washington where her California colleague Dianne Feinstein was hosting a reception for Chinese president Jiang Zemin. She called numerous press conferences to rail against President Clinton and his policy of closer engagement with China. She announced on the House floor in 1998 that Clinton would be "on the wrong side of history" when he visited Tiananmen Square during a trip to China in June. "What do you expect me to say?" Pelosi asked from the floor. "That it's not OK for a Republican president to coddle dictators, but it's OK for a Democrat?"

She has argued against almost all trade agreements with China, including Most Favored Nation status and China's entry into the World Trade Organization. She opposed permanent normal trade relations with China, which were granted by President George W. Bush in 2001, saying that such relations take away any sort of leverage the United States had to push for improved human rights in China. Why will Beijing care about our demands for rights progress, Pelosi asked at the time, if they know we're not going to do anything to hurt our business prospects in the emerging market of 1 billion people? "I predict that the trade deficit will soar [it has], the human rights violations will intensify [they have], the proliferation of weapons of mass destruction will continue uncurbed [no definitive evidence of that]. The only lever we had was free trade."

But with Pelosi in charge of the House, the Democrats in Congress turned up the heat on China to do more about human rights, slow down its flood of cheap imports, and revalue its currency. In May of 2006, she met with Vice Premier Wu Yi for a frank discussion of intellectual property rights violations, the undervaluation of China's currency, the genocide in Darfur, and human rights in China and Tibet. "I believe that the Chinese government can do more in each of these areas," Pelosi said afterward. Still, in 2007, China continued to buy two-thirds of Sudan's oil exports despite more and more evidence that the Sudanese government was contributing to the mass killings in Darfur.

In June of 2007, the U.S. Treasury refused to label China a currency manipulator, and in response, Pelosi pledged that Congress would step in to pass a measure to prod China to raise the value of its currency. In an interview on Bloomberg Television's *Political Capital with Al Hunt*, she said her colleagues were finally joining her in her concern about the impact of the weak yuan on U.S. manufacturers. Pelosi is planning to use the approaching Olympics Games, to be hosted by Beijing in the summer of 2008, as a lever for increasing pressure on China. On June 4, 2007, the eighteenth anniversary of the bloody Tiananmen crackdown, she entered a statement into the *Congressional Record* saying that the human rights situation in China remains poor. "In fact, the Chinese government is becoming even more sophisticated, using new technology to monitor and apprehend those who criticize the government or worship freely. There is new disturbing evidence of a pre-Olympic crackdown on peaceful activists including journalists, lawyers, and human rights defenders. The 2008 Olympic Games in Beijing should provide an opportunity for more free expression, not less."

Over the years, Pelosi's ardent advocacy for human rights has raised her profile in Congress and began to showcase her leadership abilities. For more than a decade afterward, she and Representative Chris Cox, a Republican from Orange County, became what conservative columnist E. J. Dionne described as "a two-person congressional freedom squad fighting for the rights of dissidents all over the world." Pelosi made appeals to anyone who would listen in the international community on behalf of a long list of Chinese dissidents, often with surprising success.

"Nancy found her niche in China, in fighting for human rights," Lemons said. "People could see that she could whip votes, they saw that she could lead on an issue, they saw her tenaciousness in fighting, first of all, for the visa bill. It was the beginning of the rest of the caucus seeing her leadership. People realized from then on that she was a force to be reckoned with," Lemons added. "And a voice that will be heard."

CHAPTER 6

THE BOYS' CLUB

*A lady Congresswoman is supposed to be demure, winsome and follow the leader-
ship of the males.*

Drew Pearson, Washington newspaper columnist, 1897–1969

Call it the walk of the Valkyries. On October 8, 1991, just four years after
Nancy Pelosi had first won office, seven women on Capitol Hill decided they'd
had enough. In a scene reminiscent of Akira Kurosawa's *Seven Samurai*, or the
American remake, *The Magnificent Seven*, Congresswomen Pat Schroeder,
Patsy Mink, Louise Slaughter, Jolene Unsoeld, Nita Lowey, Barbara Boxer, and
Eleanor Holmes Norton marched shoulder to shoulder over to the Senate side
of the building to demand action on Anita Hill's charges of sexual harassment
against Supreme Court nominee Clarence Thomas. The photograph of the
seven women climbing up the steps of the Capitol—armed only with outrage,
purses, and folders of facts—became a galvanizing image for women across the
country. The effort to very publicly impose their will on the Senate was something no other members of the House had done in the history of the two very
separate branches of government. More than any other event in recent times,
the Hill-Thomas hearings would serve as a wake-up call for women on the
importance of electing more women to Congress and to leadership positions
therein. It was a starting gun that would launch a decade of gains for women in
numbers and seniority and lead directly to Pelosi's election in 2002 as House
Democratic leader, a prelude to the Speaker's chair four years later.

The seven congresswomen marched right up to Majority Leader George
Mitchell's office and insisted he reopen the confirmation hearings to hear law

professor Hill's claims. A few days earlier, just after the Senate Judiciary Committee's hearings into Thomas's confirmation had closed, reports surfaced that Hill had told FBI agents Thomas had sexually harassed her when she worked for the nominee as an aide some 10 years earlier. The report had been sent to the Judiciary Committee, but members had ignored it, or failed to read it, or decided it was unimportant, and sent Thomas's nomination to the full Senate for a vote anyway. Women of the House were outraged. They demanded that Hill be allowed to testify publicly before the vote.

One of the seven marchers, Eleanor Holmes Norton, was the District of Columbia's nonvoting member in the House. She had written sexual harassment guidelines for the Equal Employment Opportunity Commission as its chair, guidelines Thomas was familiar with because he succeeded Norton as chair of the commission in 1982. Norton presented a statement to the Speaker of the House that day about her experience: "We wrote the guidelines," she said, "to give women the courage to come forward, as Professor Hill now has done, and by doing so to deter the most widespread form of sex discrimination in America today."

At the time, Pelosi made the point that although no one knew whether Hill's accusations were true or not, they still had to be taken seriously. "They are men," she said of the senators on the judicial committee. "They can't possibly know what it's like to receive verbal harassment, harassment that is fleeting to a man and lasting and demeaning to a woman. These allegations may not be true. But women in America have to speak up for themselves and say we want to remove all doubt that the person who goes to the Supreme Court has unquestioned respect for women. What's the rush? We need a little more time to follow up on allegations so that we can send a signal to women in America that we take sexual harassment seriously."

Pelosi and many other women lawmakers issued petitions to the Senate leaders demanding that the Thomas nomination be reexamined. Many women in Congress at the time made the point that if the committee had had a single woman on it, things would have turned out differently.

"What disturbs me as much as the allegations themselves," Barbara Mikulski told her 98 male and 1 female colleagues, "is that the Senate appears not to take the charge of sexual harassment seriously."

"The times they are a-changin' and the boys here don't get it on this issue," said Schroeder at the time. "They don't really understand what sexual harassment is and it's not important to them."

The seven congresswomen won their bid to reopen the hearings from a reluctant Mitchell, and Anita Hill was summoned to testify before the Senate Judiciary Committee in a matter of days. But only hours before her scheduled testimony, the committee granted a request from the Bush White House to let Thomas testify first. The Supreme Court nominee got off a preemptive strike against Hill, portraying her as the sexual aggressor and as a delusional liar. He also played the race card, even though the charges came from a black woman. He called himself the "victim of a high-tech lynching." Hill followed with graphic testimony about Thomas's sexually vulgar and offensive language. She testified that, after she rebuffed his advances, he described pornographic scenes to her involving bestiality and rape, many of which included her. But polls after the hearings showed that 47 percent of the public believed Thomas's testimony, while only 24 percent believed Hill. A Republican campaign to question Hill's credibility, and hostile questioning from the all-male judicial committee, had worked. The next day the Senate voted 52 to 48 to confirm Thomas for a lifetime appointment to the Supreme Court.

Thomas won the face-off but women outraged at the patronizing, rude, and dismissive hearings mobilized as never before. Barbara Boxer plastered photos everywhere of her and the six other women marching on the Senate. Dianne Feinstein mounted a campaign for the Senate in California with a fundraising letter that spoke of her "sense of rage" at what the Senate did to Hill. Harriet Woods, executive director of the National Women's Political Caucus, promised that the senators involved in the hearings would answer for their actions at the polls. "I can assure you, we are going to fire up, and if necessary we will find a woman to run against every one of these guys."

The *Washington Post*'s Judy Mann wrote: "No matter what comes out of these hearings, there is one overriding lesson for women. And that is that they cannot depend on men to protect their interests. Women have to run for the House and they have to run for the Senate and they have to win. If there had been a couple of women on that committee, this debacle would not have happened."

New York congresswoman Bella Abzug, one of the women pioneers in Congress, thought the Thomas-Hill episode had set off a "tidal wave that will open the House and Senate to 50 percent women."

Ellen Malcolm president of EMILY's List, which raises money for women candidates, said: "The Anita Hill hearings opened up for men and women both how few women there were in Congress. People were pretty unhappy with what was going on in Congress so there became this absolute passion to elect women because they would be different."

Women became the hot prospects as political candidates in 1992, Malcolm said. "EMILY's List went from 3500 members to 24,000 in one year, because we became the focal point for women."

There were also 88 open seats in 1992 because it was the first election after redistricting across the country, and when the boundaries of Congressional districts were changed, many incumbents opted to retire. "It was a perfect storm, it was a total convergence of all the political factors," said Malcolm. "There was a lot of open seats, there was momentum for change, there was incredible financial resources for women candidates, and we cashed in."

That fall, 24 new women were elected to the House, a record number for one entering class that nearly doubled the number of women in Congress overnight. Five new women were elected to the Senate. Pundits dubbed it "the Year of the Woman." Pelosi and Schroeder were ecstatic to have some company. "The cavalry has arrived," said Schroeder.

The Year of the Woman was one of the most important in a series of breakthroughs that have conditioned American voters more and more to the idea of women political leaders. Each and every time a woman has accomplished some sort of "first" in politics, her example has inspired more women to try.

Boxer, one of the seven walkers who is now in the Senate, said there's "absolutely a connection" between 1992 and Pelosi's rise. "Nancy's election is a definite outgrowth of the long struggle we've had as women for equality in the workplace and in politics," she said in an interview. "It's a huge moment for us, and it's a moment along the way."

"There is no one who understands more the importance of having women in office and the changes that have taken place than the Speaker," added Malcolm.

Cindy Simon Rosenthal, director and curator of the Carl Albert Congressional Research and Studies Center at the University of Oklahoma, believes a continuum of gains for women over the years paved the way for Pelosi's rise to a leadership position. "It's been a slow, at times glacial, incremental process. I think you can go back to some of the women who served a long time ago, in the 40s and 50s. Edith Green, Margaret Chase Smith. There were certain things they added to the picture. The legitimacy of their candidacies. The respect they earned. Their ability to rise in their own caucuses at that time to certain levels."

When Pelosi, as minority leader a few years later, was the first woman ever asked to meet with other congressional leaders at White House breakfast meetings, she paid tribute to the groundbreaking done by other women.

"For an instant, I felt as though Susan B. Anthony, Lucretia Mott, Elizabeth Cady Stanton—everyone who'd fought for women's right to vote and for the empowerment of women in politics, in their professions, and in their lives—were there with me in the room. Those women were the ones who had done the heavy lifting, and it was as if they were saying, At last we have a seat at the table."

One of the few places in the Capitol that women have not just a seat but their own table is the Lindy Boggs Congressional Women's Reading Room, which is named for the first woman from Louisiana elected to Congress who served as the unofficial hostess of the Democratic Party in Washington for years. Boggs was one of Pelosi's inspirations. The reading room, just off Statuary Hall, has divans and couches, lush drapes, a fireplace, and a chandelier. No dark walls, no leather, no cigars. The carpet is a pale salmon, and the walls are beige. It's also got the closest women's bathroom to the House floor, so women are constantly in and out. (The men's room is much more convenient, not surprisingly. It's just a few paces away from the floor, while the women's room is down through a hall where tourists cluster.) Very few men ever enter the reading room. It's becomes a hive for women in Congress—it was the meeting place of the first Women's Congressional Caucus in 1977. And on the walls are photographs of every congresswoman who has ever served: Jeanette Rankin, Barbara Jordan, Bella Abzug, Clare Booth Luce, Geraldine Ferraro, Anna Eshoo, Barbara Boxer, Nancy Pelosi.

Interestingly, the photos only date back to 1916. The slow accumulation of firsts that finally landed Pelosi in the Speaker's chair didn't even really get started until the twentieth century. During America's first 135 years, the Constitution assumed women would be represented well enough by their husband's votes (completely discounting the political value of all unmarried women.) It was Elizabeth Cady Stanton who first demanded the right to vote for women at a famous meeting in Seneca Falls, New York, in 1848. Stanton was an abolitionist who believed the fight for the rights of slaves ought to be broadened into a fight for women's rights as well. The leader of the abolitionists, Frederick Douglas, attend the meeting in Seneca Falls and rose in support of Stanton. "This cause is not exclusively women's cause. It is the cause of human brotherhood, as well as human sisterhood," he announced. The gathering set off a wave of women's rights meetings around the country and the suffragist movement was born.

It was Stanton who came up with the idea of trying to win women the right to vote out in the western territories first with the hope that voting rights would be grandfathered in when those territories became states. The territories had so few voters that they were willing to let anyone go the ballot box. The suffragettes' strategy was to slowly build up a critical mass of states until the whole country had to follow suit. So the first firsts for women in politics came out West, far away from the tradition-bound East, where a flinty independence made for fertile ground for emancipation. The realities of frontier life meant women worked just as hard as men, dashing the citified notion that women should somehow be dependent. The territory of Wyoming gave women the right to vote in 1869 and became the first state to do so when it was granted statehood in 1890. Colorado, Utah, and Idaho followed in the next few years. The first nine states that gave women the right to vote were all in the West.

Although she never held political office, Susan B. Anthony, who led the fight for woman's suffrage at the turn of the twentieth century by lecturing, writing, and constantly getting arrested trying to vote, has to be counted as one of Pelosi's political godmothers. At one point she and her sister suffragettes stormed the Capitol to demand equal rights for women. "We ask justice, we ask equality, we ask that all the civil and political rights that belong to citizens of the United States, be guaranteed to us and our daughters forever," she wrote in the Declaration of Rights for Women in July of 1876. She died 14 years before her goal was achieved, but most women give Anthony the lion's share of the credit for paving the way for the Nineteenth Amendment. The first picture on the wall in the Lindy Boggs Congressional Reading Room shows a driven, haunted woman from Montana, Jeanette Rankin. An early suffragette and liberal activist, the westerner won a seat in the House in 1916, four years before women in the rest of the country would gain the right to vote. Rankin was the first woman elected to any national representative body in the world, a breakthrough she attributed to the egalitarian, pioneering spirit of the American West.

"We got the vote in Montana because the spirit of pioneer days was still alive. Men thought of women in the same terms they thought of themselves," she said. On the House floor, Rankin introduced a constitutional amendment to give women the right to vote, and it passed in 1918 after her unrelenting advocacy despite warnings that it would "produce masculine woman, feminine men and the decay of civilization."

When the Senate killed the bill a few months later, angry woman across the country mounted campaigns to oust antisuffrage senators. A group called the Silent Sentinels staged a protest in front of the White House continuously for 18 months. After the 1918 elections, most members of Congress were pro-suffrage. On the day of the vote on the amendment in the House the next spring, suffragettes made sure all the representatives who were in favor of voting rights made it to the Capitol. One representative was at his wife's deathbed, but she had wanted him to vote so he left her side to cast his ballot. He had to attend her funeral when he got back.

On May 21, 1919, the House passed the amendment 304 to 89, and two weeks later on June 4, the Senate passed the amendment with one vote to spare. When the tally was final, a voice rose up out of the galleries, singing the hymn *Praise God from Whom All Good Things Flow*. By the end of the song, the entire Senate had joined in.

The next year, as one state after another voted for ratification, suffragists descended on Tennessee, which looked like it could be the 36th and decisive state to ratify, making the amendment law. At first it didn't look like the activists had enough votes, but Harry Bird, the youngest member of the state legislature at 24, decided at the last minute to change his ballot from no to yes after receiving a letter from his elderly mother in the mountains. "Be a good boy Harry. Do the right thing," the letter said. On Aug. 18, 1920, the Nineteenth Amendment became law.

It was Rankin who first introduced the amendment, but she is probably remembered most for her steadfast opposition to war, leaving later women politicians the legacy of a pacifist stereotype that they either embrace or find hard to shake. On the day after Japan attacked Pearl Harbor, hers was the lone vote against declaring war against the Axis powers.

"As a woman, I can't go to war and I refuse to send anyone else," Rankin said. The unpopularity of her stance essentially ended her congressional career.

Other spiritual ancestors of Pelosi's include Victoria Woodhull, the first woman ever to address Congress and the first woman to run for president, back in 1872. She also started the first Wall Street firm run by a woman. Her views advocating sexual liberation for women probably doomed her presidential bid in the starting gates, however.

Attorney Belva Lockwood, who gained prominence during the suffrage movement, was the first to make the case to Congress that women lawyers be allowed to practice in federal courts. She became the first woman to argue a case before the Supreme Court, and was the second woman to run for president, nominated in 1884 by the National Equal Rights Party. She ran on a platform calling for property rights for women, equal pay for women in government jobs, and uniform marriage and divorce laws in all 50 states. She collected 4,000 votes.

Clare Booth Luce, the well-known writer and editor for the magazine *Vanity Fair*, pioneered the way for many women in Congress in 1943. The author, journalist, playwright, lecturer, and social activist was one of the first Americans to sound alarms about the threat of communism to American interests. Among many other accomplishments, she helped create the Atomic Energy Commission and later served as an ambassador to both Italy and Brazil.

Republican Margaret Chase Smith's photo is displayed in the hallway of the reading room. She was the first woman to serve in both the House and the Senate, and became one of leading hawks in Congress during the cold war. She helped expose Senator Joseph McCarthy during his witch hunt for communists and briefly ran for president in 1964, dropping out after a fifth-place showing in the New Hampshire primary. (In the same year, Polly Bergen starred as the first woman president in the film *Kisses for My President*.

Bergen resigns the office after finding out she is pregnant, much to the relief of her hapless, threatened husband, Fred MacMurray.)

Shirley Chisholm, the first African American woman elected to Congress, in 1968, used to say it was much easier to be an African American in Congress than it was to be a woman in Congress. She ran for president herself in 1972, garnering as much as 7 percent of the vote in 12 primaries. "I met far more discrimination as a woman in the field of politics," she told Eleanor Clift of *Newsweek*. Chisholm said black men told her she shouldn't run, that if a black person was going to run for president, it ought to be a man.

Edith Green, elected to Congress from Oregon in 1954, pushed through the legislation that would become known as Title IX, the law that banned sex discrimination at colleges at universities.

It was often said that Bella Abzug was "born yelling." The fiery congresswoman from New York was an early advocate against the Vietnam War and one of the main sponsors of the U.S. Freedom of Information Act that opened up hundreds of thousands of secret government proceedings to public scrutiny. She broke with tradition in the House when she insisted she be allowed to wear her hat on the floor, and flamboyant headwear became her trademark. In 1971, she and Shirley Chisholm organized the National Women's Political Caucus to encourage more women to participate in politics.

Though her photo isn't in the reading room, Malcolm laid many stepping-stones for Pelosi through the creation of EMILY's List in the early 1980s. "EMILY" stands for "Early Money Is Like Yeast," meaning that early financial support can help women candidates to rise in the polls like baking bread. Like so many of the early movers and shakers in the woman's political movement, Malcolm also attended an all-woman's school, Hollins College, in Roanoke, Virginia. There she got involved in the antiwar movement during the 1960s and changed her voter registration from Republican to Democrat. Malcolm's great-grandfather was one of the founders of IBM, so she had a fortune at her disposal which she used to support groups dedicated to the advancement of women. Malcolm created EMILY's List after the Democratic Party let down a woman she was working hard to get elected to the Senate, Harriet Woods, in 1982. The party threw its financial backing behind a banking lobbyist, whom Woods beat in the primary despite her lack of funds. Woods lost in the general election to Republican John Danforth by 27,000 votes, and Malcolm thought more money could have made all the difference. Twenty-five years later, in 2007, the EMILY's List Web site featured a photographic history of hundreds of women it has helped lift into office, and at the end of the slide show the images all coalesce into a single picture, of Nancy Pelosi.

"It is the hardest job in politics to put newcomers into office, and particularly in the House," Malcolm said in an interview. "Ninety-eight, ninety-nine percent of members of Congress who run for reelection are reelected." Since most of those incumbents are men, EMILY's List only targets open seats when they hand out money to women candidates. "That means we only have 15 to 20 opportunities where we can begin on an even playing field trying to elect women to office," said Malcolm.

EMILY's List was pivotal in electing Pelosi's friend Barbara Mikulski to Congress in 1986. Inner-city Baltimore, with its gritty row houses and stevedore tastes, seems an unlikely place to have spawned two huge American firsts concerning women in politics. Not only did Baltimore produce America's first female Speaker of the House, it can boast that it sent the first Democratic woman to Senate as well. Just six months before Pelosi arrived in Congress on June 9, 1987, her Polish American neighbor was sworn in on the Senate floor. "For many of the women senators, when we first got elected we were viewed as novelties," Mikulski said in an e-mail interview. "At times they wanted to turn us into celebrities." The tenacious, 4-foot-11 Mikulski was part of a surge of women candidates spurred to run for office in 1986 by the breakthrough vice presidential candidacy of Congresswoman Geraldine Ferraro.

In 1984, Walter Mondale picked the Democrat from New York to join him as the first woman vice presidential candidate on a major party ticket. When Ferraro's candidacy was dogged by questions about her husband's finances, and Ferraro and Mondale suffered a humiliating loss to Ronald Reagan, women involved in politics realized that if they really wanted to see a woman vice president or president someday, they were going to have to work for it themselves. No man was going to hand it to them as a gift. Although Mondale probably would have lost to Reagan no matter who was on the ticket, Ferraro hadn't boosted him with women voters as much as he'd hoped. Many campaign strategists believed that voters weren't ready for a gender-balanced ticket yet and weren't quite comfortable with the notion of a woman in power at the highest levels of government. No woman has been picked for the ticket in the 23 years since then. But just the fact of Ferraro's candidacy gave women a tantalizing taste of what might be possible. You can't be what you can't see, Pelosi once said.

"Role models are exceptionally important in politics," said Larry Sabato. "As a teacher, I see that all the time. Why do so many of the children of politicians go into politics? It's the life they know, and they can easily imagine themselves living that life since they've seen it. People like their family are in the profession."

In the very next election, in 1986, inspired by Ferraro's candidacy and frustrated by her fate, a record 54 woman ran for the House and six women ran for the Senate.

Congresswoman Lindy Boggs was the first woman to chair a national political convention. "Though of course, she wasn't in on the actual vote, I have no doubt that I have Lindy Boggs to thank for privilege of being the highest-ranking woman ever in congressional leadership," Pelosi said in a tribute to Boggs in 2002. She said Boggs taught her two important principles: "Know Thy Power," meaning that women, children, and everyday Americans should realize how much power they have to sway Congress, and "Never fight any fight as if it's your last fight." "No matter how right you think you are, no matter how passionate or angry, you always take off your gloves and shake hands after it's over and come out fighting on the next round," Pelosi explains.

Back in California, Dianne Feinstein plowed up the soil in San Francisco for Pelosi to flourish in later. Feinstein's career rivals Pelosi's in the number of firsts she's achieved: She was the first woman elected president of the powerful San Francisco Board of Supervisors, the first woman mayor of San Francisco in 1978, the first woman elected senator of California in 1992, the first female member of the Senate Judiciary Committee, and recently she became the first woman to serve as the chair of the Senate Rules and Administration Committee.

And of course it was a woman's endorsement that got Pelosi into the House in the first place. If Congresswoman Sala Burton hadn't designated Pelosi as her heir apparent it's uncertain whether Pelosi would have ever run for office, let alone win a competitive special election or rise to Speaker. Pelosi is Exhibit A for the case that the only way for women to reach the top echelons in politics is through the committed assistance of other women.

Certainly Madeline Albright's high visibility as the first female secretary of state in President Bill Clinton's cabinet helped men in Washington get more comfortable with the idea of women in high political places. When she was sworn in in 1997, she became the highest-ranking woman ever to serve in the U.S. government. Senator Elizabeth Dole's tenure as the first female Secretary of Transportation in President Reagan's administration, then Secretary of Labor in President George H.W. Bush's cabinet, and her brief presidential bid in the 2000 election helped crack the door a bit more for Pelosi. Since the Coast Guard reports to the Department of Transportation, Dole was the first woman to take charge of a branch of the military. After that, Condoleezza Rice's competent run as President Bush's secretary of state and national security advisor from 2000 to 2008 propped the door wide open for Pelosi.

Barbara Kennelly, a fellow Trinity grad of Pelosi's who hails from Connecticut, is probably the woman who most directly prepared the way for Pelosi's bid for leadership in the House. Kennelly achieved the highest rank in Congress of any woman before Pelosi, serving as chief deputy whip of the House Democratic Caucus in the 1980s. She also was the first woman to serve on the House Intelligence Committee, as Pelosi would do later, and the first woman to serve on one of its subcommittees. She was only the third woman in history to serve on the powerful House Ways and Means Committee. "Barbara Kennelly laid the groundwork, and got as far as she could go in the institution," said Professor Rosenthal. "And because of Kennelly's successes, Nancy Pelosi could take the next few steps. It's a step-by-step process."

One picture on Mikulski's office wall shows Kennelly, Ferraro, Mikulski, and Albright arm in arm, all wearing red. When Ferraro was campaigning with Mondale, she lent her apartment to Kennelly, with the stipulation that Mikulski could sleep there when she had to work late. A bond formed that continues to this day. Like Pelosi, all four were taught by nuns in all-girls Catholic schools. In fact, when Pelosi first arrived in Congress, 40 percent of the women there had gone to women's colleges, where most of the presidents, faculty, and student leaders were women. Today, when there are more women in Congress and fewer women's colleges, the number is still at 15 percent, and includes presidential contender Hillary Clinton. Kennelly broke ground for Pelosi by running for chair of the Democratic Caucus in 1989. She was persuaded to run for a leadership post in the House by promises of votes from fellow members, votes that mysteriously evaporated when it was time to be counted. Maryland's Steny Hoyer took the post instead.

"None of the women would have stayed in those races if they didn't think they had more votes," said Schroeder. "Having worked for Ferraro and [Ohio Congresswoman Mary Rose] Okar and Chisholm when they all wanted to run for office, I remember everyone saying they would vote for them and then they didn't." Schroder blames the secret ballot for perpetuating a kind of duplicitous double standard over the years. "The boys don't really want us there, they just didn't want to tell you that," she explained. "With the secret ballot, they figured nobody would every really find out."

Back in 1992, Kennelly was asked by a *Washington Post* reporter who the most powerful women in Congress were. "Why, none of us," she replied.

"Sometimes I think it's harder to become Speaker of the House than president of the United States," Pelosi said in a recent interview. Schroeder and Barbara Boxer said the same thing. Schroeder wasn't sure a woman would ever win the top job in the House, at least not in her lifetime. "You can't go out and get more voters," explains Pelosi. "You know, I always say, as long as you can go get more votes, you can win. When you have a finite voting base, of which a fifth are women, that's not going to do it for you."

The male dominance of Congress has made for some outrageous moments for pioneering women. When Schroeder first took office in 1973, she was only one of 14 women in a 435-member fraternity. "I felt as if I had broken into and entered a private club," Schroeder said. "Most of my new colleagues considered me a mascot or novelty, as if in Denver voters had mistakenly thought 'Pat' meant 'Patrick.'" She was often told that only congressmen could use the House parking lot. "They'd always say that secretaries can't park here. Or you can't get on the elevator. I had to show my ID everywhere I'd go."

One of the worst insults she endured was from F. Edward Herbert, the old-school chairman of the House Armed Services Committee, when she was named to the committee in 1973. The Democratic leadership at the time wanted Ron Dellums, an African American representative from California, on the committee as well. Schroeder said Herbert didn't appreciate the idea of a "girl and a black" being forced on him, so he added only one chair to the committee room and made Dellums and Schroeder share it.

But for Schroeder, the most glaringly sexist thing she remembers during her early days in the House is how she was introduced to people, which was so different from how her male colleagues were introduced. Tip O'Neill was among the worst offenders, she said. So once she turned the tables on him when it was her turn to introduce him at a Washington function.

"This is Millie O'Neill's husband," Schroeder began. "She literally is the cultural maven of Boston. And of course the most important thing in his life are his four wonderful children, and on and on and on."

"To his credit, he looked at me and he said 'Pat, I get it.'"

Old habits die hard on the Hill. It wasn't until the early 1990s that women were even allowed to wear pants on the Senate floor. In 1985, Barbara Boxer and two representatives from Ohio, Marcy Kaptur and Mary Rose Oakar, led a hard-fought battle to get women access to the House gym and fitness facilities. The men had modern exercise equipment, a swimming pool, and a basketball court that were off limits to the women. Before a meeting of the House Democratic whips, the three gentleladies belted out a singing protest to the tune of "Has Anyone Seen My Gal?" (We're not slim, we're not trim/Can't you make it hers or him/Can't everybody use your gym?) It took a while, but it worked.

When Oakar later became vice chair of the Democratic caucus, she had to demand that Tip O'Neill get her invited to White House congressional leadership meetings. Finally included, she was given a seat at the back of the room, against the wall, rather than at the table. She walked out. An aide chased her down, offered her a seat *at* the table, and she returned.

When she arrived with the Class of '92, Lynn Schenk noted that Congress, which she thought ought to be *leading* the country, was actually behind the changes in American society and failing to keep pace. "Out in the real world, we took care of a lot of these basic issues between men and women years ago," Schenk said at the time. "But this place has been so insulated, the shock waves of the '70s and '80s haven't quite made it through the walls."

Once women got to Congress and started making some inroads, men often took the credit. New Jersey Congresswoman Marge Roukema and Pat Schroeder initiated the Family Leave Act requiring employers to grant up to 12 weeks unpaid leave each year to an employee for the birth of a child or the care of a family member with a serious illness. The landmark bill passed Congress in February 1993, just weeks after the new crop of congresswomen were sworn in, but at the presidential bill signing, only male members of Congress shared the stage with President Clinton and Vice President Al Gore. At the time, Schroeder observed: "Often you see women start the issue, educate on the issue, fight for the issue, and then when it becomes fashionable, men push us aside. And they get away with it."

Schroeder believes things have changed a lot in the country since those formative years for women. "The Congress has changed a lot, too. Even the men have changed. Men are much more involved in their children," she said. "Kids used to be campaign props, who were to be seen but not heard. Now men boast about their family commitments, more so than women in office." But not everything has changed. Pelosi and others say sexism, intentional or otherwise, is less crude now on Capitol Hill but in many ways more insidious because everyone thinks it's gone.

"It's still happening. It's happening to different women in different ways," remarks Marie Wilson, founder of The White House Project. "There's still a built-in paternalism, which means women still have to walk the tightrope of being tough as nails and warm as toast, as Anna Quindlen used to put it, all at the same time."

"Do we still experience sexism?" asks Anna Eshoo. "Sure we do. Not just here, we all do." But no one really thinks Congress is sexist anymore, especially now that a woman is in charge, so complaints of sexism are falling on deafer ears.

Anita Hill observed recently that when women or minorities try to cross lines and assert themselves in new places that aren't part of their defined roles, such as becoming preachers in black churches, "It's even harder now because the pretense is that these lines no longer exist. But there are many, many invisible lines."

Congressman Leonard Boswell, a Democrat from Iowa, said he still hears a lot of objections to the idea of women political leaders there.

"Occasionally I'll run into people in the district and out around the country who just won't support a woman. You know that, we all know that." You mean, they won't support a woman for president? he's asked. "Or about anything," Boswell answers. "And they'll say something derogatory about Nancy and I'll say, 'Why do you say that?' Maybe you know something I don't know so tell me, why do you say that?' And I've never got a response," said Boswell. "It's emotion. The same thing happens with Hillary. And it's the same kind of people."

Wilson and others think the country's entrenched paternalism plays out a little differently for Hillary Clinton and Nancy Pelosi. "The way it plays out with Hillary is to demonize her power. The way it plays out with Pelosi is to minimize or infantilize her power. But they both have the same effect. That's what patriarchy has been about: Women are evil, or they are childish." Wilson isn't sure whether it's intentional or not. It may just be the way many men are trying to reassert some authority over newly powerful women.

The day after the 2006 election, President Bush acknowledged Pelosi's victory and then quipped that he had sent her "the names of some Republican interior decorators who can help her pick out the new drapes in her new offices." When Pelosi took a trip to Syria to meet with the controversial president there a few months into her tenure as Speaker, Vice President Dick Cheney scolded her for "bad behavior."

"It's so 'my little girl.' The drapes are about 'my little woman.' The bad behavior's about my little girl," said Wilson. "A good girl would never pick up and go to Damascus. I thought it was fascinating from that standpoint. And he chose that language so carefully. Imagine him saying about a male Congressman 'bad behavior.'" If Steny Hoyer had been elected Speaker, would Bush have told him he'd send somebody by to cut the drapes? Or that it was bad behavior for him to go to Syria? "Not unless he'd been a dog-catcher," said Wilson.

When Geraldine Ferraro ran on the ticket with Mondale back in 1984, the sexism was blatant and unapologetic. "It was so sexist, it was stuff like she has beautiful legs, she has nicer legs than her opponent. I want to see her in a wet T-shirt contest with her opponent," said Wilson. (These were the days before sexual harassment was defined in the workplace . . . or the campaign trail, for that matter.) "People said all that kind of stuff because it was OK. The ways we've come are harder to deal with. Because, you know, if the Republicans were saying 'Did Pelosi go over to Syria to have a wet T-shirt contest?' somebody would cream them. But if you just say it was bad behavior, then the reaction is 'Well, he didn't say anything, he just said it was not the right thing to do.' What you do is you do it subtly, and the subtlety is what really creams women."

A few exhibits of this double standard in media coverage of Pelosi:

- Leslie Stahl, when doing interviews for a profile of Pelosi in 2006, said the first thing every man said about Pelosi was that "she was an attractive woman."
- In 2002, House Republican majority leader Dick Armey actually meant well when he recycled an old stereotype in an interview with the *San Francisco Chronicle*: "One of the reasons Nancy's abilities are not appreciated is that she is a beautiful woman."
- MSNBC's Chris Matthews questioned whether Pelosi would "castrate" her majority leader Steny Hoyer. He also asks frequently how Pelosi and other women leaders can be tough or effective. "How does she do it without screaming? How does she do it without becoming grating?"
- Right-wing radio talk show host Michael Savage claimed that men from the Middle East justifiably don't like America because we have "loud-mouthed, foul-tempered" women like Pelosi, Hillary Clinton and Boxer "bossing men around."
- MSNBC telepundit Tucker Carlson once said the Democratic Party was controlled by "grouchy feminists with mustaches."
- *Wall Street Journal* writer David Rogers, on November 15, 2002, criticized Pelosi's "leadership style," mocking the "den-motheresque whip letters—full of team spirit and kudos for individual members," letters he said that "sometimes gush."
- On the November 16, 2006, edition of CNN's *Newsroom*, political analyst Bay Buchanan said that Pelosi's "judgment is based on emotions not good sense."
- On November 18, 2006, anchor Contessa Brewer wondered if Pelosi's "personal feelings [were] getting in the way of effective leadership" and asked whether men were "more capable of taking personality clashes."
- After Pelosi's nomination of John Murtha for majority leader, the *New York Times*' Maureen Dowd said: "She plays like a girl."
- Dennis Miller, in a rant on October 26, 2006, said: "Every time I see Pelosi in her little Chanel suits—a latter-day 'Wacky O'—regurgitating the Democratic talking points that she had to learn phonetically because the word 'grasp' is not even vaguely in her vocabulary, I shake my head so badly you could blend paint colors in my mouth."

"When there are only a few women in real positions of power in the country, the press treats them through the lens of gender," worries Wilson. "If there were more women in power, gender would be less of an issue. They're starting with her hair, what she's wearing, instead of her issues, instead of the positions she takes. The problem is it whittles you down softly, it's killing you softly. And so it whittles down your authority. It happens in companies, too."

Pelosi herself has a huge capacity for simply tuning the chauvinism out or turning it to her advantage. She's known for a thick skin, and "she knows how to charm men, especially chauvinistic men," said one acquaintance. Even so, if Congress was so Cro-Magnon in its outlook toward women in power during her rise, how did she make it? How did she get where she got? Sure, Congress is different now, but what was her shield from the prejudices of men during her early days?

The answer may be Jack Murtha.

In 1987, when Pelosi arrived, the former Marine had a reputation for male chauvinism that stood out even in the boy's club of Congress. Murtha fought in both Korea and Vietnam, and hails from Pennsylvania's rugged coal country. He works the House floor with a booming voice and no-prisoner's approach to politics. And he and Pelosi have been allies and friends for 20 years.

"There's a lot of chauvinism in the Congress. And there's a lot of men . . . that . . . will just not vote for a woman," Murtha said in an interview. "Of course, that's where I had some influence." Murtha's backing "was the answer to sexism in the place," an aide to Pelosi told a reporter. "If he didn't have any problem with a woman in leadership, no one else would either." The counterintuitive pairing makes some sense from a psychological standpoint: A man who spent 36 years in the military and was awarded two Purple Hearts is probably secure enough in his masculinity not to be threatened by much of anything, including a powerful woman. "As the only girl among five brothers, we know she learned how to negotiate with the guys at the family dinner table!" said Mikulski. Several of Pelosi's most ardent allies are alpha male guys, including George Miller, John Burton, and Illinois Congressman Rahm Emanuel. Murtha and Pelosi became such strong friends that he went on to manage her campaign for whip and minority leader and now heads up her effort in the House to get the country out of the Iraq War.

"When I'd go to meetings during this time she'd have all the women in the House in there and just a few men," Murtha recalls. "They would always talk about women's issues. And I said, 'Look, there's a hell of a lot more men in here than there are women so you'd better think about broadening your . . . base.' And she did."

CHAPTER 7 ✦

THE GLASS CEILING

You can't break the glass ceiling unless you know where it is.

—Ann E. W. Stone, Republican activist and one of the
founders of the National Women's History Museum

On Tuesday during her formative years in Congress, Pelosi's calendar often carried the simple notation, "Gang Dinner." It meant the Tuesday Night Dinner Gang was getting together for pasta, California wine, and camaraderie. The small circle of lawmakers included several Californians—Barbara Boxer, George Miller, Leon Panetta, the congressman from Santa Clara County, and, a little later, Anna Eshoo—all of whom became close friends with Pelosi during the long plane rides back to their districts each week. Tom Downey, a congressman at the time out of Long Island, often hosted the gang at his row house on D Street. Downey's wife, Chris, loved to cook for everyone. His children knew Pelosi so well they called her Aunt Nancy. Marty Russo and Dick Durbin of Illinois usually joined them, as did Chuck Schumer of New York and Sam Gejdenson, a former Connecticut lawmaker. Sometimes the gang would get together at Marty's American Bar & Grill on the Hill. Sometimes Miller had everybody over to his frat-like townhouse for orphaned congressmen on Capitol Hill, though the lady lawmakers always complained a bit about the Cheetos crumbs on the floor. Miller, Durbin, and Schumer once hosted a fundraiser for Boxer at the group home during which guests received pairs of custom-made "Barbara Boxer shorts."

During one of the dinners at the Downey house in 1989, a massive earthquake hit San Francisco, severely damaging many buildings, roads, and bridges and killing 67 people. The temblor came to be known as the World Series Earthquake because it struck right before the start of a series game in Candlestick Park. "Nancy and Barbara were naturally worried because their husbands and family members were all at the game," Downey told the *San Francisco Chronicle*. "I had a big satellite dish at the time, and we were able to get the San Francisco news feeds to see what was going on." Millions of viewers could see the motion and the destruction of the quake as it was happening, including the swaying girders in Candlestick and sections of the Bay Bridge collapsing onto cars underneath. The final damage was more than $6 billion. Nancy and Barbara's families, however, escaped injury that night.

"We had the earthquake in '89, Tiananmen Square, the Gulf War," said Pelosi's chief of staff at the time, Judy Lemons. "When I retired I said, Nancy, we've been through everything. We've been through earthquakes, wars, everything in the world."

Pelosi cemented some of her most important friendships on gang nights, forming her "California Kitchen Cabinet." Boxer would move over to the Senate eventually, becoming one of Pelosi's fiercest allies and defenders there. Russo would go on to form the most lucrative lobbying house in Washington, Cassidy & Associates, reinventing the way Congress doles out money via a little innovation of his called "earmarks." As head of Pelosi's policy committee, Miller is now Pelosi's right hand in Congress. Anna Eshoo is probably her closest confidante in Congress. Panetta became chief of staff for President Bill Clinton in 1994, and Schumer and Durbin are both now senators.

"Those dinners were like having your family over," says Boxer. "You would talk issues, strategy, politics. I'm one of these people who believe that getting together with friends like that makes you better at what you do because you get to test out ideas." Boxer often organized the event and still does, though infrequently now. "Once a month we'll get nostalgic for one another's company so I'll call up," she adds. Nancy still attends whenever they get together. All remain good friends.

It was at those early gang gatherings that some of her friends started to think Nancy might be House leadership material.

"Over the years, amongst the gang, and there were a lot of political stripes in there, and they saw what Nancy was," said Eshoo. "We were always amazed at what her observations were, about everything. They saw what a sophisticate this women was and is . . . what a decisive leader she was.

She's not a white-knuckle leader. She's not afraid to make decisions, and boy, she makes 109 of them a day."

When Boxer was still in the House in the late 1980s, she remembers talking to Pelosi about future leadership possibilities. "I remember one day we were sitting on the plane and I think I said something to Nancy about how great she was at fundraising. And that I thought that she could be the first female chair of the DCCC [Democratic Congressional Campaign Committee]. And she does not remember this, but I remember her saying, and this is very early on, in the '80s, 'Well, I really want to be Speaker.' And I said: 'I really want to be senator.' Each of us thought the other one was dreaming."

"I always thought that she was destined for something great," says Eshoo. "I just thought so. People leave trails. Nancy has never left any broken glass behind her. How she has treated people. They love her."

What spurred Pelosi to go after her dream and mount her own bid for leadership, however, was the Democrats' surprise loss of Congress in 1994 during President Clinton's first term, the first time the party had been out of the majority in 40 years. "This should never have happened," she used to say. She soon felt the party leaders weren't doing enough to retake the majority. And she told close friends such as Lemons and Miller that she did not come to the House to sit in the minority.

"I think when we lost the House, she knew that we had to mobilize, generate support, recruit good candidates, and do all the things necessary," said Lemons. "She really made it a priority and really focused on that. And she became a player." Pelosi had always been energized by grand moral causes and difficult quests, especially campaign-related ones. Over and above her legislative work, this became her grail: to win back the House. Adds Lemons: "She had a cause."

Newt Gingrich and his Republican Revolution had capitalized on the perception that the House Democratic leadership was calcified and corrupt, much the same way Pelosi and the Democrats benefited from what they dubbed a "culture of corruption" among Republicans in 2006. Clinton and his presidency, including a failed attempt at creating universal healthcare—a proposal that was spearheaded by Hillary Clinton—were rallying points for resurgent conservative voters as well. The opposition party historically makes gains in Congress in the midterm election of a president's first term, but this was a much bigger shift than usual. Fifty-four House seats swung from Democrat to Republican, and eight Senate seats.

Gingrich had reinvented congressional politics during the fall election. His "Contract for America" was a specific list of actions the Republicans said they'd take if they won the majority in Congress. Essentially, Gingrich was allowing Americans to vote on proposed legislation themselves for the first time. The contract included institutional reforms for Congress, welfare reform, term limits, tougher crime laws, a balanced budget law—and a promise to bring all of the proposed legislation up for a vote in the first 100 days of Congress. Just six weeks after Gingrich introduced his contract promise, Republicans gained 54 seats and returned to the majority for the first time since 1954. And Gingrich kept his promise: all major legislation in the Contract was brought to the floor within the first 100 days. But most of it didn't get passed, or got bogged down in the Senate, and many of the items were vetoed by Clinton. Still, Gingrich had set a precedent, turning what had been a loosely confederated group of local elections into a truly national campaign. Pelosi and Rahm Emanuel used a similar model in 2006 when they nationalized the vote around Iraq. And Pelosi borrowed a page from Gingrich with the Six for '06 agenda she vowed to pass in the first 100 hours of Congress if she took control back.

Thirty-four Democratic incumbents were defeated in the 1994 vote, including House Speaker Tom Foley, the first Speaker to lose his district since the Civil War. In other words, the Democrats were left flat-footed and dumb-founded, spoiled over their years by their sizable majorities.

"They didn't see fully what was coming," said Eshoo. "Inside the Beltway, I mean this is like the Old Country, the thinking here. The heavy-weights in this town were loaded down by their weighted thinking. It's a place that's somewhat blinded by the weight of the past. And the past is marked by page after page after page of . . . 'the old way of thinking.' It's just the way this place is."

Pelosi and other Democrats thought it was time to inject some new blood into the Democratic Party leadership. In an interview with C-SPAN in 2001, Pelosi said she decided to seek a leadership post "because I thought it was important for us to have some different thinking that perhaps isn't at the table." She made the point then that, in 200 years, there had never been a woman, or a Californian, or an Italian American in a leadership position in the House. Right there, she said, she brought three different things to the table.

Though she did think it was important that the leadership of the House include a woman, she said right off the bat that she was not emphasizing her gender in the contest. "I didn't run as a woman," Pelosi said later. "I ran as a seasoned politician and an experienced legislator. It just so happens that I am a woman and we have been waiting a long time for this moment." Boxer said much the same thing about her friend: "I would not say at all that the reason Nancy is where she is because she's a woman. The reason Nancy is where she is because she's Nancy, and she has an amazing combination of skills." Yet much of the discussion about Nancy's bid for leadership, a discussion driven by Pelosi and her allies and the growing number of women in Congress after 1992's Year of the Woman, was about how a woman's candidacy would speak to the strong base of woman voters in the Democratic Party. There's no question that her gender was part of her appeal for many members. "To be frank, gender helps account for her rise to speaker," said Corey Cook. "The support of women Democrats partly elevated her. Initially, how she got into leadership is innately related to that." Cook, an authority on California politics, Congress, and the impact of gender on politics, says that historically, a woman's role politically has been seen in part as cleaning up the messes. "There is a sort of dimension of women as reformers, which is a strand throughout American political history. That's a pretty well-established historical trend." Men are often regarded in modern politics as the status quo and women as agents of change. In troubled times, voters want agents of change. And in the late 1990s, times were troubled for the Democrats.

Personally, Pelosi thought her geography was her biggest advantage as a candidate. She believed a West Coaster could shake up the East Coast establishment a bit. Not only did California have a huge delegation—32 votes, most of which Nancy could count on from the start—but the country's most populous state gave her a huge base of campaign contributors as well. Pelosi used to say nonchalantly, "I have the biggest base of supporters, individual supporters, of anybody in Congress." She also believed her outsider status as a westerner was an advantage in bringing some fresh thinking to a caucus that had just lost the Congress.

"It's mostly the western perspective. The entrepreneurial spirit is in the air, it's in the water," she said. "It's the attitude that people have that anything is possible. Let's not wed ourselves to old ways of thinking. Then you come back to Washington and boom, you hit that wall of resistance, which again I think is wedded to older ways of making decisions. It doesn't mean we shouldn't be respectful of our decisions. But we must also spring from them into fresher, newer approaches."

Her husband, Paul, was well versed in the new technology-based economy and the entrepreneurial forces driving it when Nancy launched her bid for leadership. You might say she is the first leader to emerge from the creative soil that spawned the high-tech revolution in Silicon Valley and the expansion of the Internet. Call it Politics 2.0.

"She's infused and motivated by California," said Eshoo. "California is the home of Nobel laureates and Levi laureates and disruptive thinking and innovation. And, in our region, most especially in my district [Silicon Valley], you don't count unless you have failed. Where here [in Washington], it's damnation. It's over for you here. How many times have they said: she shouldn't have done this, it's over. There's proper way to do things."

Miller, another of the Tuesday Night gangsters, has called Pelosi "a political disruptor." The terms "technological disruptor" or "disruptive innovation" are popular in Silicon Valley and refer to a technological innovation that supplants the existing dominant technology, as CD-ROMs replaced floppy disks, or digital photography is displacing film. The art of "disruption" is seen as a key to innovation and progress, a kind of new lingo for "creative destruction." Pelosi has said in speeches that she welcomes "an opportunity to disrupt, an opportunity to make a difference" in Washington.

In her early discussions with other members about the possibility of her bid for the Speakership, she also made the point that San Francisco's free-for-all, popcorn-popper politics was a great training ground for the job. "It's just the most magnificently diverse district, with people from all over the world. It's also a place where people are respectful of each others' point of view. I think the public expects us to have a certain civility in our debate here."

Others involved in San Francisco politics second the notion that the city's diversity is a good training ground for professional politicians. "San Francisco's politics are at an intensity that most places around the country don't share," says Alex Clemens, a longtime campaign operative and political handicapper in San Francisco. "A lot of it has to do with the nature of the city," argues Cook. "The politics in San Francisco is different than the politics in other places. The stakes are higher, the expectations are greater. People pay more attention in San Francisco."

Clemens thinks that San Francisco values, so derided in attacks on Pelosi over the years, are just a preview of America's future values. "We're a city of immigrants," says Clemens. "We think of ourselves as a shining city on a hill. We are a place that hosts many natives, but also a vibrant band of immigrants who show up because ideas are welcomed here, because being gay is welcomed here, because we're a very diverse city racially, because you can be who you are in San Francisco. That constant melting pot of ideas and new immigrants both from other parts of the world and from other parts of the country keep us on the cutting edge of many different debates. And the nation is going to go through them eventually. We tend to export our political struggles to the state of California 6 to 8 years after we go through them and then to the rest of the country 15 to 20 years after that. We are the place to go if you want the preview."

When San Franciscans speak of diversity, they are not just talking about economic or ethnic diversity, Cook points out. "You know we have this national reputation as being this leftist outlier, much of which is well earned. But the thing that folks don't realize is how fractured the city is politically. How many hundreds of different groups there are. We don't have handful of single-interest groups, we have a thousand single-interest groups. There is not one Democrat Party, there are dozens of different Democratic parties."

San Francisco is seven miles wide by seven miles long. It's a city of 800,000 in a state of 36 million, yet it dominates the state's politics, at least for now.

"A political figure like Gavin Newsom, he's a relatively small-town mayor," Cook says. "This isn't being mayor of New York. On the other hand, I think our political environment is probably as challenging or more challenging than New York given the ideological diversity, the interest diversity, the economic diversity, the ethnic diversity, the language diversity, all of that. You're being forced to manage all these competing demands in a high-pressure political environment."

With its progressive bent, California was also ahead of the country in sending women to Congress and in placing women in high political positions. "For the last 30 years, San Francisco has been a national leader in placing female politicians in leading roles," said Clemens. "We had Mayor Feinstein starting in the late '70s. Starting in the late '80s, we had a majority female Board of Supervisors. Six women, five men." When Pelosi was thinking about a possible leadership bid, both the state's senators—Barbara Boxer and Dianne Feinstein—were not only women, they were women from San Francisco. Talk about role models. Nineteen of California's members of Congress were women at the time, or about 36 percent of the delegation.

It's within that context that Pelosi began to think of herself as the possible answer to her party's woes. "I looked around and thought one day . . . I think I can bring that thinking to the table. I think I can win," Pelosi said.

"When she figured out that she's raising a lot of money and she had to argue to get an extra $15,000 to some candidate in California, while she's out raising more money than anybody else at that time except for maybe Dick Gephardt," that's when she decided to make a bid for leadership, says John Burton. "So it's just like, if I'm going to do this, if I'm going raise this money, if I'm going do this work, I want to make sure I've got some input on what's going on."

But the party's old thinkers resisted. Pelosi feels that many in the Democratic establishment didn't take her desire for leadership seriously because of her far-left base and because she was a woman.

"I think women are always underestimated in terms of being in a new position. Or at least it's a question . . ." Pelosi said in a recent interview in her office. "It's such a male-dominated institution. It's sort of a pecking order that goes back over 200 years. And all of a sudden you're saying wait I minute, I have another idea about how this should be."

"She's always been underestimated, undervalued," says Eshoo. When well-known political analyst Charlie Cook, author of *The Cook Political Report*, raised Pelosi's name as a prospective running mate for the Democratic nominee in 2000, *San Francisco Chronicle* columnist Marc Sandalow said: "Vice President Pelosi? Have the political cognoscenti lost their minds?" For a time, she felt like the Democratic leadership of the House was working directly against her. "They couldn't control me, so they tried to take me down," she told *Time* magazine in the late 1990s. Her father felt the same way about the Democratic leadership in Maryland: The Democratic political bosses forced him to run as an outsider in his first few elections as well. That role as an in-the-system outsider, crusading against the system from within, seems to fuel Pelosi's passion for politics.

"If Nancy Pelosi had been the minority leader right after Gingrich and those guys took over, the Democrats would have gotten the House back 8 to 10 years ago," says John Burton. "I know."

With the burgeoning woman's caucus and friends like Burton egging her on, Pelosi dedicated herself to helping bring about the return of the Democrats—partly to prove her own worth as a potential leader and partly to prove the worth of women as leaders. That sense of disenfranchisement, of being perennially undervalued, became another piece of her cause, friends say. It gave her the drive to stay with her single-minded odyssey for the next 13 years. Pelosi's latter-day protestations that "she never intended to run for public office" seem a bit disingenuous in that light. They may just be a vestigial Victorian reflex that women should not show ambition too obviously lest they be considered unwomanly. There's just no denying that Nancy is ambitious. To stick with a three-year campaign to promote yourself to your friends and colleagues as the single best hope for your party takes a fairly impressive ego. It turns out, of course, that she was right. Her success, ironically, may clear the way culturally so that other women don't have to be so coy about their interest in achieving power. When asked if she had any advice for a precocious six-year-old girl bent on being president of the United States, Pelosi said: "Go for it."

With a safe seat in San Francisco, Pelosi went for it herself by putting all of her influence and skills and Rolodex of donors into the service of electioneering. She started doing for Congress what she did for the party in California: raising money, helping identify and recruit good candidates, hop scotching around the country making campaign appearances for other Congress members, and generally doing everything in every two-year cycle she could to try to win back the House, aides say. "I think people saw all that," said Lemons. "They saw: 'My god, she's a whirling dervish, a fighting devil who's just out there fighting.'"

Pelosi began to convert her reliable base of hundreds of wealthy California donor friends into a national network. Many of the Pelosis' friends were wealthy, wanted to support her, and could afford to be generous. They also wanted to support good causes and good things, and Nancy became the conduit. She had a knack for appealing to their social consciences, for getting them excited about how much good they could do by giving to the Democratic Party. They trusted her instincts—and her ability to make things happen. And they saw results. One of her own political action committees, which Leo McCarthy, the former state lieutenant governor, had help set up, had raised more than $1 million in a year's time. Between 1999 and 2004, Pelosi's political action committees, PAC to the Future and Team Majority, gave nearly $3.8 million to help other members of Congress win races. At the Democratic Congressional Committee headquarters, her staff keeps a database of more than 29,000 donors Pelosi has personally contacted over the years. It's no different, really, than the yellow sheets of paper her father made to keep track of favors he did in Little Italy, scaled to national proportions. Call it the Favor File 2.0.

The Favor File got Pelosi into trouble in 2003 when Team Majority was fined $21,000 for accepting donations over the federal limits allowed for members of Congress. The problem was Pelosi had two PACs, and federal law says that PACs under the control of the same person are considered affiliated and must adhere to limits as if they were one. PAC contributions to candidates are limited to $5,000 per election, as are donations to PACs from individuals. Pelosi gave more than two dozen candidates the $5,000 maximum contribution from Team Majority and PAC to the Future during the 2002 campaign. Following her usual protocol when there is an appearance of impropriety in her finances, Pelosi paid the fine, gave back more than $100,000 in donations that were collected in access of limits and disbanded Team Majority.

But given Pelosi's outspoken advocacy of campaign finance reform, many Congress watchers were asking why it happened in the first place. In 1998, she said: "The greatest enemy to our democracy is foreign and domestic money poisoning our system." She has repeatedly said Washington has become "a swamp of special interest money." Yet what are PACs if not special interest money?

McCarthy candidly admitted to Roll Call that the "main reason" for setting up the second PAC was to "give twice as much hard dollars" to candidates. McCarthy and Brendan Daly, Pelosi's communications director, both said the FEC had approved the arrangement in a phone call, though it is the FEC's policy that so-called Advisory Opinions be obtained in writing.

The fine was a result of a complaint by a small private Congressional watchdog, the National Legal and Policy Center based in Virginia. If they hadn't unearthed the violation it might never have been publicly known. Reacting to the fines, NLPC Chairman Ken Boehm said: "We are delighted that the FEC has acted favorably on our complaint. No member of Congress has ever set up a second leadership PAC to evade contribution limits. Pelosi has been caught violating the clearest and most basic law of all, the limits on contributions. Talk about hypocrisy." In 2006, Boehm spent months looking into Nancy Pelosi's financial records, campaign contributions and legislative records, trying to sniff out other improprieties. Boehm has probably scrutinized the Pelosi family finances more than any other person on earth. Yet in an interview with the San Francisco Chronicle he said: "There was no sign that she enriched herself personally by her official actions. She didn't cross the line as far as I could tell."

Some Congress watchers believe that if Pelosi were serious about ending the influence of special interests in politics, she could lead by example as Speaker, dismantling her PAC as a symbolic stand against all special interest PACs and their outsized influence on politics. But then of course she wouldn't have the influence she holds over other members that the donations have given her. In the first 7 months of 2007, she had already raised more than $15 million to dole out to other Congressional candidates.

Berkeley's Bruce Cain, a longtime observer of California politics, thinks Pelosi represents a new kind of political export from the Golden State: the legislative enabler.

"We have a completely money-driven politics" in California, said Cain. "The party is a fund-raising mechanism." That's what the national media didn't understand about San Francisco politics when Pelosi was elected, Cain thinks. "So much now about leadership in Congress is about enabling other politicians, with money and power. That's what California politics have been about for 20 or 30 years. Leading politicians are not masters of legislative craft, they are not policy wonks. We think of them as *legislative enablers*." Pelosi represents a new kind of political template the whole country will be seeing more and more of, Cain believes. "This is the politics of leadership PACs, winning elections, electoral politics. In California we've had expensive electoral politics for a long, long time. That's where Nancy cut her teeth. Increasingly, that's what it takes. She represents this new model of legislative enabler, fundraiser, coalition builder."

Nancy got noticed by party titans in the late 1990s not for some signature piece of legislation or superior legislative expertise. She got noticed because she had expertise and skill working inside the party apparatus.

"She knows the nuts and bolts, and it's not the nuts and bolts inside legislation, it's the nuts and bolts of raising money, preparing the party for elections, a political consultant kind of politics," says Cain. It's a politics modeled more on the dot-com venture capitalist system so prevalent in Northern California, only in this case the seed money goes to promising candidates rather than tech start-ups. Call it Venture Politics, and Pelosi is its Google. Are there better policy wonks than Nancy in the Democratic Party? Certainly, though colleagues say she's one of the best informed. Are there politicians who are better on TV? Undoubtedly. Are there better legislative craftspeople? Pelosi would concede that point herself. Are there even people who are better at articulating the Democratic message? Probably. But nobody's better at helping other candidates win races.

The race for House Whip officially began on July 13, 1999, when Representative Loretta Sanchez hosted a small dinner for Pelosi at Barolo's restaurant on Capitol Hill. At the time, Pelosi was betting the race would last just a year and four months, until November 2000. In every election since 1994, the Democrats had gotten closer and closer, and Pelosi thought the Democrats had a good chance of winning back the House in 2000. If that happened, Dick Gephardt would become Speaker of the House, David Bonior of Michigan would become majority leader, and the whip's job would open up. Pelosi wanted the job. There were also rumors that Bonior had started talking about running for governor back home in Michigan because his congressional seat was being redistricted out from under him. And Gephardt was talking about running for president again in 2000. If both those things happened, and the Democrats won in 2000, the new whip would actually become the new Speaker of the House. That was something worth running for.

"Once those rumors started flying, you locked in, you locked in right there on what you were hoping to do," said Lemons. In other words, you had to decide you wanted it, and decide you wanted it bad. In 1998, Pelosi conducted an informal survey of House Democrats to see if there were enough votes to make her a contender. With 40 women in the House, 17 of whom were Californians, and 52 delegates total hailing from California, Pelosi had some healthy built-in constituencies. Unlike the men in Congress, women tended to vote as a bloc, as did Californians. Pelosi found 80 votes in that very first survey. The magic number was 108.

Pelosi made it clear to the 25 guests at Barolo's that she wanted it. She held two more dinners quickly afterward. Complaints started to come from other possible candidates, including Maryland's Steny Hoyer and John Lewis of Georgia, that it was far too early to start an in-House campaign for leadership, especially given the fact that the Democrats hadn't even won the House back yet. Pelosi dismissed the complaints as the grumblings of an old boy's network trying to hang onto its power. "In order to buck 200 years of history, if I have to start earlier than someone else, so be it."

So began months of dinners, campaign appearances, letters to caucuses, team lunches, impromptu lobbying sessions in the hall. Lewis, a leader of the civil rights movement in the 1960s, was an early casualty. When he pulled out in the summer of 2000, he blamed Pelosi for starting the contest too early and said he didn't think he had the stamina or support to stay in the marathon race for the duration.

That left a single opponent, Steny Hoyer. Patrician, silver-haired Hoyer looks like one of the faces on Mount Rushmore and gives stem-winding, rafter-ringing speeches on the House floor. He's a lot like Pelosi in many ways. They both grew up in Maryland and both interned in the office of Maryland's senator Daniel Brewster after college. He was also inspired during his college days, like Pelosi, by John F. Kennedy, whose bust graces his office. In 1959, a Pontiac convertible passed him on the University of Maryland campus carrying Kennedy, and Hoyer impulsively followed it to the student center. Inside, Kennedy gave an inspiring, idealistic speech asking students to get involved in government to change the world. The next week, Hoyer changed his major to politics and decided to heed Kennedy's call. "It was just like that," Hoyer says. Later, in Congress, Pelosi and Hoyer were on the Appropriations Committee together, and both became dealmakers and nuts-and-bolts pragmatists who knew how to get things done in the Capitol Hill labyrinth. His signature piece of legislation was the Americans with Disabilities Act, which he shepherded into being under a Republican president in 1990. He also endeared himself to other members by fighting for pay raises over the years. The two were friends: Pelosi backed him in his first bid for whip.

In the race against Pelosi, the friendship turned into an intense rivalry. They became what the tabloids would call "frenemies." There was no clear front-runner at the beginning of the contest, although Hoyer had the experience and visibility of having run for a leadership post before. Hoyer cast himself as the more moderate candidate, pro-defense and pro-trade, and thought he could appeal to a wider range of Democrats than Pelosi could. Pelosi cast her self as a vote for diversity, for "the new."

The job Pelosi and Hoyer were after was the number-three leadership post among Democrats in the House. The majority "whip" is the party's chief nose-counter, charged with persuading colleagues to back the party line on legislation they are trying to pass, sometimes with carrots, sometimes with a whip. "Whipping" party members into shape requires managing floor debates, spreading the party position, and counting and delivering votes. A giant leather bow whip is usually displayed prominently in the winner's office. It's a thankless job—you constantly have to be the disciplinarian and bad guy—but it's considered the stepping-stone to the jobs of majority leader and Speaker. "We pretty much figured the winner would be the next leader and the speaker of the House," Representative Bob Matsui of Sacramento told the *San Francisco Chronicle*. Hoyer had tried for the job before, but lost to David Bonior after some of the senior members decided to throw their weight his way. This time around, Hoyer was making sure he locked up all the party titans early.

When Lewis pulled out and threw his support behind Hoyer, the race for whip became a high-stakes two-person poker game, played with a deck of 215 cards (the number of Democrats in the House). The object of the game was to collect 108 of those cards. The contest becomes Texas Hold 'Em–like in the machinations involved in figuring out which supporters your opponent has, which are firmly in hand for you, and which could go either way. Some support is clear at the beginning of the game. The 32 California cards, for example, were all in Pelosi's hand; much of the East Coast in Hoyer's. Early counts made public by each of the candidates showed a pretty close show-down, between 80 and 85 votes for Hoyer, 65 for the upstart Pelosi. At this stage, your opponent knows who many of your supporters are, suspects who some of the others are, and has no clue about a pack of Congress members who haven't revealed themselves one way or the other to either of the players. The trick is in divining how many of these "community cards"—members who could go either way—will help you and how many will help your opponent. The game is complicated by a whole slew of wild cards, however. The fact that a bloc of supporters, the conservative Blue Dog Democrats, for example, may follow their caucus leader once he decides what his vote is makes getting those wild cards extremely important. Two or three wild cards in your hand and the game is up. And since no want really wants to be on the wrong side of the person who ends up winning, there's quite a lot of bluffing involved. One veteran of the games told the *Washington Post:* "People say what they want to say and people hear what they want to hear. Obviously at the end of the day, somebody gets lied to."

The game requires a constant counting and recounting of the cards you hold. "Every Wednesday we would have a team lunch," said Judy Lemons. Pelosi and her staff had assignments for everyone who came and "lists, lists, lists." "We had this little formatted card that gave each member who came to that team luncheon three people to work that week. And then the next week you'd have a report. Slowly you could start to pull together all of these pieces and information about where all of the members stood," said Lemons. One of the enticements to join Nancy's team was great food, Lemons joked. "People would come just to eat. They were just sandwiches, but they were good sandwiches, grilled salmon, tomato, mozzarella: She always says: 'First we eat.'"

Pelosi asked her oldest and most powerful ally, Jack Murtha, to be her campaign manager. "I agreed because I felt like she had a talent for politics, a talent and a vision," Murtha said in an interview. "It wasn't just politics, it was a vision for the country that I was interested in." Denver's Pat Schroeder, who was in Congress at the time, said their operation was to die for. "They put on a whip operation that was very good. They really did. Eat your heart out. I wish I'd had that."

Lemons said Pelosi never countenanced a negative strategy against Hoyer. "One of the things that she ran on for whip was that she saw the caucus as a huge force of creative talent. And that every individual in that caucus had a role to play and she intended to utilize the creative thinking and the resources of the caucus and to showcase every aspect of the caucus."

This was Texas Hold 'Em with high stakes: The betting in this case was the money raised for other candidates in the 2000 elections. Venture politics was coming of age. One candidate, rookie Brad Carson, wasn't even in Congress yet when he received donations from both Hoyer and Pelosi. Eventually he got $25,000 from Hoyer and $22,000 from Pelosi on his way to winning his race against a retiring Republican in Oklahoma. By the time November rolled around, Hoyer had wagered $1.5 million on Democratic candidates, five times what the majority leader Bonior had given to candidates in the entire last decade. Pelosi, however, had wagered $3.9 million, an amount that simply stunned the rest of the caucus.

Yet the Democrats failed to win back the House in 2000. They trimmed the Republican Party's margin to six seats but still fell short of fulfilling Pelosi's quest. That meant there was no job to fight for anymore. Without a majority, the Democrats didn't need a third party leader. They already had Gephardt as minority leader and Bonior as minority whip. The game was paused.

Later that year, Bonior started making noises again about running for governor back in his home state of Minnesota, and by next spring the game was on again. At that stage there were roughly 24 undecideds who were the key to the now two-year-old contest, and Pelosi and Hoyer began massaging egos vigorously.

After losing another election, the Democrats were more determined than ever to shake things up, and the appeal of new faces, such as Pelosi's, grew.

"You know, Steny had been here, he'd run before, against Bonior, and a lot of people were looking at a woman, a liberal who could cross all the boundaries and get Blue Dog support," said Lemons. "Bit by bit by bit Nancy was able to demonstrate that she had the votes to win in the public letters supporters sent her. If you kept those letters and counted, you'd start to see this huge groundswell that Nancy was amassing in support of her candidacy for whip."

By September, Pelosi claimed 100 public backers and 20 private ones. Hoyer counted 77 public, 23 private. If everyone was telling the truth, somehow Congress had swelled by 5 members since the last count. Meanwhile, Bonior decided to make the announcement of his retirement as whip official on September 11. And then the world stopped.

Pelosi was in a meeting with Dick Gephardt and Democratic members of the Appropriations Committee when the first plane hit the World Trade

Center. They were watching on a television when the second one hit. "I thought it was a simulation of the first," Pelosi told C-Span. A bomb scare forced an evacuation of the Capitol, which had been the original target of the plane that crashed into the Pentagon not long after. No one knows why the terrorists who had hijacked American Airlines Flight 77 changed their minds at the last minute and turned off to hit the Pentagon instead. That night, and for weeks after, the area around the Capitol looked like a war zone, with armored Humvees and National Guardsmen on every corner. Not far away, a truck carrying antiaircraft missiles stood ready on the street. Working at the Capitol and everywhere in Washington in the weeks and months after became an exercise in anxiety.

As the ranking Democrat on the House Intelligence Committee, Pelosi had the opportunity to visit Ground Zero soon after the attacks, and she toured the site for a long time. "Nothing can prepare you for the amount of devastation," she said then. The attacks on New York and Washington brought the whip race to another halt as Pelosi and Hoyer focused on the response. Pelosi dove into the job of accurately assessing the terrorist threat and investigating the breakdown in intelligence that allowed the attacks to happen. She wrote a bill creating the independent 9/11 commission that investigated the response efforts before and after the attacks. As the top Democrat on the House Administration Committee, Hoyer began working on evacuation plans for the Capitol.

Within two weeks, however, both were quietly campaigning again. As of October 8, Pelosi claimed to have 102 public supporters and 120 commitments overall; Hoyer said he had 78 public votes and 105 overall. The vote to succeed Bonior was set for October 10.

As election day dawned, nearly three years after the campaigns had begun, Team Pelosi made wake-up calls to supporters. "We had a huge operation for getting members there, not missing any votes," remembers Lemons. "We had walkie-talkies for tracking every member. That's total Nancy Pelosi style. Details, details, details. Don't leave anything undone."

The lawmakers filed into the Cannon Caucus Room at 9 a.m. for one last pitch from the candidates. Hoyer spoke for himself, swinging for the fences rhetorically as he quoted Adlai Stevenson and Bobby Kennedy and extolled members to build a "new world society." Pelosi asked Murtha to speak for her, and he emphasized the huge amounts of money Pelosi had raised for many of the people sitting in the room and how she had personally helped gain four seats for the Democrats in California in the last election.

It was Politics 1.0 versus Politics 2.0, face to face.

When the secret ballots were counted, Pelosi had won decisively. The 118 to 95 tally made her the highest-ranking woman in the history of Congress.

Congresswomen Maxine Waters recognized the earthquake that had just happened. "When Nancy Pelosi enters the leadership, it will be a dramatic for the Democratic Party. This goes way beyond Capitol Hill."

Hoyer attributed Pelosi's win to her fundraising prowess, her gender, and the 32-delegate head start she had as a candidate from the most populous state. But Pelosi said her win was "about the new; it's not about male or female." The election put her second in the House Democratic hierarchy after Minority Leader Gephardt. "We made history, and now we have to make progress," she said in an acceptance speech, promising to make good on her pledge of helping Democrats retake control of the House.

Team Pelosi celebrated their victory at the Phoenix Park Hotel near Union Station that night. "I've thought of what poets and philosophers would say," she told the ebullient crowd. "But when you win a hard-fought fight like this, I think of what Jackie Gleason once said: 'How sweet it is.'"

She says the historic significance of her win didn't really hit her, however, until her first meeting as whip the following February. "I thought, I'm attending a meeting that no other woman had attended in my capacity," she said. In an interview with C-SPAN after her victory, she was no longer shy about taking credit for making history. It was a hard-fought battle, and she won. "I think there was a glass ceiling in politics. I think I did break that," she said.

Two Republicans came to her swearing-in ceremony in the Capitol's Statuary Hall. One was Ralph Regula, who was key to Pelosi's efforts to pass the public-private partnership deal to preserve the Presidio. The other, lurking behind a column during the ceremony, was none other than Majority Whip Tom Delay.

"He always liked Nancy. He always admired her," said Judy Lemons. They had become friends during her early years when Nancy would arrange trips for members to go out to San Francisco for fact-finding tours on the AIDS crisis. "They had this great relationship of mutual respect and understanding," said Lemons. Both leaders kept black leather whips in their offices, and Delay promised to show her how to "pop" hers. In the kind of twist of fate that happens only in Washington, Delay would become one of the poster boys of the "culture of corruption" that helped the Democrats take back the House in 2006.

"When she was sworn in as whip, she actually read a poem about imagination, about the power of imagination," said Marie Wilson. "I kept it on my desk because I thought it was interesting that she was interested in the importance of the imagination. That was the theme of the whole piece, and I thought good, because that's not something people think of."

The night after the swearing in, 300 fans mobbed Pelosi at a celebration at the National Postal Museum. Bob Weir and Mickey Hart, former members of her favorite band, the Grateful Dead, along with rocker Steve Miller, were there to perform for Pelosi's party. When Hart was asked why he came all the way across the country for the celebration of a political insider post most people in America had never heard of, Hart echoed a memorable Clinton campaign line, saying "It's the women, stupid."

CHAPTER 8

CHOCOLATE AND THE GAVEL

Any jackass can kick a barn down, but it takes a carpenter to build it.

—Sam Rayburn, former Speaker of the House, 1882–1961

For days after her victory, Pelosi's spacious new office under the Capitol Dome filled up with gift baskets of chocolate, tins of chocolate, chocolate chip cookies, chocolate-covered coffee beans, gold-foil-covered Godiva boxes, chocolate, chocolate and more chocolate. The gifts from well-wishers competed for space with the bowl of homegrown Ghirardelli that Pelosi keeps on her desk. Friends say the entire Pelosi diet consists of four basic food groups: milk chocolate, dark chocolate, white chocolate, and truffles. "She eats a lot of chocolate," Judy Lemons said. "As far as I know she doesn't drink caffeine or alcohol. She sleeps about five hours a night. She's like a hummingbird that can't find its nest. Constant, constant, constant." Her favorite meal is reportedly chocolate mousse. Pelosi's nine-year-old granddaughter, Madeline Crowda, once asked a crowd at a tea in honor of her grandmother: "Do you know she eats chocolate ice cream for breakfast?" She's rumored to keep a stash of candy bars in a filing cabinet outside her inner office for late-night legislative sessions.

As Pelosi made her way up through the ranks, she often delivered chocolate cakes to supporters or helpful staff members. Her meetings are always punctuated by bowls of Ghirardelli chocolate. She's also the queen of thank-you notes and the remembered birthday and dozens of other grace notes that have endeared her to her colleagues. Aides say they often see her curled up in a corner writing personal notes to people when there's five minutes of downtime.

Chocolate can be said to be part of her leadership style. After she entered the leadership of the House, one Democratic aide said she used the "chocolate and the gavel" to bring party members along. She ran the House floor like an Italian mother, checking up on members' children, always making herself available, sending those chocolate cakes, making everyone feel warm and welcome. Pelosi is a strong believer in the small gesture, more brass tacks than big picture. "She has this kind of nurturing thing where you're family, everybody has a voice, everybody gets involved, everybody has a place at the table," said Lemons. "Everybody's welcome. Maybe it's an Italian thing."

Colleagues also applaud her for sharing the spotlight in a way no other speaker has. Her press conferences are rarely solo events; she's always pushing other members forward to announce new legislation or bills passed. Pelosi once told an interviewer for Vogue magazine: "It's amazing what you can get done if you're willing to give other people credit for it."

Congressman Bart Gordon thinks Pelosi brings a kind of refined civility to the halls of Congress, conducting meetings in a different air. "She's very much a lady," he said. "When she's in a meeting or you're with her. She doesn't say straighten up, or don't chew gum, or don't curse, but you want to act better. You want to act better, because you know you're in the presence of a lady."

At the same time, in her first months as whip she immediately insisted on a stricter discipline in the House, rewarding loyalty and punishing dissent. "People know not to mess with me," Pelosi once said. "You don't see it too often, you don't want to see it, really," Gordon said of the tougher side of Pelosi's personality. "But it's there, and that's the other part of this consensus building. When she's not happy with someone, they know it. She stays unhappy for a while."

"I call it The Grandmother Look," said Ellen Malcolm. "I've gotten that grandmother look, and when you get that look from Nancy Pelosi you do what she says. You sit up straighter in your chair and you say yes ma'am."

Her emphasis on holding people accountable was a break from the leadership of the immediate past, congressional observers said. "She is not afraid to tell people what she wants them to do and hold them accountable," said one aide close to the Speaker. This is the "gavel" part of her leadership style.

She made a point of waving that gavel even before she was elected, when she contributed $10,000 to Lynn Rivers in a Michigan primary against the longest-serving House member, John D. Dingell, who had announced his support of Hoyer. Dingell complained that it was unprecedented for a member of the House Democratic leadership to favor one candidate over another in a primary.

Pelosi's staff defended the donation by saying at the time it was given, it wasn't clear that a new redistricting plan would pit Rivers against Dingell. The donation was handed out in September 2001, one day before the new district borders were signed into law. And it didn't help Rivers much: Dingell won the primary anyway. Some of Pelosi's allies, however, said she was clearly sending a message about loyalty, much the way she would a few years later when she backed her longtime ally John Murtha for majority leader, even though she probably knew he was going to lose. For many in the caucus, the contribution announced in no uncertain terms there would be retribution for disloyalty.

"This is the toughest political turf that you could fight on," Pelosi said in an interview at the time. "A limited number of votes, a zero sum game. People are either for you or they are not, and you can't go anywhere else for votes." That with-me-or-against-me mentality sounds a lot like a certain president she criticizes to no end. "Her biggest weakness is she views the world in two camps: 'those who are for me and those who are against me,'" a House leadership aide told *Roll Call*, a Capitol Hill newspaper, back then. "She'll have to get over that if she's going to succeed."

Many of those who work most closely with her said she sees the world in a lot more hues of gray now, taking a somewhat softer approach as Speaker. Although Pelosi is known to carry a grudge, it's never for long. And she has a talent for patching things up with former rivals. At a House Democratic retreat shortly after beating Hoyer, she danced cheek to cheek with her opponent of three years. At a later retreat, she dragged Dingell out to the dance floor when a band starting playing a Motown tune. "She's as good a dancer as she is a leader," said New Jersey congressman Bob Menendez. "The party that dances together, stays together," quipped Brendan Daly, Pelosi's communications director. Dingel went on to swear Pelosi in as Speaker in 2007. Burying the hatchet for the sake of unity has become one of Pelosi's signatures. Rivals are not enemies, she has said. Congress is a place where egos dare: People inevitably are going to disagree and oppose each other on issues and offices, but it doesn't mean they are opposed to each other personally. The point is to disagree without losing civility, she tells her caucus.

Lemons explains Pelosi's leadership style this way: "She'll build coalitions. She'll listen to people who disagree. And she'll take their suggestions into consideration. In the end she will compromise, but she will not compromise her principles. She has principles. She will not violate them. And if she thinks someone is asking her to or if someone is questioning her principles, she will flatten them."

But Pelosi said she also believes in a bubble-up kind of leadership rather than a top-down kind. She's more wheedle and cajole than command and control. She said it's essential that the Democrats respect their own diversity and take advantage of it. She doesn't waste a lot of time lamenting decisions that don't go her way, and believes more than anything in forward motion. In action. In getting things done.

"Here's what I tell people, and now I benefit from my own advice. I learned this at my father's knee: You have to act, you have to be intuitive," Pelosi told a reporter. "The minute you falter, people will be taking away your options."

The diversity of the caucus she inherited as whip was extraordinary. Democrats in the House had gained a reputation for their contentiousness, for their inability to agree on much of anything. Their diversity may have been their strength, as Pelosi said, but it was also the source of their disunity. If Pelosi was going to succeed as whip, she needed to show a talent for unifying the Democrats so that they spoke with a single voice, a voice that was clearly different from that of the Republicans and that challenged their agenda forcefully.

"We have an extremely diverse caucus, we got the Blue Dogs, who are the moderates, the fiscal conservatives; we got the new Democrats; we got the Hispanic caucus; we got the black caucus," said Leonard Boswell, a Blue Dog Democrat from Iowa. "We've got all these different groups, and then we got the basic, the far left, Maxine Waters." There were other dogs as well, the remnants of the Yellow Dog Democrats of the South, also know as the Dixiecrats, who often voted together and voted more like Republicans than Democrats on several issues. Later came the Blue pups, moderate new members of Congress who made it a point of pride to deviate from the liberal party line.

The whip's job has been likened to herding cats in recent years, but it's really more like herding a rambunctious pack of dogs, many of whom are purebred herd dogs with no intention of being herded by anyone. The term whip originated in rural England, where the "whipper-in" kept the hounds together on a fox hunt. Members of Parliament, many of them ardent fox hunters, adapted the term to describe their own jobs and shortened it to whip. All members of Parliament go by the name now. As whip, Pelosi and her lieutenants were going to have to keep a lot of different breeds from peeling off from the pack. Other dogs were going to snarl and bark every step of the way. Some she was going to have to keep on tight leashes, others very long leashes. She's also got attack dogs like Jack Murtha and David Obey and George Miller to intimidate the other dogs into submission. Wes Allison of the *St. Petersburg Times* made the point that the liberal dogs in Pelosi's case want to bolt ahead of the pack and she has to rein them in. The moderate dogs she has to tug and pull at to get them where she wants them to go. It isn't always pretty, but it moves the pack along.

Pelosi's own metaphor for how a whip gets legislation through the House is a prettier one, that of chief kaleidoscope turner.

"I call it a great kaleidoscope," Pelosi said in 2001. "On some issues, some of us will all be in the design together. And then on some issues, you'll just turn that dial, and some people will just have to go to each other." On each vote, said Pelosi, it's a different design.

"What people saw when she became whip was someone operating at a level way beyond what most people had experienced," said George Miller. "This is a 24/7, this is an all-out commitment. People are constantly astonished by her work ethic. People bitch and moan about working on a Friday or coming in on a Monday, and what have you. Then somebody will recount her schedule. This place wasn't operating that way. To do the things that are necessary to win back the House, that meant campaign, that meant policy, that meant messaging, working with the members, the whole package."

"She has a wonderful way of bringing people along," said Anna Eshoo. "She understands very importantly what motivates each person. If you're going to go and talk to someone, you're gonna need to know not only them, their district, the issues that are there, what they need, all that, but also what motivates that person."

Hers is the politics of consensus. Members of Congress say Pelosi is respectful of the balancing act they have to contend with, constantly calibrating what she calls "the 3 Cs:" Conscience, the Constitution, and Constituents. (It's hard not to add a fourth C to the list today: Cash) One senior Democratic staff member said she tells members that she'll listen to what they need, she'll make changes in legislation to accommodate them, she'll make her best effort to understand the politics of their district or their committee, "but we came here to get some things done, and we're going to have to do it, and that may involve taking some tough votes. We have to do that."

The strength of that approach is a willingness to wade into tough decisions and ruffle feathers if she has to. Over the years, many men in Congress, including John Kennedy, have referred to that quality as courage. Right away as whip, Pelosi took on tough decisions that some caucus members felt Richard Gephardt was too wishy-washy to take on himself. She would not delegate the tough decisions to anyone else.

"She has no fear," said Lemons. "She will stand up for what she believes in. And I think that's another riveting thing that people see in Nancy is that. You want a fighter, she'll show you a fight. She'll be out there fighting for what the caucus believes in. She has no fear."

Chief among those tough assignments facing her immediately as whip was responding to September 11. The same day she was inaugurated, the

House and Senate Intelligence committees announced an unprecedented joint investigation of the attacks. Pelosi was the senior Democrat on the House committee and became a leading player in the effort to document what went wrong. Leonard Boswell served with her on Intelligence and remembers being impressed with her attention to detail and her intellectual candlepower during the hearings. "The first time I worked with her on an individual basis was on the select intelligence committee. And that's when I got to see her up close and in action. She's extremely bright," he said. Eshoo reinforces the impression of Pelosi's smarts. "She's extraordinarily bright. This is a great intellect. She never forgets anything."

Pelosi called the joint investigation "an unusual step, but the events of September 11th called for unusual measures." She promised the panel would assess the performance of both the intelligence community and Congress in its oversight role.

It was in her role on the Intelligence committee that Pelosi first took on President Bush in a way unlike any leader before. After September 11, the mood of the country was such that all questioning of Bush's decisions on protecting Americans seemed tantamount to treason. Even the usual watchdogs in the press were partially muzzled by a resurgent patriotism and strong national resolve to fight the war on terror with a united front. In a statement on the House floor, Pelosi, too, felt the need to emphasize House Democrats' backing of the president. "For the past 13 months, we have stood shoulder-to-shoulder with President Bush to remove the threat of terrorism posed by Al Qaeda. Our work is not done. Osama Bin Laden, Mullah Omar and other Al Qaeda terrorist leaders have not been accounted for. We have unfinished business." But she also was determined not to relinquish her constitutional oversight role, promising accountability for members of her caucus, the intelligence agencies, the president.

The first signs of her willingness to hold Bush's feet to the fire, no matter how high his popularity, came during the Intelligence committee hearings into the attacks on September 11. The first public hearings began on September 18, 2002. By November, members of the committee had found that the FBI and CIA had known that Al Qaeda operatives were planning a strike of some sort in the United States. Pelosi wanted to know if that information had been shared with the National Security Council, which might have been able to connect the dots among the various reports and prevent the attacks. The National Security Council includes the president, vice president, secretary of state, CIA director, and other higher-ups involved in reviewing intelligence. In essence, Pelosi wanted to know if Bush had known about the possibility of an attack ahead of time. But the Intelligence committees did not have the authority to review

National Security minutes, and the Bush administration refused to authorize their release, setting up the first of many clashes between Congress and the executive branch and, more specifically, between Pelosi and the president.

On NBC News' *Meet the Press*, Pelosi said: "Unless the National Security Council minutes, and other communications between the National Security Council and the intelligence community are made known to the committee, we will never have answers . . . . The Congress is responsible. We have oversight responsibilities, we cannot have this gap." It was later revealed that an August 6, 2001, intelligence report delivered to the president included information "acquired in May 2001 that indicated a group of [Osama] Bin Laden supporters was planning attacks in the United States with explosives." *The President's Daily Briefing*, however, did not say when or where.

When the information came out, Pelosi reacted to it strongly. "We were never able to get much of the material we requested from the National Security Council," she said. "The nation was not well served by the administration's failure to provide this critical information." When Pelosi's panel issued its final report, the joint House-Senate committee called for punitive measures against the intelligence and law enforcement officials whose mistakes may have failed to stop terrorists on September 11. Pelosi and other committee members reported that the FBI and CIA officials did not pursue leads or share information that might have allowed them to unravel the plot. But because of the difficulty getting access to information, the report left many questions unanswered. In late 2002, Congress created the National Commission on Terrorist Attacks to conduct a wider investigation, not just of the intelligence failures before September 11 but of all the circumstances that led to the attacks. Pelosi was named to that panel too. After more than a year's time, the commission issued a tough report filled with damaging accusations that are still causing ripples. The findings led, among other things, to the appointment of the country's first intelligence czar overseeing all the separate intelligence agencies. Pelosi and Bush went head to head again over the secrecy issue when the 850-page report was released with 28 blank pages—pages that the administration had classified. Pelosi charged that Bush was protecting Saudi Arabian citizens who had likely aided and abetted the attackers. "Classification should protect sources and methods, ongoing investigations, and our national security interests," she averred. "It is not intended to protect reputations or people or countries."

Pelosi had shown a new face for the Democrats in Congress, that of a real opposition party. Her willingness to take on the bulletproof Bush administration less than a year after September 11 would also take her on a collision course with her own party leader, Dick Gephardt, in her freshman year as whip. In hindsight, it's difficult to believe someone so new to the job, the person charged with maintaining unity in the marbled halls of Congress, would break with her boss so cleanly and so publicly less than a year after joining his leadership team. But for Pelosi, it was a matter of principle.

On September 20, 2002, President Bush asked Congress—the branch of government the Constitution has entrusted with the power to officially declare war—for unlimited authority to use military force against Iraq without any further congressional consultation or approval. Sixty-one percent of the country was in favor of a preemptive strike against Iraq, according to polls at the time. Most lawmakers on Capitol Hill were in favor as well, including Pelosi's boss Dick Gephardt, Hillary Clinton, John Edwards, John Kerry, and many of the other prominent Democrats on the Hill. Al Gore was a forceful opponent, but not in public office at the time. Neither was Barack Obama, though he opposed the war as well. The Bush administration had made its case that Iraq was an imminent threat and that its weapons of mass destruction could fall into terrorist hands. In its promise to keep America safe, the Bush administration had committed itself to sniffing out terrorism and thwarting its designs preemptively before it became a threat to this country. Another Bin Laden was not going to happen on their watch.

In the White House-drafted resolution, Bush cited "the high risk that the current Iraqi regime would use weapons of mass destruction in a surprise attack against the United States."

The staunchest opposition to the resolution came from Nancy Pelosi, who had begun to emerge as the leader of a faction of Democrats strongly against military action in Iraq.

"There was a misrepresentation of the war, and she never believed it from the start that the intelligence could justify us going to war," said Jack Murtha.

"The case of using force in Iraq has not been made," Pelosi said the day the Bush resolution was introduced. She thought a war with Iraq would undercut the war on terrorism. "I don't like this resolution," she added. "If the administration brings us the evidence and makes a compelling case to the American public that a threat is indeed imminent, or that Saddam Hussein was actively involved in the tragedy of last September 11, we may very well come together in agreement. We are clearly not there yet."

Pelosi said she had reviewed the intelligence on Iraq and Saddam Hussein thoroughly as the ranking Democrat on the Intelligence committee. Surprisingly, what she had seen in the past had persuaded her that Saddam Hussein *did* possess weapons of mass destruction. "People associate her with traditional women's issues, such as education and health care," her spokeswoman at the time, Cindy Jimenez, told the *Washington Post* in 2001. "But she was the first person in the House to talk about weapons of mass destruction." As far back as December of 1998, when President Clinton authorized a fourday air war against Iraq to destroy alleged nuclear, chemical, and biological weapons facilities, Pelosi had believed the attacks were justified. In a statement read on the House floor in 1998, Pelosi said:

> As a member of the House Intelligence committee, I am keenly aware that the issue of chemical and biological weapons is an issue of grave importance to all nations." She added that "Saddam Hussein has been engaged in the development of weapons of mass destruction technology which is a threat to countries in the region and he has made a mockery of the weapons inspection process.

In 2002, she said much the same thing about the likelihood of weapons of mass destruction in Iraq:

> Others have talked about the threat posed by Saddam Hussein. Yes, he has chemical weapons, he has biological weapons, and he is trying to get nuclear weapons. There is a threat not only from Iraq, but from other countries of concern in the past.

As it turned out, Pelosi, Bush and everyone else who thought there were weapons of mass destruction in Iraq were wrong, of course: There were none. But in both 1998 and 2002, Pelosi was as convinced as everyone else by the available intelligence that the weapons were there. Which raises the question: Why did she support a Democratic president's attack on Iraq over weapons of mass destruction but not support a Republican president's war? Partly it was partisan. Pelosi was determined to demonstrate the differences between Republicans and Democrats in her new leadership role, but her argument against Bush's war was more about its costs than whether it was justified. Clinton's attack, which began on the eve of his impeachment hearings over the Monica Lewinsky case, was a limited air assault aimed at destroying the facilities for making weapons of mass destruction rather than a ground invasion meant to overthrow Saddam Hussein. Rightly or wrongly, Pelosi believed "containment" was justified but invasion was not. "So let us do what is proportionate, what is appropriate, which mitigates the risk for our young people," she said during debate on the House floor in 2002.

Her argument against Bush's strategy was that the first priority had to be the war on terror, and an invasion of Iraq would dilute that effort. No such war existed in 1998. In 2002, America barely noticed Clinton's attack because the impeachment trial overshadowed it completely. There was no serious talk then of Saddam's ability to retaliate, and indeed he never did.

Here's what Pelosi said in 1998:

> The responsibility of the United States in this conflict is to eliminate weapons of mass destruction, to minimize the danger to our troops and to diminish the suffering of the Iraqi people. I believe in negotiated solutions to international conflict. This is, unfortunately, not going to be the case in this situation where Saddam Hussein has been a repeat offender, ignoring the international community's requirement that he come clean with his weapons program.

And then in 2002:

> I come to this debate, Mr. Speaker, at the end of 10 years of service on the Permanent Select Committee on Intelligence, where stopping the proliferation of weapons of mass destruction was one of my top priorities. I applaud the President's focusing on this issue, and on taking the lead to disarm Saddam Hussein.
>
> It is from the perspective of 10 years on the Intelligence committee that I rise in opposition to this resolution on national security grounds. The clear and present danger that our country faces is terrorism. I say flat out that unilateral use of force without first exhausting every diplomatic remedy and other remedies and making a case to the American people will be harmful to our war on terrorism.

It's interesting to note that in 1998, Pelosi felt that "negotiated solutions"—that is, diplomacy—were worthless with Saddam, but that in 2002 diplomatic remedies "hadn't been exhausted." Her answer to that inconsistency is that intelligence in 2002 showed that war would make things worse, that it might trigger an attack on the United States that wasn't likely if we did not attack.

Here's what she said on the House floor:

> I want to call to the attention of my colleagues a letter that was just declassified about Saddam's use of chemical and biological weapons. The letter refers

to a question asked by a Senator to George Tenet, the Director of the Central Intelligence Agency. The question was: "If we initiate an attack and Saddam thought he was threatened, what is the likelihood that in response to our attack that Saddam Hussein would use chemical and biological weapons?" The response was: "Pretty high," if we initiate the attack. Force protection is our top priority on the Intelligence Committee. We must protect our men and women in uniform.

Pelosi argued that many other costs of the war were too great to justify invading Iraq. Some of her arguments in 2002 turned out to be prophetic by 2007:

- She predicted rightly that the cost to U.S. diplomatic alliances would be great, saying that the United States risked endangering cooperation from over 60 nations that were sharing their intelligence and helping us in the war on terrorism. "We cannot let this coalition unravel," she said.
- She warned that the cost in American lives would be too high for the American public to stomach. The number of American lives lost stands now at more than 3,500—higher than the toll on September 11—and public opinion polls consistently show that 70 percent of Americans want troops home within the year.
- She warned about the costs to the budget: "This cost can be unlimited. There is no political solution on the ground in Iraq. Let us not be fooled by that. So when we go in the occupation, which is now being called the liberation, could be interminable and the amount of money it costs could be unlimited—$100—$200 billion, we can only guess." Here Pelosi was way off. The two best-known analyses of the war's costs so far show the amount of direct spending at $700 billion and counting. Linda Bilmes, at the Kennedy School of Government at Harvard, and Joseph Stiglitz, a Nobel laureate and former Clinton administration adviser, estimate the total cost will be more than $2 trillion when the economic impact and healthcare costs are factored in. The nonpartisan Congressional Research Office reported in July, 2007, that the war was costing $12 billion a month and that Congress had approved $610 billion in war-related funds since 9/11, about the same amount of money spent on the Vietnam War.

Pelosi concluded her floor arguments back in 2002 with an ardent plea to her Democratic colleagues to vote against the resolution.

These costs to the war on terrorism, the loss of life, the cost to our economy, the cost in dollars to our budget, these costs must be answered for . . . . If we go in, we can certainly show our power to Saddam Hussein. If we resolve this issue diplomatically, we can show our strength as a great country . . . . Let us show our greatness. Vote no on this resolution.

Though many of Pelosi's objections to the war do seem prescient and obvious now, they received very little press at the time—none of the antiwar debate in the House did—and the vote passed, 296 to 133. Although Gephardt had helped craft the resolution and thrown his weight behind it, the majority of House Democrats followed Pelosi's lead, voting against the resolution 121 to 81. The vote was the beginning of the end for Gephardt's reign. His resignation as majority leader was still a month away, but the war vote marked the real beginning of the Pelosi era in Democratic politics.

"You got to remember, Gephardt's the one who put this authorization together," Murtha said. Gephardt called the ex-Marine a number of times for his support, and eventually got it. But Murtha has since rescinded that support and become a leading voice against the war. "This authorization was so broad you could drive a truck through it. You could do anything with this authorization. Hell, I voted for it, but I expected them to do inspections, do diplomatic efforts, because that's the way it started out." But Pelosi, Murtha said, has been unwavering in her opposition. "She recognized that it wasn't justified," Murtha said. "And then as it went on, she recognized it was not getting better. All the things that have come about she foresaw and recognized."

In the 2002 election on November 5, Gephardt failed for the fourth consecutive time to bring the Democrats back into the majority in the House. The party actually suffered setbacks in both the House and the Senate as the country rallied round the wartime president. Analysts and party officials blamed Gephardt for not distinguishing Democrats from Republicans better on both domestic and international issues, something Pelosi had just done in dramatic fashion on the House floor. Democrats opposed to Bush on the war and on his tax cut policies had run better than those who had compromised with the administration. The party wanted a leader who could take on Bush, and Gephardt read the writing on the wall. A day after the elections, he announced that he was stepping down as leader of the party in the House.

One year after breaking one 200-year-old glass ceiling, Nancy Pelosi was about to break another.

CHAPTER 9

THE MARBLE CEILING

There never will be complete equality until women themselves help to make laws and elect lawmakers.

—Susan B. Anthony, women's rights pioneer, 1820–1906

As minority whip, Pelosi never put pictures on the wall of her office; she didn't plan to be in it for very long. Pelosi assumed the Democrats would take back the House in 2004 and she would become majority leader that fall, second in command to Dick Gephardt, whom she thought would take over the job of Speaker of the House. Instead, she was about to become the first woman to lead her party in Congress *because* the Democrats did not win the majority back. She wasn't going to be majority whip, but after Gephardt stepped down she would become the highest-ranking Democrat in the House.

The race for whip had taken three years; the race for minority leader took about 36 hours. A day after Gephardt announced he would be relinquishing the minority leader's job to focus on his presidential bid, Pelosi confidently proclaimed: "If this election were today, there's no question I would win." She had 111 public commitments and needed only 104. One pretender to the throne, House Democratic caucus chair Martin Frost of Texas, pulled out of the race quickly after he botched his first press conference as a candidate by vehemently criticizing Pelosi for being too partisan. Harold Ford Jr., a 32-year-old representative from Tennessee, jumped into the fray late saying Pelosi was too liberal and prone to "obstructionist opposition." He bragged about how he could work closely with Republicans, noting that he had supported President Bush's war resolution. At a press conference later that day, Pelosi made her case eloquently that the Democrats needed someone who could distinguish them from the Republicans, not become them. "I told them never again will Democrats go into a campaign where we don't have a message as to who we are and what we stand for, how we are different from Republicans," Pelosi recalled.

The caucus saw it her way. On November 14, 2002, House Democrats voted 177 to 29 to make Pelosi their new minority leader, breaking another glass ceiling in the House and in American politics.

"She's a fresh face, and a positive difference," Representative John Spratt, a Democrat from South Carolina, told *Roll Call* after the vote. "That is vitally important to a party that has lost several elections in a row. She clearly has this spirit about her that gets communicated to all of us."

In reality, Pelosi had secured the votes long before that November through her generous donations to many of her backers. In the 12 months since she had became the minority whip, Pelosi had campaigned for Democratic candidates for Congress in 30 states and 90 congressional districts, aides said. The *San Francisco Chronicle* noted that in one 72-hour span, Pelosi flew 3,678 miles, traveled 14 hours in rented vans, shook more than 600 hands, visited 6 congressional districts, raised more than $50,000 for fellow Democrats, and visited three grandchildren. She once traveled from Washington to Hawaii and back on the same day to make a campaign appearance for a candidate. In 2000, Pelosi had raised nearly $4 million for other candidates. This time around she had upped the ante to between $7 million and $8 million, distributing the largesse to more than 100 candidates, according to the Center for Responsive Politics. Pelosi personally gave other candidates $722,000 from her leadership PAC and her own campaign funds.

Pelosi was starting to get some attention outside of political circles by this time. In 2002, the Gallo family of Napa Valley—yes, those Gallos, the ones who sell wine by the jugful—gave several of the maximum individual donations of $5,000 to Pelosi, as did several members of the Haas family, owners of Levi-Strauss, the jeans maker. Barbara Streisand, Kirk Douglas, and novelist Danielle Steel were among the Southern California celebrities who contributed as well. "And these people, they're not political action committees, these are just people who believe in what she believes in, people believe in her," said former California congressman John Burton. She was receiving celebrity fan mail and in airports was frequently asked for autographs or pictures. She was also diligent about appearing on the Sunday talks shows, more so than any other member of Congress, and therefore becoming the face of the opposition. *Glamour* honored her among its "Women of the Year." *Time, Newsweek, Women's Wear Daily* all did pieces on her. She appeared on the cover of *Parade* magazine when it ran a feature speculating about the first woman president. *Elle* magazine observed that "Nancy Pelosi is a Babe."

Something different started happening under Pelosi's leadership in the House as well. She took a hands-on, people-focused approach to her new job. "She works from sunup to way past sundown. Person by person: phone conversations, horse trading, adding language to a bill to satisfy a specific concern of one of the members, pep rallies, ice cream, whatever it takes," said George Miller. She paid close attention to the interests of individual members, something that members complained Gephardt had stopped doing as much as he focused more and more on his run for president. "She's extremely focused on her members, but not in a fawning sort of a way," said an aide close to Pelosi. "And she will do anything to help the members get what they need to succeed." The chocolate and the gavel were starting to make a difference. The Democrats were starting to show signs of something that hadn't shown in a few decades: unity.

"She understands in a very sophisticated and profound way what unity is," said Anna Eshoo. "It's not that it begins and ends with party discipline, to be loyal to a party, but that if you are not unified, the doors in front of you will be locked. You can't do anything unless you bring a unified position to whatever you are doing. I think that members at this stage know that when Nancy walks through the door, wherever she's going, when she walks through the front door of the White House, when she walks through the door to meet with chairmen of committees, whoever she's meeting with, she takes all of us with her. In other words, it's not about her. That's a rarity in this business. People who are in this business will generally stipulate that it's a selfish business, because you come into this business promoting yourself. You're required to. Where does the promotion end? It's ongoing. Nancy is not about promoting herself. And people know that."

By 2005, a study by *Congressional Quarterly* found that "over the past half-century, Democrats in the House were never more unified" than they were under Pelosi, voting together a record 88 percent of the time. A woman in the minority leader's chair had achieved something five decades of male leaders hadn't. That unity bought Pelosi a great deal of loyalty. "I think that people admire the fact that even when we were in the minority we had the best voting record of any Democratic caucus in Congress in 50 years," said a Democratic operative.

Her ambition was to create a true opposition party that would thwart the majority on as many votes as possible and highlight its scandals, its mistakes, and its overreaching. She'd maintained unity in part by sticking with her strategy of pursuing a confrontational policy with Bush and the Republicans in her desire to offer voters a clear alternative. She offered up an unabashedly partisan economic stimulus plan, a partisan prescription drug plan, and an alternative budget. Many members said the Democrats in Congress had not differentiated themselves well enough from Republicans in so many years that many Americans were saying there wasn't much difference. Pelosi, a daughter of the New Deal, wasn't just repositioning or repackaging; she believed in her DNA that Democrats were the chosen party. She saw Republicans as the dark side, destroying the country. "She really hates this president with a passion," said Pat Schroeder. "Everything he has stood for and he and [Vice President Dick] Cheney have done is the antithesis of what she believes in."

Donna Brazile, Al Gore's campaign manager in 2000, may have put the allure of Pelosi best: "What we need is a bold strike—we have to come back fighting. Nancy is our best answer: someone who is willing to take a risk. She is not a cautious leader."

Both Democrats and Republicans seemed excited by Pelosi's ascent. Conservatives drooled at the prospect of a leftward swing in the party when the country as a whole was tilting rightward. "I want to know where to send the flowers," said Republican consultant Nelson Warfield. "I am ecstatic. She'll be a working poster board for what's wrong with the Democratic Party. Across the board, she is a plus for the Republicans."

The biggest risk she continued to take was her criticism of the decision to invade Iraq. Pelosi visited Kuwait and other parts of the Middle East just 10 days before the war started. She told her longtime ally Murtha that "even though I voted against going to war, I want to make sure the troops understand I support them 1000 percent." Yet her opposition to the war intensified after the trip. It was an opposition that was still at odds with public opinion and was splitting the party. When U.S. troops entered Baghdad 30 days after the start of the war and the giant statue of Saddam Hussein was toppled, Pelosi said she hoped the United States wouldn't live to regret the day. Brendan Daly, her communications director, said she took a tremendous amount of criticism for the statement.

In the two years after the last election, Pelosi had raised $30 million for Democratic candidates, traveled to more than 25 states and 115 cities, and attended more than 130 fundraisers. She was already starting to see some enthusiasm for the idea of the first woman Speaker on the stump. "Fathers of daughters are coming to these events, and bringing their daughters to these events," she said. "They are excited about the idea of the first female Speaker. It's sort of overwhelming to me to see the response."

But it wasn't enough. In the 2004 election, the Republicans were able to capitalize on the mixed signals coming out of the Democratic camp on the Iraq issue, portraying it as a sign that the party was weak on national security. It was wartime, and voters were inclined to stick by the wartime commander in chief. Iraq hadn't become the quagmire it is today. Some 60 percent of Americans still supported the war. Even though it was a politically unpopular stance at the time, Pelosi hadn't compromised her principles on the issue, a consistency that would become one of the hallmarks of her credibility later. President Bush won reelection handily, and the Republicans kept their majority in the House.

Personally, Pelosi was devastated by the results. She said she truly believed John Kerry was going to win the presidency and sweep Democrats into the majority in the House. But politically, she was pragmatic about the first loss on her watch. Before the election, she had said that retaking the House might take four years, given that the GOP had a 12-seat advantage and Democrats had gotten too comfortable with minority status. After 2004, however, she was determined to reinvent the way Democrats campaigned for Congress, starting from scratch if she had to. She also wanted to re-create the way the Democratic Party presented itself to the country.

So, shortly after losing the 2004 elections, she went out and found a secret weapon to unleash in 2006: Rahm Emanuel.

Rahm Emanuel is a former ballet dancer with the heart of a pit bull. He practices politics with the sheer will of Mr. Incredible and the manic energy of the Tasmanian devil, relentlessly pushing himself and his family of candidates toward the finish line, refusing to stop until he gets where he wants to go. During the 2006 campaign everyone called him Rahmbo, or "the Enforcer." Pelosi simply called him "field marshal." He lost a finger in an Arby's meat slicer when he was young and has come to relish the tough-guy image it has endowed him with. It's an image he gilds by frequently employing the f-expletive in conversation—as noun, verb, adjective, and punctuation. He once sent a pollster he disagreed with a dead fish in a mahogany box. "Rahm just may be our skinny, nine-fingered, Jewish, Chicago version of LBJ," said Paul Begala, who served with Emanuel in the Clinton White House. He's a myth in the making, and colleagues believe he'll wind up as Speaker of the House someday himself.

A verbatim quote from Emanuel after advisers told him to exercise more leadership during the 2006 campaign: "I am exercising it, with every fucking fiber in my body. If you don't see what you like, I highly recommend you pick up the fucking phone and do it yourself. I *am* fucking relaxed, but I'm telling you I'm trying to get it done."

Naftali Bendavid, a political editor and reporter for the *Chicago Tribune*, embedded himself at the Democratic Congressional Campaign Committee during the 2006 election season, where he got to watch Emanuel at close range. "He's a very intense guy who likes to come at you 100 miles an hour," Bendavid said in an interview. "It's his personality but also his strategy to come at you with great force, and knock you off balance. He'll question you relentlessly until you feel like there's something you need to do, maybe what he wants you to do." He does it with everyone: staffers, people he's trying to solicit money from, reporters. He was constantly pushing Pelosi as well. "Well, I never said Rahm was a diplomat who spends a lot of time schmoozing," said Pelosi. "He's abrupt with me all the time."

"The alliance between her and Rahm is no match made in heaven, but she knew he was what the party needed," said Bruce Cain, a congressional scholar at Berkeley. They needed someone new, someone assertive, someone with relentless drive. They needed a field commander who fought as ruthlessly and vigorously as the Republicans did.

"Rahm is a politician who is really a political consultant disguised as a politician," said Cain. He cut his teeth for 20 years on party politics much the way Pelosi did in California. He was a senior adviser and chief fund-raiser for Richard Daley's winning campaign for mayor of Chicago in 1989, and served as the finance director of President Bill Clinton's first campaign in 1991. He is an extraordinary fundraiser, a master planner, and knows how to read polls and run campaigns, all qualities that describe Pelosi as well. They'd known each other long before either of them won an office, and it was his work as a campaign operative rather than his record as a neophyte congressman that attracted Pelosi.

After the 2004 Republican victory, some conservative pundits were talking about the prospect of a generation of Republican rule. They gleefully described a tectonic shift in the American political landscape. Grover Norquist, an influential conservative activist, told PBS *Frontline* that "Republicans have the House until at least 2012, but probably another decade. They have the Senate indefinitely." But Pelosi wasn't buying it. A month after the vote, she called Emanuel and asked him to head up the

2006 campaign for the congressional Democrats. Emanuel, who'd been a Congressman for less than two years when Pelosi came calling, thought it would take two election cycles to get back to the majority and didn't want Pelosi to say they were going to win; Pelosi was adamant that they could do it in one. She wanted to start yesterday.

Rahm was a choice that immediately ruffled feathers, given his lack of Congressional experience. But Pelosi said she picked him to run the campaign because he'd be "cold-blooded enough" to win. When people complained about his abrasive manner, Pelosi would have none of it. "I said to them: 'We're here to win this election. What is this conversation about? I don't think we can be better served than by having Rahm at the DCCC.'"

The dynamic between Pelosi and her campaign manager quickly became one of dog walker to big dog. "She was kind of restraining him," said Bendavid, who was there to see and hear the two leaders interact during the 2006 campaign. "He came off as this very able but very zealous subordinate who always wanted to push harder and do more and do whatever it was immediately. He was always coming out with four-point plans for tackling the Medicare issue, or three-point plans on stem-cell research, how they should stage a debate on the House floor and have a series of press conferences and urge the candidates to have town hall meetings. He was always coming up with memos and ideas, and Pelosi's reaction generally seemed to be, from what I saw, 'Yeah, some of those ideas are good, some of those we should do a little bit later.'" She had to keep in mind the interests the whole party had, not just a few House seats, like Emanuel. "A lot of things that might have looked like problems if they had lost look like creative tension with the vantage point of victory," Bendavid added.

Bendavid never saw any real argument between the two headstrong leaders. It doesn't mean it didn't happen, but certainly there was less tension between Emanuel and Pelosi than there was between Emanuel and Dean, who had a knock-down, drag-out blowup over Dean's 50-state strategy during one meeting early in the campaign.

"His impatience with the leadership and how slowly they moved, in his opinion, was abundantly clear," said Bendavid. "But Emanuel's very careful to stay on her good side and make it clear that he's not taking her on, but rather pushing the leadership in a certain direction." A lot of people compared him to Newt Gingrich in 1994. But when they did, Emanuel was very quick to say that the difference between him and Newt was that Newt was fighting the leadership of his own party, which he wanted to get rid of as much as he wanted to get rid of the Democrats. "'I am not trying to get rid of the leadership of my own party.' That was a message that he very much wanted out there, that he was not trying to fight against the leadership," Bendavid said. He did chafe sometimes at his subordinate position, though. During one party function, Emanuel referred to himself jokingly as Pelosi's "valet."

The magic number was 15.

That's how many new seats the Democrats needed to take back the majority. Emanuel personally took charge of 50 of the congressional races, throwing himself into the task with a ferocity to match Pelosi's. Congressional campaigns are, in many ways, much tougher to manage than presidential campaigns. "You've got to keep track of dozens and dozens of candidates," said Bendavid. "You have to know their strengths and weaknesses, psychology, fundraising for all these different candidates, and what you do in one race affects another race." By early 2005, Emanuel had assembled a team of young, battle-tested congressmen and congresswomen to serve as his brain trust. They began by trying to recruit the best candidates he could find, especially more moderate or conservative candidates who might be able to win in traditionally Republican districts. He would call potential candidates such as Heath Schuler, the former Redskins quarterback, as many as five times a day trying to talk him into jumping into the race. He personally persuaded 30 of the new candidates to throw their hats into the ring, including Schuler and Tammy Duckworth, an Iraq war vet who'd lost both her legs in combat. Duckworth was one of more that 40 military veterans the Democrats encouraged to run for office in the mid-term elections. "We needed an outreach program so that veterans would know they have a home in the Democratic party," said Christine Pelosi, Nancy's daughter, who helped the Democrats organize the effort to reach out to veterans. A year and nine months before the vote, the battle was joined.

"I think that they were very good at finding candidates who could win in places where Democrats had not won before," said Bendavid. "They worked very hard at not writing off certain parts of the country and not adhering to a specific Democratic orthodoxy, so that if a candidate violated that they wouldn't get any support." This was the key to their strategy: Enlarge the Democratic tent to include moderate candidates and antiabortion candidates, and even candidates who supported the Iraq war.

John F. Kennedy said victory has a thousand authors. That was certainly true with the Democrats' victory in 2006. Although Rahm rightly got the lion's share of credit for the hard-fought campaign, there were hosts of other things happening that Pelosi and her staff were involved with and that other members were doing. Rahm was one of the campaign's four-star generals, and Dean, chairman of the Democratic Party, was the other. Dean had his 50-state strategy and Rahm his laserlike focus on races where he thought Democrats could gain Republican seats. The differences in those two approaches meant a clash about the priorities of the campaign, but it was a tension that Pelosi was somehow able to take advantage of and channel into victory. To this day, both Rahm and Dean say it was their strategy that won the day.

"I don't want to take anything away from Rahm, he played a huge, huge role," said an aide who was involved with the campaign. But Nancy was the one who hired him and who came up with the winning battle plan, the aide said.

"They all made contributions," said Bendavid. "Pelosi was the larger visionary person, but Emanuel was the campaign manager."

Representative John Murtha lays all the credit at Pelosi's door. "There's nobody who can take credit for changing from the minority to the majority but her. She just worked at it tirelessly, raising more money than everybody else, talking to more people, listening to advice about the war. She did all the right things."

Pelosi saw a sequence to her leadership. Once the Democrats were voting with a high degree of unity, she could focus more intently on the party's message. "What we haven't done well as a party is distilling that message," she said in June of 2005. "That's where we haven't made steps forward." Pelosi wanted a simple, clear message that people would associate almost automatically with Democrats. In other words, she wanted a Democratic "brand."

According to aides and campaign officials, the campaign analysis went like this:

1. Democrats always want to tell you everything they're for.
2. Because of the party's history, Democrats are inclined to define their objectives in terms of programs. And when they define programs, they define government. And when they define government, they define taxes and spending, and suddenly they're right into the soup of tax-and-spend and big government, so they end up reinforcing the negative impression, or brand, that the Republicans have labeled them with. (Most of this has little to do with the facts, Pelosi's people argue; it just has to do with the branding.)

What Pelosi wanted to do was step away from that traditional methodology of running a campaign. In 2004, she told her close aides, and the staff of the DCCC: Let's ask ourselves what we would do if we were in the private sector trying to market Democrats to the American people.

"Four years ago, Nancy asked what would be the reason people would be interested in the congressional Democrats?" said George Miller. "That was the question she posed." She wanted to rebrand the Democratic Party. She wanted a new New Deal, or a return to the greatness of the Great Society. She told her team that she didn't want to abandon the things Democrats believe in, but she wanted to take the things Democrats wanted to do and talk about them in a way that people were going to understand. "As opposed to 'we really want to tell you about HR3145, after the market is done, and we go to the 302B allocations, you'll be able to see as amended . . .'" said John Lawrence, Pelosi's chief of staff. "People don't know what the hell you're talking about."

In 2004, the Republicans were better at it. The GOP could tell people in six words what the Republican Party was for: lower taxes, smaller government, strong defense. That's it. That's what Arnold Schwarzenegger did at the Republican convention in 2002 in what was regarded by people on both sides of the aisle as a great speech. No matter what the reality of the Republicans' record, their brand remained intact. If a person was for those three things, he or she was a Republican.

Before 2005, the Democrats were in the field with a spokesman and a message for a year out of every four years in a four-year cycle, Howard Dean said. "The Republicans, with their grassroots effort, which they began after Barry Goldwater's defeat [in 1964], were in the field four years out of a four-year cycle and they started the next day after the four-year cycle was over for the next four years." In presidential campaigns, Dean said, Democrats began years ago to focus only on the 25 states with the most electoral votes so that the national Democratic infrastructure in the other 25 states began to collapse, and was pretty much nonexistent by 2004. "So it's not surprising 25 years later it is socially unacceptable to admit that you're a Democrat in about a third of the counties in the country," Dean said at a fundraiser. "It is not surprising that people think things about Democrats because all they've heard about Democrats is from people like Rush Limbaugh, Dick Cheney, and Bill O'Reilly. So basically this was a party that was shrinking and shrinking and shrinking. So we needed to make some changes."

"We started off in 2003, 2004, we started thinking about this," said Lawrence. "How do we get a different brand for Democrats? And how do we undercut their brand that they [Republicans] successfully if inaccurately patented and imprinted on the public mind?"

Pelosi took the initiative on the rebranding effort. She wanted to do it not only with the House but with the Senate, with state and local officials and with governors, so that there was some consistency of message. She didn't want the national party in Washington off talking about one thing and Democrat candidates in Peoria talking about something else. Like Newt Gingrich had done in 1994, Pelosi planned to nationalize the congressional elections in 2006 around a set of shared issues, around a brand.

And to that end, she brought in people from the private sector: business execs, Internet entrepreneurs, PR pros. She wanted the party to talk to voters the way a church talks to its parishioners, or neighbors talk over the back fence, or the Nordstrom's shoe salesman talks to women buying pumps.

"She had us working on some of that as early as 2004," said Lawrence, who was Miller's chief of staff at the time. "I was working with people on the outside and with [Senate Majority Leader Harry] Reid's staff, the governors and others. We did a lot of emphasis on people who didn't do political. Because most people don't spend a lot of time thinking about politics. The things we talk about here [in Washington] are really pretty foreign, and if you listen to Republican messaging, they didn't talk about Washington either."

"She had these huge resources outside the Beltway," adds Miller. "She really is not a product of the Beltway. Most people fail to understand this. She isn't on the pundit circle. She isn't on the talk-show circle. She's out engaging with people in Chicago, in Houston, Texas, in Jacksonville, Florida, about this agenda for the nation that the Democrats can lead on. It's very different than anything I've been associated with in my 33 years. Because she's outside the Beltway. She's not sitting here folding in with the same people who brought you the losses of last year. New people, new thinking . . ."

What the corporate people told them to do was differentiate Democrats from Bush, and take Bush down. They advised an aggressive campaign to tell voters what was wrong with Bush's leadership and what was right with the way Democrats would do things. The brand they focused on was "New Direction for America," which conveyed a notion of change. Pelosi believed Americans were ready for a change. She, more than any other leader in the party, believed the country was growing weary of the war, weary of Republican rule. "People want a change," she told *Roll Call* on June 27, 2005. "People want a change from a policy standpoint and an ethical standpoint." She said poll results showed "devastating things" about how the Republicans were running the country.

But where would that "new direction" lead people? That's where the short-hand Six for '06 came in. The New Direction and Six for '06 were inseparably linked. Six for '06 was a page right out of Newt Gingrich's book as well. Vote for the Democrats and you're voting for specific legislation, practically bypassing the members of Congress, who were never a very popular bunch anyway.

"So we say to people, if you elect Democrats, we are going to raise the minimum wage and we're not going to have any congressional pay raises until we do, because we mean it," said Lawrence. "If you elect us, we are going to pass a stem-cell bill, we are going to pass the 9/11 commission recommendations, we are going to rescind the $12 billion in subsidies they [Republicans] gave to the oil companies last year when the oil companies were having their highest profits in history, and we're going to take that money and put it into alternative energy. We said we'll do that, and we'll do that with Republican votes, but we won't have a chance to do that if you don't vote for Democratic leadership because these bills will never come to the floor."

Six for '06 told people what the Democrats were for in clear, simple, unambiguous terms, and it attempted to differentiate Democrats from Republicans. Pelosi's team purposely focused on a small number of issues, emphasizing that they were the first steps, that Six for '06 wasn't the entirety of what they wanted to do.

In late September 2005, on the eleventh anniversary of the Gingrich's "Contract for America," Pelosi and other Democratic leaders kicked off a political crusade called "Campaign for Change." On a new Web site launched for the campaign, Emanuel asked prospective contributors and volunteers to "take back America for the people." The leadership team trotted out their campaign piece by piece. They had a big rollout of lobby reform, and one for an ethics reform package in January of 2006. They did one on national security that had to do with veterans' assistance, strengthening the military, and changes in Iraq policy. And after each rollout they did the press events and gave each member of Congress background information so they could say what they would do if they were in charge. "That's the only thing that people wanted to know was, what difference does it make if you guys win?" said Lawrence.

The party also set out to recruit 50,000 new campaign volunteers and was running a series of management and leadership training sessions for candidates around the country to improve their chances of winning. Christine Pelosi directed some of these boot camps, personally working with over 40 candidates, 12 of whom are now in Congress.

"Our Boot Camp offered leadership trainings showcasing the best practices (and lessons learned) in message, management, mobilization and money for over 40 challengers across America," Christine said in an interview. (Christine shares her mother's love for alliterative campaign bromides, such as "people, politics, policy," "conscience, constitution, constituents" and "idealism, intellect and integrity".) "Candidates and their campaign managers attended regional round tables and participated in virtual trainings and conference calls with elected officials and policy advocates between September, 2005, and May, 2006," Christine added. The training sessions focused on the best way to get out a Democratic message on Katrina, ethics in Congress, Iraq and immigration.

The Democratic campaign machine was humming like it hadn't hummed in years. In addition, Pelosi, Emanuel, and Hoyer were barnstorming the country headlining fundraisers. In an 80-hour campaign-a-thon from Friday, June 23 through Monday, June 26, Pelosi visited four cities, attended five fund-raisers, made three media appearances, went to two official meetings and a charity event, hosted members of Congress in her home in Georgetown and raised $1 million for House Democrats. She alone was responsible for an astonishing $60 million for her candidates in the 2006 election cycle. From 1990 to 2000, Gephardt raised approximately $2.5 million for candidates. From 2000 to 2006, Pelosi raised more than $140 million. Venture politics had come of age.

Pelosi, Emanuel, Dean, Hoyer and their staffs were going gangbusters recruiting candidates, raising money and delivering The Message. And then they got some help, a lot of help, from the most unlikely place: the Republicans themselves.

The turning point in Pelosi's 12-year quest to win back the House was President Bush's proposal to privatize Social Security at the beginning of his second term in 2005. Pelosi held a tough line against the legislation in the House, refusing to let other members propose their own alternatives that might give the Republicans a target. She wanted the country to associate the reform completely with Bush; she didn't want any shared authorship because polls showed as many as 75 percent of Americans were opposed to it. The plan never made it to the House floor.

"At one point Bush announced to Pelosi, 'I'm going out on the road on this one. I'm gonna fight you in 10 states,'" one of Pelosi's staffers said. "So he went out on the road. Everywhere he went his numbers dropped. He came back and they had the conversation again, and he said 'I may go back out' and she said, 'I'll pay for your ticket.'"

Pelosi considers the defeat of the Social Security initiative her greatest legislative victory in her 20 years in the House. "It was important for us to take him down, destroy [Bush's] brand," Pelosi said in June of 2005. "We've done that. . . . He's now perceived as the guy who wants to cut my benefits."

In rapid succession after that came the bungled response to Hurricane Katrina in New Orleans; the controversial government intervention in the Schiavo family's decision to remove the feeding tube from comatose Terry Schiavo and let her die; the indictment of majority leader Tom Delay on charges he broke campaign finance laws back in Texas; the Jack Abramoff lobbying scandal; and the congressional page scandal involving Republican representative Mark Foley. On top of and above all that was the dramatically worsening situation in Iraq. A throw-the-bums-out mentality was growing across the country.

"They handed us a few that were doozies," said Lawrence. Pelosi and other true-believer Democrats saw the mismanagement of the Katrina crisis—the slow response during the first days and the government red tape many of the country's poorest citizens became ensnared in—as a parable for the way in which the Bush administration ran government. "Hopelessness. Indifference to the poor. Government can't really do much of anything," said one Democratic operative. "It sort of reminds you of Herbert Hoover during the Depression. And I think it drove home the notion that there was a constructive role for government to play."

The Democrats had the opportunity to talk about cronyism within the administration when some of Bush's political appointees appeared to lack the experience to deal with Katrina, having gotten their jobs through party loyalty rather than job expertise. The same issue came up with the early appointees to the interim U.S. government in Iraq. The Democrats had tried to make hay out of what they saw as rampant cronyism in the Departments of the Interior and Energy even before the devastating hurricane, but their accusations didn't have a much of a hook that middle Americans could relate to their daily lives. Katrina gave cronyism a hook.

Still, if Pelosi, Emanuel, Dean, Charles Schumer, who headed the Democratic Senate Campaign, and Hoyer hadn't put things into place, all the different scandals and problems would have been interesting but may not have added up to a majority in Congress. Pelosi and her lieutenants hammered the Republicans relentlessly about a "culture of corruption" for six months and worked hard to make sure voters viewed every new scandal or development through that lens. "The Foley thing would have been very quickly isolated as one rogue, but instead we were able to show, which was true, that a whole host of people high in the Republican hierarchy had knowledge of what was going on and decided not to become engaged," said one aide close to the leadership. Pelosi knew how to take advantage of the shifting tide because in her heart of hearts, she's a campaign person.

"The Iraq War and the problems the Republicans inflicted on themselves played the biggest role in the outcome [of the 2006 elections]," said Bendavid. "But the Democrats did a better job than they had done in recent memory of positioning themselves to take advantage of the situation. To that degree you have to give them some degree of credit." When Al Gore ran for president in 2000, and even when John Kerry ran in 2004, many political analysts felt that the conditions were very favorable for Democrats to win, yet Gore and Kerry didn't close the deal. So what did Pelosi and Rahm do differently that brought home the blue ribbon?

"Seems to me, from what I saw, there was a psychological change in the Democratic Party," said Bendavid. "I think for years [President Bush's Deputy Chief of Staff] Karl Rove did a number on them, and they just started to feel like no matter what they did, he was going to pull out a victory. I think the Democrats were kind of spooked. One of the more significant things that happened in the last election was that, because of Pelosi and Emanuel, they tried to change that psychology, with some success. They believed they could win. I tend to feel like psychology is underestimated in politics. There is something about really believing you can do it, and therefore putting the resources and energy into these races."

Pelosi had been a true believer for 12 years. By summer of 2006, thanks in large part to her vision, a remarkable psychological shift was taking place within the Democratic Party. They were acting like winners, and the Republicans started to get spooked. "In this election, they were the ones who were freaking out," said Bendavid. They started obsessing about Pelosi, and especially about Emanuel, releasing press release after press release about the bad things he was doing. "It's something you see in sports sometimes," said Bendavid. "He freaked them out somehow."

Republican campaign ads countered the Democratic assault by obsessively targeting Pelosi herself. A television commercial put out by the National Republican Congressional Committee against Vanderburgh County Sheriff Brad Ellsworth in Indiana is a prime example: "Pelosi and the other Democrats want to raise your taxes, cut and run in Iraq and give amnesty to illegal immigrants. So remember: a vote for Brad Ellsworth is a vote to open the floodgate of ideas that are bad for America and expensive for you."

The problem was, most people in the country didn't really know who Pelosi or Emanuel were. A June 2006 poll showed that only about 25 percent of voters in Indiana's Eighth District recognized Pelosi's name. National

Republican Congressional Committee communications director Carl Forti said that didn't matter. "You didn't have to know who Nancy Pelosi is to understand what liberal San Francisco values mean," he said. "She's the face of the party. She's the one with the liberal voting record, so she's the one to use this way."

In late September, Pelosi said she thought the focus on her was a sign of desperation. "I think it's going to be a hard sell for them to say 'It's not about George Bush and his failed policies in Iraq and in the economy and what that means for middle-income families. It's about Nancy Pelosi'—somebody most [people] have never heard of."

Democratic officials believe this was the biggest mistake Pelosi's opponents made in the 2006 election. They thought they could characterize her as a left-wing San Francisco liberal nut. What they didn't understand, the officials said, is that she's a *Baltimore* politician. And she learned her politics in the wards of Baltimore. She just happens to live in San Francisco. "This notion that you were just going to take her and portray her as out of touch—not a chance. People deluded themselves with that for years, and you've seen it only more so lately," said one aide. During the 2008 campaign, in fact, the NRCC launched a series of ads that try to link moderate Democratic freshmen congressmen in vulnerable districts with the radical left-wing politics of Nancy Pelosi. It remains to be seen how effective a strategy it will be now that Pelosi has a higher profile, but Democratic strategists think the NRCC is looking for a "magic button" in Pelosi that just isn't there. "You can become obsessed in this business that there is a magic button in politics," said one strategist. "If you just hit one thing you can win. It can work that way to an observer, who's on the outside, who says gee, everything just fell into place. But you've got to put the pieces in place, and putting the pieces in place is a decidedly unglamorous part of the business. Pelosi knows that business."

"In the last nine months you've seen a real reversal of that idea that California is not attached to the rest of the country," said Berkeley professor Bruce Cain . "The eternal hope is that she'll have a Jane Fonda moment that will show the country how out of touch Democrats are. She's way too savvy for that."

As the 2006 midterm election neared, Pelosi obsessed over an enormous binder full of notes detailing every contested race in the country.

She continued to keep tabs on 60 to 65 candidates by phone, aides said. A week before the election, she and former president Bill Clinton headlined a fundraiser in San Francisco that brought in $2 million. Pelosi and Emanuel met constantly in the last week, repeatedly going over all the races district by district, state by state, like two generals playing a war game over a map of the country.

"It's the last thing she's doing when she goes to bed at night and the first thing she does in the morning," Brian Wolff, Pelosi's political director, said at the time. "She's very detail-oriented. If she doesn't know about it, it's not being done."

By election night pundits who just a few months earlier had predicted small gains for Democrats were saying that the party had a chance to take back both the Senate and the House. Pelosi and family and friends went to the nondescript DCCC headquarters on Capitol Hill to await the results. Pelosi's youngest daughter was overdue with Pelosi's sixth grandchild, and Pelosi thought she might have to make a choice later in the night between celebrating at headquarters or being at her daughter's side. If that happened, she told a reporter, "I'll be in the hospital."

Attached to one of the walls of the cubicle-laden building was a giant whiteboard that had been divided into 80 squares. Each square represented one of the House races where the Democrats had a chance to win—or lose—a contested seat.

The first results came in around 8 P.M. and looked good. Sheriff Brad Ellsworth won in Indiana, and staffers whooped and clapped, according to Bendavid, who was there. The cheers started coming faster and more frequently as the night progressed. At 10:47, Schuler had won his race in North Carolina. Staffers were screaming and exchanging high-fives with each new victory. After Schuler's win, the Democrats had 11 of the 15 seats they needed. At 11 p.m., the political staff in the *Washington Post* newsroom was projecting that the Democrats could pick up as many as 25 seats, maybe more. Then at 11:08, CNN projected that the Democrats had retaken the majority in the House of Representatives.

Bendavid said that minutes afterward, Pelosi walked into Emanuel's office at the DCCC. "Fellas," roared Emanuel, "Madame Speaker!" They hugged each other for a long time, Bendavid remembers, rocking back and forth as a staffer called out "Mission Accomplished!" Barack Obama called to congratulate her, and then she began to walk back to her office, saying she had to call her brother Tommy. As she walked past the staffers, a few began to clap. Then more started applauding, and more, until the entire staff rose to its feet, many of them whooping. They gave Pelosi a standing ovation.

Soon afterward, Pelosi headed over to a celebration shindig at the Hyatt Regency on Capitol Hill. Bendavid saw Senator Charles Schumer, head of the Democrats' Senate campaign, teasing Paul Pelosi in a private room as they waited to go onstage. "The First Man of the House!" he pronounced. "The First Gentleman!" Out in the hotel lobby, where a giant TV screen was set up, a newscaster announced that the Democrats likely would pick up 30 seats total, which would mean a 232 to 202 majority in the House and the nation's first woman Speaker. That's when the dancing started.

Well after midnight, Pelosi took the stage. Supporters were chanting "Nancy! Nancy!" and then switched to "Speaker! Speaker!" as she climbed up the steps with Senate Democratic leader Harry Reid. They joined Emanuel and Senator Charles Schumer on stage for a group hug, then clasped hands and raised their arms together as red, white, and blue ticker tape came cascading down.

Representative Kendrick Meek of Florida eventually introduced Pelosi at the victory rally, calling her the person who put everything together. "We've been waiting a very long time for this night to get here. And it's here now," said Meek. "This outstanding leader from California has led the House Democrats into the most unified caucus that we've ever been in recent years on behalf of the American people, fighting Republicans and special interests at every corner. She's courageous—nails for breakfast. She fights on behalf of all Americans, our leader, Democratic leader Nancy Pelosi."

After a few more rounds of thunderous applause, Pelosi asked the crowd: "Are you ready to make history tonight?" That got more applause, much more.

It'd been exactly 90 years since Montana's Jeannette Rankin had been the first woman elected to Congress. The gains for the Democrats were the biggest since Watergate, and it was the first time since 1922 that a party hadn't lost a single Congressional seat, incumbent or open "You talk about the glass ceiling. This is the marble ceiling," Pelosi said the next day.

In the end, her daughter Alexandra graciously waited a week after the election to give birth to Paul Michael, named after her dad. President Bush called to wish all congratulations, and Pelosi joked that "Paul" just barely beat out "George" as her new grandson's name.

CHAPTER 10

INAUGURATION DAY

To those who question whether women would change the nature of political power, or whether political power would change the nature of women, there can be only one answer—let's try it. Let's find out.

—Congresswoman Bella Abzug, 1920–1998

Though it was a straight party-line vote, 232 to 202, it took nearly two hours for the 110th Congress to elect Pelosi Speaker on Monday, January 4, 2007. Members didn't spend that time deliberating about whether she was the right person for the job. Rather, many of the lawmakers, moved by the history-making occasion, had a short speech they wanted to make while casting a ballot.

"For more than 200 years, the leaders of our government have been democratically elected. And from their ranks, our elected leaders have always selected a man for the responsibility and honor of serving as speaker of the House. Always, that is, until today," said Representative John A. Boehner, the previous majority leader who handed the gavel over to Pelosi. "Whether you're a Republican, Democrat or independent, today is a cause for celebration."

"Just as the biblical Esther was called to save the nation, I cast my vote for another woman called for in such times as these," said Representative Bobby Rush, the Chicago Democrat and former Black Panther.

"This vote is for the future of all our grandchildren and for world peace," said Representative Lynn Woolsey (D-Calif.).

"It's cool," said Caroline McCaul, 10-year-old daughter of Republican representative Michael McCaul.

Pelosi spent the two hours of the vote on the floor of the House surrounded by her grandchildren. Children were everywhere that day. Pelosi had one or more of her grandchildren on her lap for most of the two hours, and when she wasn't sitting she was standing up holding her six-week-old grandson, Paul Michael, swaddled in his white receiving blanket. The visitors' galleries were jammed with women and children, too. Young girls, businesswomen, women's rights activists and many daughters and grand-daughters of congressmen and congresswomen. While she waited, Pelosi greeted a steady stream of her spiritual ancestors with hugs and kisses, including Senator Barbara Mikulski (D-Md.), and former Colorado representative Pat Schroeder.

When the vote was finally official, cheers drowned out the announcement of the tally. Pelosi, still holding Paul Michael, lit up in a maternal smile and bowed repeatedly in all directions as the crowd around her filled the room with applause. She kissed her way to the rostrum up a gauntlet of well-wishers. At 2:08 P.M., Boehner handed her the wooden gavel with a hug and a kiss. (It was a day of air busses as well.) And then, while Representative John Dingell, the longest-serving member of Congress, issued the oath of office, Pelosi did something none of the 59 speakers who had come before her had done. As she held "the hammer" high overhead in what is usually a moment of raw political power, she gathered a welter of children around her in front of the high-backed leather Speaker's chair. As she held up her right hand to take the oath of office, she held a grandson's hand tightly in her left.

"For our daughters and granddaughters, today we have broken the marble ceiling," Pelosi announced to raucous, roaring cheers. "For our daughters and granddaughters today, the sky is the limit."

Like a fair-minded first-grade teacher on a field trip, she then gave each and every child a turn with gavel.

Although the scene had the look and feel of giddy spontaneity, Pelosi had orchestrated the tableau with great care, as she had her 20-year climb to get there. The maternal image projected from the dais and the elaborate four-day celebration of her election—one pundit dubbed it Pelosi-palooza—were all choreographed to soften her image a bit and introduce Pelosi to average Americans as a sort of national grandmom while the media spotlight was full on. Nancy Pelosi had achieved an American first, but many people across the country didn't know much about her until that media moment, and now she would be forever remembered in association with those preschoolers on the rostrum.

This was a classic "money shot," a public relations term for a single visual that can instantly shape and frame a politician and an agenda. A money shot works just as well with the sound turned off, emotionally and contextually branding Pelosi in viewers' minds. It was an image aimed at hearts more than heads. The video appeared on every major television network and cable news station, and the still photo ran on hundreds of front pages around the country, including the *New York Times* and the *Washington Post*. Her popularity and name recognition leapt in the next week. The image—and news of Pelosi's ascension—resonated around the world, eliciting an outpouring of jubilation among women of all walks. Pelosi's communications teams reports receiving good wishes via e-mail and letters in the thousands.

Cindy Simon Rosenthal, author of *When Women Lead* and *Women Transforming Congress*, had this to say: "I thought it was a brilliant way to put a exclamation point on the theme which she embraced for her Speakership, which is about change. What better way to illustrate that than to have grand-kids on the podium. It was an image that especially resonated with a lot of women, Republican and Democratic. It was the exclamation point that something has really changed. Nancy Pelosi is Speaker!"

Ellen Malcolm of EMILY's List thought it was a positive image as well "When she was sworn in and there was such excitement about electing the first woman Speaker, I think the combination of her holding the gavel of power yet surrounded by children on the podium told a tale to a lot of people that is a different day in America," Malcolm said.

One of the most succinct tributes came from Pelosi's eight-year-old granddaughter, Madeline, at a women's tea honoring Pelosi: "Because my Mimi got this job I think more women will get jobs like hers."

Pelosi wasn't one to presume false modesty. She herself called it "an historic moment for women of this country. We waited for many years of struggle to achieve our rights. But women weren't just waiting; women were working. We worked to redeem the promise of America, that all men and women are created equal."

At an afternoon tea party that turned into a Women's Power rally the day before, Pelosi said: "America's working women, women working at home, whatever they choose to do, they have a friend in the Capitol of the United States." Five hundred women all sported Rosie the Riveter buttons with Pelosi's face superimposed above the slogan "A woman's place is in the House . . . as Speaker." Pelosi obliged by flexing her bicep for the crowd.

The jubilation among many women across the country that week and that day was spiced with just a dash of confusion, and some disagreement, about the symbolism of the children on the podium. "Powerful" and "mommy" is a new and unfamiliar combo plate in political leadership, at least in the United States. What did those children tell us about the state of gender politics in America? Was this a step forward or a throwback for women? Was it a purely calculated move to attract the family values vote or an unadvised show of lightness when the moment called for seriousness? No matter how choreographed it was, the image was remarkable in its unfamiliarity. It was truly something new: a visual redefinition of what true power is, or might be.

"When Pelosi got into leadership, she didn't act they way people expected," notes Marie Wilson. "She surrounded herself with family, which was an enormously unusual thing for a woman leader to do."

Katrina vanden Heuvel, editor of the progressive political magazine *The Nation*, wrote on her blog: "I wonder why Pelosi, a woman I admire, seemed so keen to use her first day as a speaker to portray herself as a traditional, family-first kind of woman. Many of the women I spoke to worry that the photo fed the image of women as one-dimensional."

In her blog, attorney and commentator Lisa Nuss worried that the imagery "takes us back to the 1980s. No one should think the media response to this is entirely benign or that it doesn't contribute to a public perception gap about which gender is better left in charge of children and which the legislative agenda."

Berkeley's Robin Lakoff said her first reaction was "Oh God, I wish she wouldn't do that, because it just sort of deprofessionalizes the business."

But Lakoff had a second reaction. "Thinking about it again, it opens up a whole new range of possibilities. Because when you say 'Well I wish she wouldn't talk and act like a woman,' that's just going back to old prejudices."

She elaborated in a telephone interview: "Whenever there are women in positions of power, they play like they are sort of honorary men. Margaret Thatcher is a case in point." Women in political leadership roles have had, in the past, to prove they were "man enough for the job. "But Pelosi's experiment, if it should bear long-term fruit, is much more important and exciting for all of us, because it offers us a whole new, effective way of doing democracy (small d)," Lakoff said. "We've never had women in positions of real power. This is such an intriguing question. What would it be like? How would women do things differently? Surely once every 10,000 years you could try new ways of doing things." Pelosi refused to follow any male role models in her new position.

Pat Schroeder, who briefly explored a run for president and who has fought a few battles of her own against stereotypes and sexism, said it was an unsettling image because, for the first time, the county had a powerful leader who also understood what a woman's life and a mother's life is like. She thinks it was a breakthrough. "She has a very different style. It's soft but firm, embracing, but again, if you aren't going to give respect back, if you aren't part of the team, then you're on your own. She's saying I'm powerful *and* I'm a mommy."

Wilson saw the image as a breakthrough for Pelosi herself, too. "I don't think she's somebody who's been seen as a strong leader. But she stood up and with that vote said I am a strong leader. And I'll show you how strong. I'm just going to surround myself with my family. You're not going to take a thing away from me." In a single moment, Pelosi may have widened the country's definition of "leader" and its respect for the role motherhood plays in sustaining a society's civic life.

"We all say children are our future," said Senator Barbara Boxer, "but she took it to that next step of making a visual statement."

The inauguration was the crown jewel of a week of events deliberately planned to highlight select parts of Pelosi's life story. The kids at swearing-in stressed her family ties, a move that was seen by some analysts as a staged effort to rehabilitate the Democratic Party's image. A day after the ceremony, Pelosi returned to Baltimore's Little Italy in a photo op that certainly showcased her blue-collar roots. She attended Mass at the Catholic women's college where she studied political science in Washington, which certainly made it clear that religious values are important to her (and Democrats). And later she dined at the Italian embassy as Tony Bennett sang "I Left My Heart in San Francisco," a party that highlighted her Italian American heritage. That event also may have happened to remind people of her party's image as a champion for ethnic minorities. Kathleen Hall Jamieson, who teaches political communication and rhetoric at the University of Pennsylvania, called it all a strategic repositioning, a map of where she wants to take the party.

"Essentially, she's trying to embody the Democratic Party that she would like to offer the nation in 2008," Jamieson told a reporter.

Others thought the inaugural events seemed like grandstanding, a bit of self-serving showmanship. Mike Murphy, a Republican political consultant and former adviser to Massachusetts governor Mitt Romney and Senator John McCain (R-Ariz.), told the *Washington Post* he thought it all a bit much. He blasted Pelosi for turning the swearing in into a coronation.

"What? No fireworks?" he asked. "She has every right to throw a new-speaker celebration, but it's 500 percent from what is normal. Nobody voted for Nancy Pelosi as Speaker; they voted for a change in Washington. It's an aggressive act to grab the spotlight and create a cult of personality."

In her column on *townhall.com*, California political commentator Carol Platt Liebau complained that Pelosi's celebration and "self-congratulatory rhetoric" were reminiscent of "a certain type of 70s-style feminism; one could almost hear the strains of 'I Am Woman, Hear Me Roar' playing in the background." She argued that, given the prominence of women in Washington, ranging from Hillary Clinton, to Elizabeth Dole, to Condoleezza Rice, to Education Secretary Margaret Spellings, Pelosi's assertions that women still were being systematically excluded from political leadership was a stretch. And she criticized Pelosi for selling herself short by forcing the world to view her achievement through the prism of gender. "She didn't win the post of Speaker of the House because of her sex or despite it. She won because of her hard work, her fundraising, her long tenure in the House and her political skills . . . . her sex was incidental—as it should have been."

Barbara Boxer defends the triumphant imagery Pelosi engineered, saying women too often stand aside for everyone else and let their own accomplishments go unmarked. "It had to be marked, and I'm so glad she marked it when she got the gavel. There's a reason for it. It's not something that can be glossed over. Sometimes these accomplishments need to be celebrated. She understood that. I was very supportive of what she did."

Pelosi has always valued a bit of style and flourish—as long as it's tastefully done. Her communications folks acknowledged beforehand that an inauguration with flair could help capture the national imagination, raising Pelosi's visibility and consequently her effectiveness as the face of the Democratic opposition to the president. And they said they hoped the image also served as a foil to the caricature of Pelosi that had been drawn in the fall by Republicans. Kate O'Bierne, Washington editor of the conservative *National Review*, told a *New York Times* reporter that the imagery was probably effective, signaling a kinder, gentler, softer approach to voters weary of war. She didn't say she thought that was a good thing.

In the national opera that is Washington politics, then, the visual cast George W. Bush as the stereotypical male: decisive, black and white, stubborn, strong-willed, and inflexible. "I am the decider," Bush has said over and over again. Pelosi is the female lead, expressing more historically "feminine" tactics: reasonableness, listening, talking nicely, being open to suggestions, strict but willing to compromise, the cleaner-up of messes. "It takes a woman to clean up the House," Pelosi often said before the 2006 election. Perhaps this is just the kind of gender power-sharing arrangement we want then: neither an Alpha Mom nor Alpha Dad completely running the show, but each checking and balancing the other so that together perhaps they get the country where it needs to go. Dad certainly is being held more accountable than he was. In the meantime, however, the power struggle is on.

Speaking of metaphoric dads and moms, Robin Lakoff's husband, fellow Berkeley linguist George Lakoff, is the one who first suggested Americans see the Republican Party as the tough father and the Democratic Party as the responsible parent. The observation has devolved of late into the shorthand of Daddy Party and Mommy Party, terms that have been bandied about liberally by blogs and pundits since Pelosi took charge. Chris Matthews was the first to use the term "Mommy Party" on cable television.

George Lakoff explains what he actually meant by the comparison in his book *Whose Freedom? The Battle over America's Most Important Idea*. He believes that both Democrats and Republicans see the bond between government and citizen through metaphors of family. Republicans generally prefer what he calls the "strict father model, which assumes a strong, dominant government that disciplines its citizen children to make them into responsible adults. However, once those children have proven that they are morally and financially responsible, the father-government should not interfere with their lives." In contrast, Lakoff argues, Democrats subscribe to the "nurturant parent model" in which "mothers" and "fathers" both try to keep the essentially good citizen children away from bad influences, such as pollution, social injustice, and poverty. (It should be noted here that Lakoff is a liberal.) Lakoff believes that most political speeches work primarily by invoking these metaphors and urging the adoption of one over the other.

But aides for Pelosi blanch at the suggestion that the maternal image projected on the dais that day was contrived, or somehow inauthentic, even if politically useful. It was just Pelosi being Pelosi, they say, pointing out that the new Speaker raised five children before she jumped into politics at age 46 and has emphasized children and the issues that most affect them for more than 20 years in Congress. The children were all her idea, not an aide's, said longtime friend Eshoo. The Speaker's inaugural celebration of children, aides argued, was a fitting culmination of her guiding philosophy.

The real question is whether Pelosi is able to continue to carry over the freshness and originality of that first-day image into a new kind of leadership that emphasizes a different agenda, different priorities, and a different style from her predecessors. Will a woman wield the power of the Speaker's office differently?

A survey conducted in 1998 by the Center for the American Woman and Politics at Rutgers University found the biggest difference between men and women political leaders came in their policy priorities. The study concluded that women were more likely to give priority to policies that relate to family, society and women's rights. And women officeholders were more likely to bring citizens into the process and open government up to public view rather than conduct business behind closed doors. They were also more responsive to groups that had historically been kept out of the lawmaking process.

For her book *When Women Lead*, Cindy Simon Rosenthal compared how women and men lead committees differently in all 50 state legislatures. She chose to compare committee chairs because that was the only place she could find large numbers of women politicians in leadership positions at the time.

"There are some differences," Rosenthal said. "It tended to be that the women were the ones who placed a higher premium on consensus. Women who placed a higher premium on trying to listen to all the different perspectives and trying to bring them together. It tended to be on average that the women were a little more likely to not be willing to just impose their vision, but work to accommodate and bring in other people's ideals and ideas." Rosenthal throws in one big caveat: Women's experiences were different depending on the kind of legislatures they served in. The kind of institutions involved and the norms they have had a huge impact on what kind of leadership women exercised when given the chance. "In a more institutionalized, professionalized institution, you tend to see more top-down and autocratic leadership," Rosenthal said, rather than the more consensual leadership favored by many women. "Congress is the epitome of that," Rosenthal added. "That's a factor to be understood as a constraint on Pelosi's own exercise of power and leadership. She will undoubtedly operate under the norms and constraints of the institution. I think she will do some things differently, but her leadership will be in part a product of that institution." Until the institution itself changes, or she changes it, it's not realistic to expect Pelosi to be able to assert a different kind of leadership.

But there are precedents for institutional change brought about by women leaders in other disciplines. Harvard professor Rosabeth Moss Kanter, considered one of the business world's rock stars, is the first person who examined how women often handle authority differently in business settings. In her influential book *Men and Women of the Corporation*, she theorized that businesswomen actually define power differently: not as the ability to get others to do what you want, but the ability to get things done. She and others have observed that women thrown into leadership positions generally get results by collaboration and compromise rather than command and control. This style of leadership may take longer, Kanter observed in her studies of women in the workplace, but the people involved ended up seeing the project as their own and themselves as having an investment in its success, so it is often more productive over the long haul. It's the old leadership adage: People tend to support what they create themselves.

Much has been written of late about this style of leadership, which has been dubbed "transformational" as opposed to the "transactional" or authoritarian style most men are thought to employ. "Transformational" leaders are interpersonally oriented, leading by example, empowering those who work for them, stressing mentoring and collaboration. In a study of business owners in 2005, management scholars Jennifer E. Cliff, Nancy Langton and Howard E. Aldrich found that male leaders wanted to be thought of "as God . . . as capable . . . as the captain of the ship who calls the shots." Women business leaders told the researchers they wanted to be thought of as "someone who's here to work for my employees . . . as a resource . . . [as having] their well-being at heart."

"Women tend to be more collaborative, no question," said Malcolm. "I don't think that's a stereotype. I think women in general look for ways to bring people together and are less likely to say it's my way or the highway and I'm going to prove it to you."

A raft of books such as *Enlightened Power* (2005), *Why the Best Man for the Job Is a Woman* (2000), *Secrets of Millionaire Moms* (2007) and *The Female Advantage: Women's Ways of Leadership* (1990) make the case that women make *better* leaders than men in general. *BusinessWeek* recently declared a "new gender gap" that might leave men as "losers in a global economy that values mental powers over might."

But many women don't buy the arguments that the cooperative, collaborative kind of leadership, rather than the competitive kind, is inherently female.

"I hate it when people say that women just innately like to bring people together. I don't think so," said Wilson, author of *Closing the Leadership Gap: Why Women Can and Must Help Run the World*. "I think it's something women have had to do to have authority."

Pelosi and other women have mastered these techniques because they've had to, not because the traits are more common to women than men, she argues. No one gave them positions of authority, her argument goes. They had to somehow work themselves up through a hostile pecking order, building a large set of supporters and friends until the guys had no choice but to give them a shot. Wilson calls it leadership from the foot of the table rather than the head. Ron Heifetz, in his book *Leadership Without Easy Answers*, takes a close look at the kinds of leadership in which people lead without authority.

Most women leaders, he argues, and leaders of color, too—outsiders—have had to build communities of trust to get the authority to lead. What may be interesting now, he said, is that that kind of leadership in companies and in legislative bodies is often preferred, whether it is executed by a man or a woman.

"And when you build authority that way, you know what you're building?" Wilson asks. "You build in loyalty because you have relationships with people. That's what I think Pelosi was able to capitalize on." When you're leading from the foot of the table, she said, you have to do it in a way that's tough but caring so you don't alienate them. "There's so little command and control behavior that works anywhere anymore."

When asked what traditionally feminine qualities have served her well as Speaker, Pelosi said: "I don't even think of it that way. But I do think that, I'm not saying this is a female trait, but I am a good listener, and many men are, too. No inference being drawn about anyone else's capacity to listen. I do try to have decisions made in a collegial way. Listening and talking it through rather than just deciding how something will be or conducting a meeting in a way that doesn't elicit honest response. But what do I bring from the standpoint of being a woman, I guess, is patience."

She has often emphasized that most of her leadership skills she acquired as a mom. One of those skills is the efficient use of time, the ability to get a job done and move onto the next one: ". . . no underutilized resource, of time, of energy, anything. How are we going to get this task accomplished? How do we involve as many people as possible? You have to listen to people to do it in a way that they will be satisfied with. And also, sometimes, when you're having some internal debates about the direction you go, just to make sure that at the end of the day, we're all united. It's not as important to win the point 100 percent. That unity is more important. As I always say to my children, never let friendship leave your voice. Literally and figuratively, in terms of leadership, that's how you do it. Because we have some heated discussions in our conference."

Pelosi had no authority when she entered Congress 20 years ago, but she steadily built a community of loyal followers, raising money for them, paying attention to their family lives, nurturing relationships with them, earning their respect by sticking to principles, showing results, and working hard in their campaigns. She developed so many ways of leading effectively from the foot of the table that she has finally gotten to the head of the table.

Malcolm believes that now Pelosi has real authority, there's no question she is leading differently than men do. "One of the ways she is leading differently is giving women opportunities and acknowledging the importance of the advancement of women," she said. "There was always this real message of women are important and matter to me and this is an achievement for women and not just me."

Call it the Old Girls Network. Pelosi and other women have built up a strong Ethernet of politically active women that may lead to greater gains in the future. Dennis Simon, a Southern Methodist University political scientist who has studied woman candidates for Congress, reports that 2006 marked the ninth consecutive election cycle in which the proportion of women running in congressional primaries has increased. Women made up 16 percent of the candidates in those primaries in 2006, an all-time high. Clearly, a dynamic was at work that favored some sort of antidote to Bush's tough, divisive leadership, and women were the beneficiaries because they were seen as clear alternatives and agents of change.

"Around the country, I've seen this very new women's political movement building," said Wilson. "I see more groups being built around recruiting women at the local level. What's happened with Pelosi, particularly coupled with Clinton, with Janet Napolitano, head of the National Governors Association, with Kansas Governor and rising star Kathleen Sibelius, with Shirley Franklin heading up the Democratic mayors and governors, with Susan Collins really being talked about as a vice presidential candidate, what you've got, at the top and bottom, is a serious new look in women in politics."

A short list of grassroots groups that have emerged in the last several years to help women run for office includes:

- An AFL-CIO–sponsored program called Stirring the Pot
- Emerge-CA
- Arizona WISH (Women in Senate and House) List and ArizonaList (A-List)
- Every Open Seat a Woman's Seat
- The Coalition to Recruit and Elect Women (CREW) in Massachusetts
- The Woman's Campaign Fund in Minnesota
- Future PAC, a national political action committee that helps fund African American women candidates
- The Vote, Run, Lead program sponsored by The White House Project
- The National Education for Women's Leadership program run by Rutgers' Center for American Women in Politics

Ruth Mandel, one of the founders of the Center for American Women in Politics at Rutgers University, put it this way: "We have a chance to see what women do when they wield real power."

"Women help each other, our successes are intertwined," Pelosi told an interviewer in 2002. She said she admires just about every woman she knows in politics. "If I just knew one woman, she'd be an inspiration. Women in this business are fabulous, they are idealistic, they glow in it. They are for families, they care, they get it. Women provide the power of example."

Larry J. Sabato, founder and director of the University of Virginia's Center for Politics, believes that power of example is what will make the difference when it comes to more women participating in politics and wielding real power. The greater the number of women in leadership roles, the more young women will get involved in politics. It's all about numbers. And since politics is often the realm of our idealized archetypes of men and women, role models in politics are even more important than in other fields.

"Role models are exceptionally important in politics. As a teacher, I see that all the time," said Sabato, something of a role model himself for political commentators. The *Wall Street Journal* has described him as the most quoted political expert in America. *Washingtonian Magazine* calls him "the Dr. Phil of American Politics." He himself calls Pelosi the ultimate role model—second in line for the presidency, top leader of the largest house of Congress, visible in the media daily, "and someone who cuts an attractive figure."

Pelosi's emergence, coupled with Hillary Clinton's presidential run and other recent gains for women in the political realm, may also signal a resurgence of sorts for a redefined feminism. Pelosi is proud to call herself a feminist, and the president of the National Organization of Women, Kim Gandy, lionized Pelosi as the first "self-identified feminist" to become Speaker of the House. But the kind of feminism Pelosi practices doesn't meet the standards many of the original feminist organizations have, however. After she wore a head scarf in Syria in deference to local custom, many feminist groups and spokeswomen complained, saying she was setting back the cause by kowtowing to an egregiously sexist regime. But Pelosi defended the scarves as a show of respect to other cultures, a when-in-Rome gesture that had nothing to do with women's rights. Pelosi called the scarves irrelevant to her commitment to feminism, which she said is strong. But she's more of a pragmatic feminist than the woman-needs-a-man-like-a-fish-needs-a-bike feminists of Gloria Steinem's day. Hers is a tactical, choose-your-battles feminism rather than an ideological one, just like her politics. Keep an eye on results, on the long-term gains, she advises. She wouldn't have ever made it to her current position if she'd practiced the politics of confrontation employed by so many 1970s feminists. What's the better strategy: fight every fight to the death, or skip some battles and live to fight another day?

Reinventing the meaning of feminism for America is going to take some doing, though. We're still a generation that associates "feminist" with bra-burner. "Well-behaved women seldom make history" goes an old feminist saw. When Republican speechwriters were describing Pelosi as a San Francisco liberal, many Americans over 40 were still hearing and seeing carryover images of feminist women from those earlier battles: outspoken, curt, confrontational activists sneering at menkind and carrying a giant chip on their shoulder pads. We've certainly striated the stereotypes in the past 40 years, so that not all empowered women are thrown in with the early firebrands of feminism. But many older men—and women—are still wary of what they're going to be confronted with when they meet a woman of power, because certainly on occasions in the past, it's been a difficult confrontation, especially in Congress.

The 1970s feminist is not remembered as a "collaborative and cooperative" personality that men, especially the traditional-family men of Congress, are eager to work with. Pelosi, in her rise through the ranks, has taken a different approach entirely. She wants people to see her as a woman who is familiar to a majority of people—a wife, mother, daughter. When she talks about her family, her upbringing, her grandkids, she's trying to expose the parts of her background people connect with. She's trying to be what Bill Clinton once tried to be: a leader who leads with humanity, whether it's to be less threatening to a man or more connected to a woman. She's deliberately trying to offset that 1970s feminist stereotype. That's not to say Pelosi isn't always enthusiastically reverent toward the Gloria Steinem gang. In fact, she has argued that Steinem's damn-the-torpedoes personality type was absolutely necessary at that time to lay the groundwork for her own more collaborative type of leadership. But feminism, Pelosi said, has evolved.

Pelosi's advocacy of a "balanced" feminism joins a larger debate raging right now about moms who leave the workforce and get back in later. The Bureau of Labor Statistics shows an increase of about 8 percent in the number of married women at home with infants from 1997 to 2004. The biggest increase was among mothers with college degrees. This is a feminism that emphasizes a range of choices but doesn't dictate what those choices ought to look like.

Another feminist complaint about Pelosi has to do with some of her bumper-sticker statements that seem to play gender politics for political gain. "Do I have to use my Mother of Five voice?" for example, or "It takes a woman to clean up the House."

Here's an exchange that took place on CNN on the subject between Pelosi and CNN reporter Andrea Koppel:

PELOSI: Maybe it takes a woman to clean house.

KOPPEL: That kind of has a sexist undertone to it? Is that deliberate?

PELOSI: Well, it is, because the fact is a woman represents what's new in politics.

KOPPEL: How is that?

PELOSI: Because it has never happened before.

The *Washington Post* described Pelosi as a "grandmother of five" in the story about her historic election. (She has six grandchildren now, with the birth of Paul Michael.) The same story described Harry Reid, the new Senate leader, as the "son of a hard-rock miner" with no mention of Reid's 16 grandchildren. If Pelosi emphasizes such old-fashioned images and uses such language, isn't she telling others that it's okay to continue using such stereotypical characterizations about women? Isn't the goal of all this some sort of gender neutrality, where women politicians are judged completely on their merits and not their gender? Don't we hope one day to have a society that is both color blind *and* gender blind? If women don't want to be passed over because of their gender, then they can't ask for special consideration just because of their gender either, can they? Either we're going to be a gender-neutral society or we're not. You can't have it both ways, depending on which side of the gender aisle you're sitting. Isn't that what the principle of all men—and women—created equal binds us to aim for?

But defenders of Pelosi's "It takes a woman" quip say such statements are completely different when delivered by a woman instead of a man.

"What's she's doing is taking it over," argues Wilson. "If you want to clean up a pattern of behavior, just take it over. Instead of letting other people do it to you, you say, yeah I'm gonna clean up the House. It takes a woman. Do I have to use my mother voice? I mean, if *she* says it, it starts to imbue it with humor and authority. She takes over the pattern."

The "takeover" strategy has been used for racial epithets as well. African American film director Spike Lee did something similar—co-opting the language of insult—in his masterpiece, *Do the Right Thing*. At one point the plot of the movie pauses while Spike himself comes onscreen, looking straight at the camera, and unleashes a string of racial epithets, with the intention of disarming their ability to insult.

Other political observers argue that the media is probably remiss in not describing personal details about the home and family life of male candidates, even what they wear. The error lies not in mentioning Pelosi's six grandkids but in omitting men's, these critics say. Certainly Pelosi doesn't mind being characterized as a grandmother of six. For her it's about respecting her right to define her own image, her own stereotype, and that's how she wants to be known, as a grandmother of six. Since so many voters make their decisions about candidates based on who the candidates are rather than what their policies are, shouldn't the media report more about their home life rather than less? More about who they are? People bring their personalities to work, they don't leave them at home; it could be argued that big decisions that people have made in their personal lives suggest the kind of character and values that they will eventually bring to their personal relationships at work. Politicians rely on those values for touchstones for whatever decisions they make with whatever authority they hold. In that light, knowing politicians' personal stories is hugely important.

Pelosi would also be the first to argue that we're a long way from gender neutrality. Even with the gains of 2006, women remain underrepresented in elective office: They make up 51 percent of the population but only 16 percent of Congress, 24 percent of state legislators, and 18 percent of governors. Women's interest groups are especially worried about the prospects of women in state capitals: Women lost ground in 20 of 50 statehouses following the November election.

Former Ohio House Speaker Jo Ann Davidson, cochair of the Republican National Committee, thinks Pelosi's high profile could help bump the state-level numbers in 2008, the way Hillary Clinton's high visibility in her husband's presidential campaign helped create a jump in 1992, the so-called Year of the Woman.

When asked whether she was happy about the record numbers of women elected to Congress in 2006, Pelosi said: "We wanted more."

"The biggest obstacle women candidates face is not about gender, it's about the lack of opportunity," said Ellen Malcolm. "Ninety-eight percent of incumbents who run for re-election are re-elected in most years . . . . The bottom line is there are very few opportunities."

Since there still aren't that many women in Congress, the built-in biases of Congress still need to be vigorously challenged and exposed, Pelosi believes, and alternative ways of managing constantly put forward. We're still recalibrating, she said, we're far from balanced. Pelosi argues that her approach to leadership is already pushing things in the right direction, creating a different dynamic within the House.

"When women are there alongside men, men are more likely to do things they need to do without being seen as sissies," said Wilson. "I mean, it helps men be able to express a fuller range of behaviors. I think that's what will change—you won't just have this kind of leadership at the table that women will be doing. Men have every bit as much capacity for that kind of collaborative leadership, but we've screwed it down in them really tight early on because it's considered just too soft. But men can do this. "Everybody's got that but we've assigned the hearts to women and the heads to men. And everybody thinks with their heart, actually, so it's good to have your heart well trained."

Senator Mikulski sees the same thing happening in the Senate. "For many of the women Senators, when we first got elected we were viewed as novelties," she said. "At times they wanted to turn us into celebrities. In the 110th Congress—we've been here for awhile. There are women Senators on every powerful committee and they hold powerful leadership positions. And we work with the men of the Senate to build coalitions. I call these guys the 'Galahads.' They work with us on everything from women's health initiatives to making sure that seniors have pensions they can count on."

Wilson readily admits that women leaders can learn from men, "because sometimes we don't make tough, clear decisions. We do ask more people than need to be in on a decision." The key, she believes, is having a mix of men and women in leadership, a balance of leadership styles and agendas. Women's voices are still too muted in the overall equation.

She cites Rudy Giuliani after 9/11 as an example of the advantages of a balanced, blended style of leadership.

"Giuliani was always a very tough kind of mayor here [New York] and after 9/11 he added a dollop of care and started actually talking differently to people. And people worshipped him because here was this tough guy who was also able to be tender. That's what people are looking for."

Pat Schroeder thinks Congress needs more women at the table so a different agenda can be enacted. In her first year in office, Pelosi has dramatically refocused the country's agenda onto what were once called "soft issues"—better daycare, better healthcare, a cleaner environment, raising the minimum wage, interest rate reductions on subsidized college loans, and expanded federal support for stem-cell research. But it remains to be seen how much of her agenda she'll actually get passed by the Senate and not vetoed by Bush.

"We have cut all the human issues out, and left those to women and called them women's issues," said Wilson. "The human piece is often missing from the equation." She thinks Pelosi might be just the person to get "human" issues out of the gender ghetto and get them front and center permanently.

Mikulski said women in Congress are not a single, monolithic block but rather a force. "We are not solo acts—we believe that every issue is a woman's issue and we work together to form coalitions to get things done. We work on not only the macro issues, but also the macaroni and cheese issues—the issues that affect American families—from foreign policy to the climate crisis and healthcare. We women set the tone for civility and respect on Capitol Hill. We want to carry that tone of civility with us in an otherwise prickly institution."

"If Americans would stop demonizing our female leaders and choose power over our fears," Wilson adds, "women just might turn out to be the best promise our country has."

CHAPTER 11

THE HUNDRED HOURS

*A woman is like a tea bag—you never know how strong she is until she gets in
hot water.*

—Eleanor Roosevelt, former first lady and social activist, 1884–1962

The desk was epic. It filled the room like the deck of an aircraft carrier.
Observers say the men who piloted the oak colossus over the years sat behind
it like they were driving a warship. It was the Man of the House on one side
and all the little people on the other. Its size was intended, of course, to humble and intimidate visitors, much the way Pierre L'Enfant designed the entire
city of Washington—with its wide lanes and traffic circles and marbled
solemnity—to humble and intimidate foreign leaders. The desk was an
expression in wood and iron of raw accumulated power, a monument to the
egos that have filled the office in the past.

The desk was gone the shortly after Pelosi took office, as were other
longtime vestiges of the House of Representatives: its smoke-filled meeting
rooms. Its three-day workweeks, its marble ceiling. Nancy Pelosi had them all
removed in her first few weeks as Speaker. She had a smaller writing desk
brought into her new office and pushed it against the wall—as more of a side
table, really—so she could get more people in for face-to-face meetings. The
office sports yellow roses, ocher drapes, and bowls of chocolate. The feng shui
of the room is more she than he, more we than me.

"We used to always laugh about how these guys had these big desks," said
former congresswoman Pat Schroeder. "Most of the women just don't do

that. I think it was a huge cultural difference. I know I slammed mine against the wall. And then when anybody came in we had a great big room where everybody could sit around. And people would be just amazed that you weren't sitting behind your battleship."

"This furniture was built for males," said Congresswoman Anna Eshoo, who also got rid of the giant desk in her office when she moved in. "These desks were massive. Built for power. Power desks. And to tell you the truth, we can't sit at these desks." Eshoo said she had to get a new one because she couldn't reach across the top. "Have you ever seen all these big chairs? I got rid of them because I was like Alice in Wonderland. My feet were dangling off the chairs."

Multiple couches fill the Speaker's office now where the desk used to be. A statue of blustery Phil Burton is also in the office, as is the "Goddess of Liberty." She has pictures of her husband, Paul Pelosi, and their five children and six grandchildren, and the picture of her with Senator John F. Kennedy when she was 16. The paintings on the walls are on loan from the Fine Arts Museums of San Francisco. The office has a balcony that overlooks the entire Mall, with a view down to the Washington Monument, the Reflecting Pool, and beyond to the Lincoln Memorial three miles away. Pelosi hosted the alumnae from Trinity in the Capitol for her forty-fifth college reunion, and she took classmates out on the balcony for photos. They all had dinner in Statuary Hall, and gathered for their class picture on the floor of the House. "Most of the girls were saying it was just like being Cinderella at the ball," said a classmate of Pelosi's.

The House has 435 members, 5,500 staffers, 25 official committees, and no fewer than 135 subcommittees. The largest committee, the Committee of the Whole, includes every single person in the House. There are 7,000 BlackBerrys in the U.S. Capitol complex, 15,000 laptops, 125,000 pieces of furniture, 5,800 parking places, and 11,500 phones. More than 200 million postal and email messages are sent to members of Congress each year. The average representative earns $165,200; Pelosi makes an extra $46,900 as Speaker. When a vote is about to happen on the House floor, bells go off around Capitol Hill, and all the representatives hustle to the floor. If they're in their offices, they get to the Capitol via a small subway under the Hill that looks more like an Epcot ride than a mode of transport. Inside the chamber, bas relief profiles of great lawgivers—Solon, Hammurabi, Grotius—watch over the proceedings. Oddly, the Democrats sit on the right side of the center aisle and Republicans sit on the left. The Speaker presides over it all from the top of a multitiered dais in a high-back leather chair.

The Speaker's office has a staff of 50 people to massage and manage all the egos. Pelosi's senior staff includes a chief of staff, John Lawrence, who worked for Pelosi's closest ally, George Miller, for 30 years. Her Deputy Chief of Staff George Kundanis, who runs Pelosi's floor operation, has also worked on the Hill for 30 years. Pelosi also has a chief of staff for dealing with California, Terri McCullough, who happens to be married to Howard Wolfson, Hillary Clinton's communications director. Pelosi also has several people who manage bills on the House floor, one of whom is Tip O'Neill's granddaughter, Caitlin. Everyone seems to know everyone else in the small town called the House of Representatives.

Ten of the 50 people who work for Pelosi work in the policy shop. If she wants an energy package by July 4, her policy people are the ones who put it together. Another 10 people man the communications shop, which includes both daily press and long-term message making. These are the people who do speechwriting, press releasing, and news monitoring. A separate three-person team handles all the Web pages and blogging, including the Speaker's own blog, The Gavel. Rounding out the staff are her schedulers, the administrative office, a few people who arrange events, and the security team that guards the Speaker. Interns do many of the administrative jobs, such as answering the phones.

There is no such thing as a typical day in the Speaker's office. On some days there are leadership meetings, other days caucus meetings. On certain days the Speaker has to spend a lot of time on the floor, especially before a big vote. Some days she is out campaigning for congressional candidates or raising money. Her top aides always try to set aside some time to bring her up to speed on floor activities, or they sit down with her and find out how she wants to handle the speech side of things. Every day the Speaker will meet with individual members; dignitaries come through regularly to chat.

Pelosi's office gets over a thousand letters, phone calls, and invitations a day, and that doesn't include e-mails. Her staff had to set up a separate letter and phone operation because the Speaker insists everybody's message be listened to, sifted, and digested, and every written message gets some sort of a response. "She wants people to just know they are being listened to and they are being heard," said a staffer.

Such is the giant unholy lawmaking machine Pelosi faced on her first day in office. And right away, Pelosi planned to sweat every detail.

"She opens the House every day," said Jack Murtha. "She understands the tradition and history of the House. Whenever a bill is passed she announces the passage of the bill. Now, Tip O'Neill used to do that. That's the way it should be. I mean, she is the Speaker of the House. I believe that's a very important part of recognizing who the Speaker is. And the power of the Speaker, and the influence of the Speaker."

A Speaker has to think in six-month segments. The first six months, she has to prove to people that her party is worthy of governing. In the next six months, the party has to close the deals that are introduced during the first six months. The six months after that begin the campaign for the next election. The fundraising really never ends. It's a permanent campaign feeding a giant, Jabba-the-Hutt bureaucracy with a life, appetite, and will of its own. Leading it, leading 435 leaders, is more a matter of keeping Jabba fed, watered, and happy than moving him anywhere meaningful. The sheer *representativeness* of Congress works directly against the *efficiency* of it. Most people are here for their home districts or for themselves; they're not especially here to pursue the greater good.

Cindy Simon Rosenthal said Congress is the epitome of the "professionalized" institution, with a long history of social norms and protocol, and such institutions tend to be top-down and autocratic and not easily changed. "So when she gets this criticism that she's playing too hardball, or she's being too loyal to her lieutenants, well, isn't that what people have done in the past?. To expect that she's going to be something totally different is not realistic. She got to the point where she is because she was successful in the U.S. Congress."

Yet even before the 110th Congress had passed a single bill, Pelosi had set a new tone on Capitol Hill, first and foremost by simply insisting the representatives come to work. With the increasing demands of fundraising and constituent pleasing, two- or three-day workweeks had become the norm, with members flying to their home districts on Friday and flying back on Monday. "Certainly there were a number of people arguing these two-day weeks were just preventing anything else responsible from happening," said Thomas Mann, a Brookings Institution scholar and co-author of *The Broken Branch: How Congress Is Failing America and How to Get It Back on Track*. "Gradually the drumbeat was, the schedule is absolutely critical and if you don't change that you're not going to have any hope of accomplishing anything."

"She's done it differently," said Anna Eshoo. "How she operates, how quickly she's become a force for change and a force for good."

Pelosi got immediate criticism for the longer workweek, as she did for banning smoking in the House and Senate lounges within the Capitol. She started her tenure with some small but tough decisions and endured some small but tough criticism because of it. But she was already showing people she was not afraid of wading into a fight. Even before she was sworn in, Pelosi was being dismissed by critics in Washington as a Speaker bound to fail. When she backed Murtha out of loyalty to him over heir apparent Steny Hoyer for the majority leader job after the election in November, CNN sported a headline "Damaged Goods?" while Wolf Blitzer, anchor of *The Situation Room*, asked "how badly is Nancy Pelosi damaged politically?" Gloria Borger in *U.S. News & World Report* said Pelosi "looks like a girl eager to 'get back' at the guy she didn't like." In a column titled "Dump Pelosi," *Slate*'s Timothy Noah wrote: "Let Pelosi remain speaker for now. But let her know that, before the new Congress even begins, she has placed herself on probation." *New Republic* asked: "How can Pelosi recover?"

Glenn Greenwald, author of *How Would a Patriot Act*, noted in his blog "Unclaimed Territory" that by the time Pelosi was inaugurated, the pundits had "already pronounced her to be a bitchy, vindictive shrew incapable of leading because she's consumed by petty personal bickering rather than serious and substantive considerations." The gist of the early criticism was that Pelosi couldn't separate the personal from the political, in both the Hoyer vote and in her objection to the appointment of Jane Harman as chair of the House Committee on Intelligence. Several media outlets reported that Pelosi opposed Harman because of a "cat fight" over the time they wore the same dress to a Capitol Hill event. Many such attacks were premised on the arcane assumption that a woman leader was going to be wholly ruled by her emotions. That was the press speaking, of course. The public seemed to have a different view. An AP-AOL News poll taken January 16—18, after Congress actually got down to business, put Pelosi's approval rating at 51 percent—higher than Congress's (34 percent) or President Bush's (36 percent). Within days of her start, caucus members were singing her praises as well. Early in the session, Representative George Miller said: "What the Democrats in the caucus are telling me is that this is the best three weeks of their life." Within months independent analysts were giving her high marks on how she was running the show, especially praising her efforts to reach out to all members, Democrat and Republican. Five months into her tenure, the *Washington Post* reported that she had surpassed her previous record of keeping the Democrats unified in voting 88 percent of the time. During the first five months of the session, they voted together 94 percent of the time. Even a few Republicans began grudgingly admitting that the Speaker had run a tight ship in the early going.

"I admire her political leadership," Representative Tom Cole of Oklahoma, chairman of the National Republican Congressional Committee, told the *San Francisco Chronicle*. "She's tough-minded, aggressive, knows what she believes in and acts on it."

When asked how she reacts to being underestimated time and time again, Pelosi said, "I don't care. I don't worry about what other people think. I have a great deal of confidence about what I am doing and how I am equipped to be the Speaker of the House." She does think some of the early criticism had to do with gender bias. But she quickly made the point that it was men who put her into office, a point reiterated by Senator Barbara Boxer. "She's had to have as her base men. The people who voted for her," Boxer said. "That's an enormous, important message. Women have come to the point where we get support from everybody."

Pelosi and the Democrats launched their Six for '06 agenda within hours of taking their oaths of office. The Hundred Hours was an accelerated echo of Kennedy's 100 days reference in his inaugural address, which was itself an echo of Franklin Delano Roosevelt's early promise for quick action to combat the Depression in his first 100 days. From the first hour on the floor, Pelosi intended to make it clear that the days of the Do-Nothing Congress were over. The Pelosi Congress had large ambitions. She and other top leaders had decided over Christmas break that breaking the logjam in Congress, getting bills passed, was more important at the outset than bipartisanship. For the first 100 hours, they ran Congress much the way the Republicans had run the chamber, locking the minority party out of making amendments or deliberating on the content of the bills. Critics quickly pointed out that after the election, Pelosi had said: "The principle of civility and respect for minority participation in this House is something we promised the American people. It's the right thing to do." In the first 100 hours, however, Democrats exchanged that promise for expediency.

"In some respects, the initial agenda in the House, Six for '06, was designed—for good or for ill—to be moved quickly," said Mann. "Once you commit to that there's no way you can have regular order and deliberation. You're basically taking bills that were drawn up in the previous Congress so that you could skip the committee stage, you take these under closed rules to the floor, so no there really isn't a chance of deliberation."

But Republicans could still vote, and many joined the Democrats in quickly passing the Six for '06 agenda, which had been carefully chosen and crafted to pick up votes on both sides of the aisle. "We've gone out of our way to put legislation on the floor that we thought was going to get bipartisan support," said a senior Democratic staff member. "We didn't try pushing just an agenda that we could pass on our own." The House's first vote was the implementation of the 9/11 Commission's recommendations on national security, which many Republicans supported. In her first 100 hours, Pelosi also pushed through an increase in the minimum wage, the first approved in 10 years; a cut in student loan rates; a rollback of government subsidies for oil companies; an expansion in stem-cell research; a requirement that Medicare leverage its buying power when purchasing prescription drugs; and a modest ethics reform package. The House also restricted spending earmarks that members of Congress use to pay for pet projects back in their home districts. By the time this book went to press, the minimum wage, the 9/11 commission recommendations, a college aid expansion and an ethics package had been passed by the entire Congress and signed into law by the president. Bush vetoed the stem-cell legislation after the Senate passed it.

In the first few months, it was all about motion. Phil Burton used to say whatever you do, keep it in motion. Keep it moving. By that criterion, Pelosi was a quantitative success. All measure of activity increased during Pelosi's first session: Bills passed, roll call votes, oversight hearings, laws enacted and signed by the president. Mann compared the 109th and 110th Congresses and found that, during the same 7-month time period, Pelosi had nearly doubled the number of hours in session, from 665 to 1032. The number of roll call votes had nearly doubled, as well, from 453 to 846. She'd increased the number of substantive measures passed from 52 to 90. She'd increased the number of oversight hearings from 393 to 605; the number of hearings devoted to Iraq from 63 to 133. The laws enacted by the president, however, dropped from 60 to 55. By the August recess, Pelosi had pushed through 68 key bills, 49 of which received some bipartisan support. President Bush also threatened more than 20 vetoes.

Mann believes a better comparison might be the 104th Congress, when Newt Gingrich and a Republican majority took over from a Democratic majority. Pelosi stacks up well against Gingrich's Contract for America, too: 90 substantive bills passed versus 52; 605 oversight hearings versus 438; 55 bills signed by the president versus 28.

"I really give her very high grades," said Mann. "She came out of the chute and stumbled on the Murtha-Hoyer leadership race. But her colleagues said she did it in good faith, to reward somebody who had really worked on her behalf, and gave her a pass on it. And I think she's been very effective thus far. She's proven to be pragmatic, but tough. She's not afraid of taking on some of her senior colleagues . . . . But then makes peace with them and they go on to work together. She's cautioned them to stay away from impeachment talks, to use the subpoena judiciously, and to try to stay away from gotcha personal scandal hearings and focus on failures of governance, and administration."

Respected Congressional Scholar Norm Ornstein, in a column for Roll Call, wrote: "We have a long way to go before Congress is truly functional. There are still major gaps in procedure and no semblance yet of a consistent regular order. The minority has a larger role, but not yet an appropriately robust role. But there are some signs at least of better times ahead for those who love Congress. And signs that Nancy Pelosi could be an exceptional Speaker."

Most Republicans in Congress, however, had nothing but scorn for Pelosi's 100-hour agenda. "The Democrats' first 100 hours were spent on watered-down initiatives that at best were ineffective and at worst were detrimental to our economy and citizens," said Congressman Phil Gingrey of Georgia. "The Democrats showed their commitment to raising taxes and expanding the federal government. They also showed their willingness to forgo debate and process for sound bite solutions that do nothing to address the real problems facing our nation."

If Pelosi had an arch nemesis in Congress during her first year, it was 31-year-old Representative Patrick McHenry of North Carolina, the youngest and most pugnacious member of Congress. McHenry has never met Pelosi, but he conducts frequent press conferences lambasting her leadership, and issues scathing Pelosi-bashing press releases almost weekly. *The Hill* newspaper has dubbed him the "Anti-Pelosi."

"Speaker Pelosi and the Democrats promised action—and delivered hypocrisy," McHenry said at a press conference he dubbed "The Real 100 Hours." "They promised an open, accountable government. They promised to end corruption in Washington. They promised to enact ALL of the 9/11 Commission's recommendations. They promised to make college more affordable. And by my count, they're 0 for 4."

"I truly believe Nancy Pelosi's liberal agenda will harm the country," he told *The Hill*. "Pelosi's style is combative and inflammatory." He argues that his own combative and inflammatory style is the only way to respond to hers. "It needs to be done," he said. After the 100 hours agenda passed, he complained that Democrats pushed their bills through without committee hearings and with no opportunity for amendments despite a promise that bills would "come to the floor under a procedure that allows open, full and fair debate consisting of a full amendment process that grants the Minority the rights to offer its alternatives . . ."

"Certainly in the first 100 days the Democrats in the House were pretty aggressive in using the rules to their advantage," said Professor Matthew Green. "But in her opening speech she said 'I'm a speaker for the entire House.' This is something that past Speakers took for granted and recent Speakers have neglected. Not just [Dennis] Hastert and Gingrich, but recent Democratic speakers as well." Green thinks Pelosi, a great admirer of O'Neill's, might be trying to emulate those bygone days, keeping one eye on history. "Sam Rayburn was much more bipartisan. O'Neill confronted Reagan, but there were times when O'Neill had the opportunity to be more partisan with House Republicans and chose not to," he added. In a column for *The Hill*, Ornstein wrote: "Pelosi genuinely believes a Speaker should govern as Speaker of the whole House, and that many issues can, and do, cut across party lines,"

After the initial burst of legislation, Democrats did promise to permit Republicans to participate more widely, a promise congressional observers and even some Republicans say they've generally made good on—to a point. "Beyond the initial agenda, the committees started going to work not just on oversight but really on marking up legislation," said Mann. "Some of it is really occurring on a bipartisan basis."

"We've had more in the way of open rules or limited open rules in the last five months than they [Republicans] have had in whole Congresses," said one senior Democratic staff member. "Open rules" allow any member to offer relevant amendments to a bill after debate is over. Under a close rule, no amendments are permitted. Limited open rules allow only those amendments specified by the Rules Committee for a specific bill. In her heart of hearts, Pelosi would like everything to get on the floor and get debated under open rules, a senior aide said. "The problem is that there are just practical limitations on time. And there's the realization that a lot of amendments are put up only for political value." There's no shame when a minority party loses an amendment because everybody expects it to lose. The only value such amendments often have is to embarrass people in the majority. "So we naturally have to cull through amendments and say, you know, if something has no chance of passing, and if it's there for no other reason than political opportunism, then that probably is going to have less of an opportunity to come to a vote than other amendments," the senior aide said.

He added that the leadership team has been far less restrictive about allowing "motions to recommit," which are a kind of last chance given to the minority party to amend or kill a bill after its final review, or reading. Such motions have in the past hampered the majority party's effort to ram through its legislative agenda unchanged. "We're not going to oppose them just because a Republican offered them," a Pelosi staff member explained. "Republicans were lockstep. They would never ever vote for any of our motions to recommit." The evidence during the first six months bears this out: House Republicans won on 13 motions to recommit, 13 more than the minority Democrats achieved during the same stretch of time in the 109th Congress. In the first quarter, the Democrats also approved more open rules than the Republicans did in the entire last Congress, according to Mann's analysis.

So after the first 100 hours, by most accounts and much to some liberal groups' chagrin, Pelosi has made bipartisanship more of a priority in her first session as leader than Hastert did before her. In 2004, Hastert instituted a "majority of the majority" policy, allowing the House to vote only on bills that were supported by the majority of its Republican members. That meant, of course, any bipartisan bills or bills backed by a majority of Democrats never made it to the House floor. An aide to Pelosi made the point that things like the minimum wage, expansion of stem-cell research, and implementation of the 9/11 recommendations would have passed the House under Hastert if he'd allowed them to come to the floor. Legislation on those issues had enough bipartisan votes to pass, but the bills didn't have the votes of a majority of the majority, so they never got voted on.

"Our whole point was, if you have a fair process—which we didn't have because of the way the Republicans ran the place, and these bills were allowed to come to the floor, they would pass," said a senior staff member. "And so the only thing that obstructed the will of the public and even the will of the congressional majority from occurring was the tyranny of the Republican leadership."

The House is more partisan than it used to be because of the narrow margins the party in power has to work within. Every vote and every issue in the House is put into this calculus: Does it help the party or hurt the party in the marginal seats? The permanent campaign dictates legislation. The dynamic at work is that each party is always angling for control and in some ways fighting for control at the same time they both are fighting about substantive issues, which makes having dispassionate arguments and real deliberation, let alone bipartisan agreement, more difficult. Even if a leader such as Pelosi wants to be magnanimous and inclusive as a policymaker, her hands may be tied by the necessity of holding on to the majority so she can do anything at all.

Still, Pelosi has made efforts, experts said. She sought Republican input when she reformed the page system, when she set up the panel on global warming, and in setting up an independent ethics panel. She asked the Republicans whom they wanted to have on those panels, and she had meetings with the House minority leader, John Boehner, to review those efforts. Ornstein sees glimmers of bipartisanship in many committees, including the powerful Ways and Means Committee, where Democrat Charles Rangel and Republican Jim McCrery helped forge a bipartisan trade pact that Pelosi has since backed away from.

Gordon said the Science and Technology Committee he heads has passed 27 bills with bipartisan support. "We've really tried to work in the committee in a bipartisan outreach way," he explained in an interview. "It's easier to do that on a committee than the House at large. Clearly in the House at large it hasn't been that good. You have structural problems. For one thing, you have a Republican minority that wants to get back in the majority."

Pelosi also has assuaged concerns within her own caucus about her liberalism by promoting many conservative Democrats to key roles and committee assignment—John Spratt of South Carolina, Sanford Bishop of Georgia, Collin Peterson of Minnesota and Mike Thompson of California. "She has issues to pursue, things she wants to help the party to achieve," said Mann. "But initially at least she appears to be more open to compromise, and I would say compromise not just within her party, but also with the other party."

Keeping her own party together is no small feat.

"She's got to manage a very heterogeneous party at a time when you have no votes to spare," said one of Pelosi's top aides. "If you look at these votes we've been winning, we win a lot of votes by two or three votes."

The caucus is much more heterogeneous than it was in 2006, before the Democratic Party went out and recruited a host of moderate and antiabortion candidates, said Bruce Cain. "There are some advantages to having a smaller, more homogeneous minority. Where there have been disappointments, it's been because she has such a heterogeneous caucus to manage." Right now, for example, the liberals in the House are unhappy with Pelosi for not ending the war sooner. Keeping the caucus together takes constant attention and engagement from Pelosi—with 233 souls. "If I wanted to have a word with Nancy Pelosi in this last hour, I could have," said moderate Blue Dog Leonard Boswell. "She's accessible. You don't have to get an appointment to go to her office to see her. I think that every member feels like, if they need to have a word with the Speaker, in a day or two you'll get the chance."

How does she do it with all her time demands? "She's on the floor constantly," said Boswell. "She comes right up and down that aisle. She's hands-on. She's not just got the whip down there working on things as you'd normally expect; she's there too." She also works 15-hour, 18-hour, sometimes 21-hour days.

"You know what it takes?" asks Lawrence. "It takes her staying in the office making phone calls until midnight. Night after night after night. Absolutely. I know, because I do it with her. She will stay here before these big votes personally picking up the phone and talking to the 15 to 20 undecideds."

Steny Hoyer, majority leader, said he and Pelosi practice the "psychology of consensus." Hoyer elaborated: "All these folks, they represent their districts, which is what they should do, they don't represent Nancy or me or the party, they represent their districts. On the other hand, we were elected as a majority. We have a certain premise of the new direction we want to take the country. One of the successes Nancy and I have worked at is reaching across the spectrum of the caucus to bring consensus."

The fact that Hoyer is perceived as leader of the moderate Democrats and Pelosi as a leader of the more liberal wing has raised sparks between the two of them over the years. But operating together as a team, working to keep their own constituencies within the big top, seems to benefit the party.

"Essentially the strength that Nancy and I bring to this is we have a broad reach between us across the whole spectrum. And I think it really helps. Nancy is a moderate political leader. And by that I mean that while she represents a district that may certainly be more liberal than some, she is a politician and a leader who understands if you are going to be successful it is because you create agreement, not just make points. It's easy to make points. What's not easy is to make policy, to move things forward. To get 218 votes. Nancy's objective is to get 218 votes."

Congressman Gordon thinks Pelosi's liberal reputation paradoxically helps the caucus keep on a moderate track. "She knows where she is philosophically, she is more liberal than the caucus, but she knows where the caucus needs to be," said Gordon. "She has the unique ability to tell the more liberal wing, if I can swallow this, you can, too. So I think she is very important, she serves a real purpose there. We can be a much more moderate caucus with her than we could be with somebody that is more moderate. She understands where we need to be, in a more middle position, and she can help keep us there."

Pelosi's biggest accomplishment right out of the gate, observers say, has been reinvigorating Congress's constitutional oversight role. Many of the oversight committees had atrophied under Hastert's reign as the Republican Party rubberstamped Bush administration policies, especially concerning the Iraq War. Within months of taking over, Democrats had hired more than 200 investigative staffers for oversight committees, opened dozens of inquiries, and begun issuing subpoenas to cabinet members. Among the topics of investigation: the firings of U.S. attorneys, the handling of the response to Hurricane Katrina, immigration reform, the prison at Guantanamo Bay, administration intervention into studies of global warming, war profiteering, war-contractor crimes, and a host other Iraq-related subjects. Pelosi assigned some of her staff to pick and choose the oversight battles they took on. Workshops were held for young staffers on how to investigate. The Watergate-era ritual of committee-room grillings on Capitol Hill returned in force.

"Oversight is just as important, if not more important, than legislation," Representative Henry A. Waxman (D-Calif.), chairman of the House Oversight and Government Reform Committee, told the *Washington Post*.

"It's the most healthy sign of vitality," said Mann. "That and challenging the president on a variety of matters having to do with the appropriate powers and responsibilities of the two branches. But what gives it substance . . . is what's going on in committees, raising important questions, holding officials to account. This is where Congress had failed so utterly in recent years."

Of course, a fresh accountability is what should be expected with the return of divided party government. Republicans were calling the increase in oversight hearings "a witch hunt" shortly after they began in earnest. But independent observers celebrated the return of checks and balances to Washington as a sign of the healing of a dysfunctional institution. "In terms of the balance of power, it's a healthy thing," said Michael Green. "I think it's unfortunate that it required a change in party control for Congress to reassert itself. I would strongly support the views of Norm Ornstein and others who said Congress should care about its power regardless of what party is in charge. Perhaps that's being naïve."

"With narrow majorities . . . and the presidential veto, the Democrats recognize the limits of what they can do legislatively," noted Mann. "But they can accomplish a lot through the oversight process. And that's where there's been just a striking reversal."

Pelosi's biggest failing during her first days, most observers agree, was her last-minute support for Jack Murtha over Steny Hoyer for majority leader.

Hoyer was already the minority whip, Pelosi's number two, and the natural heir to the majority leader title. And Hoyer felt that he had earned it, working almost as tirelessly as Pelosi had over the years on behalf of other candidates and raising busloads of money himself. After Pelosi, Hoyer is one of the best fundraisers in the House.

"It worried me quite a bit when she injected herself in the majority leader's race for Murtha," said one Democratic congressman. "Because I wanted that unity. But they've been longtime friends, so I understand that. She felt like she owed him."

It's tough to figure out how one of the best vote counters in the business wouldn't know that Hoyer had the votes to win the seat no matter what Pelosi wanted. And it's even tougher to figure out why such a meticulous planner waited until the very last minute to announce her support for Murtha if she intended to do so all along. Staffers said she didn't make hundreds of phone calls or call in favors for Murtha by threatening political futures the way she has on other appointments and issues. Some Democrats thought she was sending a message about loyalty to her caucus, much the way she had done with her support of a candidate running against Hoyer-supporter John Dingell when she became whip. Others thought she simply overplayed her hand. In the flush of her gigantic victory and the triumphant return of the Democrats to power, she may have overestimated the clout she had to pick and choose her own number two.

Pelosi herself said Murtha's credibility on Iraq made him the best candidate to push the caucus toward some sort of withdrawal timetable or benchmark legislation. She said her choice to head the House Intelligence Committee, Silvestre Reyes—who opposed the Iraq War from the start—was chosen for the same reason: to put all the strongest advocates of bringing the troops home in positions where they could make the biggest difference. If her legendary focus was completely zeroed in on doing something about Iraq, then this strategy makes sense. She argued that the main reason voters put Democrats in power was to bring the troops home, and she planned to do everything she could to fulfill that charge.

The most likely scenario, however, is that when Murtha asked Pelosi to support him, she couldn't turn down her oldest friend in the House. Nor was she going to expend too much political capital on the bid, which she must have known was a lost cause. Pelosi's no political naïf, as so many pundits believed back then. She was walking the high beam with high heels again. She knew better than anyone that Hoyer had accumulated huge amounts of loyalty and goodwill in the same way she had over the years—through fundraisers, phone calls, lunches, advice, campaigning, and friendship. His 149 to 86 victory over Murtha spoke more about his colleagues' loyalty to him than their disloyalty to Pelosi.

"Here's the deal—she's apparently been irritated by a perception that Steny has been undermining her, and it's an incorrect perception," Massachusetts Representative Barney Frank, a Democrat, said at the time. "Look, someone told me she hasn't liked him since 1963, and it has had zero effect on how well they have worked together. We don't have to guess at this. We have seen it. They can and will work well together as we move forward."

Turns out, the fallout has been relatively minor, as she must have known it would be. Right after the party elections on November 16, 2006, Pelosi and Hoyer were holding each other's hands when they came out of the caucus room to speak to the press. (During the photo op, Murtha stood behind them with his hands in pockets and his eyes cast down.) Hoyer said recently that he and Pelosi are both professionals and have moved on. "The majority leader's race was obviously a strain for the relationship but I recognized that one of her great strengths was her loyalty and her willingness to take risks on behalf of those who have been her strong supporters," Hoyer said. "And I think that's what she did in the Murtha-Hoyer race. And I respected her for it, although it disappointed me."

"If you were diagramming the perfect Speakership, you wouldn't put that play in at the beginning," said Cain. "But certainly it could have been pre-meditated. That kind of rope-a-dope is not without precedent in California. Phil Burton and Willie Brown both used those kinds of tactics."

Maryland's Elijah Cummins said it best, thought Boswell: "Here's what we need, these two," referring to both Hoyer and Pelosi. By April the two were dancing cheek to cheek at a fundraiser. "She's a good dancer," Hoyer adds with a grin. Her singing, reportedly, is not as good.

Pelosi also got dinged by the White House early in her tenure for a high-profile trip to Syria to meet with President Bashar al-Assad. Some conserva-tive columnists dubbed it "Spring Break in Syria." The *Washington Post* editorial page went so far as to accuse Pelosi of running a "shadow govern-ment." Conservative commentator Rich Lowry of the *National Review* told Fox News that Pelosi is "absurdly crazy to want to go on this Magical Mystery Tour of every rogue state in the world."

Berkeley's Robin Lakoff thought Pelosi's gender had something to do with the criticism. "Is there something about 'Well, I don't think that women have the right to do these kinds of dangerous things?' A man is tough; there is some terrible fear that a woman might give away the store. Or women have to be kept in line. Because they're so nice and everything?" She commented that Cheney's use of the words "bad behavior" to describe Pelosi's trip made it sound like the Speaker were a little girl.

Pelosi's trip makes sense within the larger framework of her general leadership style, which is one of engagement, negotiation, and conversation rather than hierarchy and pronouncement. "I think Bush really tends to do this sort of hypermasculinity business. 'I won't talk to them. I won't move an inch. I won't budge. I am the decider,'" noted Lakoff.

Historians observed that other speakers had made similar trips, including Democratic leader Jim Wright and Republican Newt Gingrich. During a trip to China, Gingrich raised eyebrows for declaring that America would respond militarily if China attacked Taiwan. (When asked for comment for this book, Gingrich refused.)

Pelosi's trip was no accident. Aides said her senior staff had decided that the Speaker had a key role to play in foreign policy and in trying to restore what they saw as America's damaged credibility abroad. "I think we're living in a very portentous time," said Congressman Boswell. "International relations are very bad. I keep in touch with a close friend in Portugal. And he said, 'Leonard, what's going on over there?' He said you don't seem to be the country you told us about. You make us nervous. In fact, you make us a little bit frightened." Pelosi's trip and future ones are meant to mend such fences and open channels of communication the Democrats feel the Bush administration has dangerously shut down. Aides also noted that the bipartisan Iraq Study Group had recommended opening talks with Syria and Iran to try to settle down the Mideast. Communications director Brendan Daly said Pelosi's trip was also a deliberate attempt to raise her profile as the face of the opposition, to make her a player on the international stage.

In late June of 2007, Representative Steve King, a Republican from Iowa, introduced an amendment to appropriations legislation that would have prohibited Pelosi from using State Department funds to travel to nations that are known to have sponsored terrorism, including Cuba, Iran, North Korea, Sudan, and Syria. King said it was likely Pelosi had committed a felony by violating the Logan Act.

The Logan Act was passed in 1799, when John Adams was president, and forbids unauthorized citizens from negotiating with foreign governments. The law gets trotted out from time to time, usually by political opponents, when private or government officials other than the president visit controversial

foreign leaders. Critics alleged that former House Speaker Jim Wright violated the Logan Act in 1977 and 1978 with his "intrusions" into negotiations
between the Sandinista government and the Contras in Nicaragua. President
Reagan accused the Reverend Jesse Jackson of violating the act when he went
to Syria to help in the release of a captured American pilot. Jane Fonda had
been accused of violating it during her trips to Hanoi. Even Richard Nixon,
when he visited China after his presidency, was a target of a complaint. But
because the language of the act is so broad, no one has been prosecuted for a
violation in 200 years. And when Democratic senators John Sparkman and
George McGovern were accused in 1975 of violating the act during a visit to
Cuba, the State Department concluded: "Nothing in section 953 [Logan Act],
however, would appear to restrict members of the Congress from engaging in
discussions with foreign officials in pursuance of their legislative duties under
the Constitution." Representative King's amendment failed, 337–84.

In some ways, it appeared that Bush administration was following
Pelosi's lead in revisiting the value of diplomacy in the months after her trip.
Within a month, Secretary of State Condeleeza Rice was in Syria for high-
level talks, the first high administration official to engage in such talks in
two years, which made all the earlier criticism of Pelosi's visit a bit moot. A
couple months after administration officials lambasted Pelosi for raising the
prospect of similar talks with Iran, the White House opened its first substantive talks with Tehran in an effort to foster better regional diplomacy
with the hope of improving the situation in Iraq. Shortly after, as lawmakers
on Capitol Hill began to consider making the 79 recommendations of the
Iraq Study Group official policy of the U.S. government, the Bush
administration suddenly took a new look and embraced many of those same
recommendations, all of which had been summarily dismissed when they
were issued in December 2006. Pelosi pushed for months for benchmarks to
measure progress in Iraq, another recommendation of the study group; the
Bush administration finally embraced them after White House talks
between negotiators for Bush and Pelosi. And by summer, when Pelosi
began to get serious about pushing global warming legislation, the administration for the first time acknowledged that something had to be done about
the issue. Suddenly the center of gravity in Washington seemed to have
shifted from Pennsylvania Avenue to South Capitol Street. A sure sign of
that shift was a spoof on the Republican National Campaign Committee's
Web site that had Pelosi listing her jobs on a resume: Speaker of the House,
Commander in Chief, Secretary of State. In the national minivan, Pelosi

was no longer telling Bush to stop and ask for directions. She had shifted over to the driver's seat.

In May, Republicans in the House jumped aboard the ethics reform bandwagon driven by the Democrats. The House voted 382 to 37 to pass a bill that would require lobbyists to disclose bundles of campaign checks they assemble for representatives. Pelosi was credited with twisting arms within her own party to get the measure to the floor after much resistance. It was the second prong of a three-prong strategy she was pursuing to keep her promise to voters to host "the most ethical Congress in history." The first prong had come right away in January, when the House enacted rules restricting gifts, meals, and travel paid for by lobbyists. An independent ethics panel was the third prong. At the same time, the National Republican Congressional Committee launched a blitzkrieg of ads and information packets to try to turn the tables on the ethics debate by pointing out all the ethical lapses of House Democrats.

"The Republicans have essentially taken the position, 'Look, we were bad. You caught us. But these guys are worse.' That's their defense," said Steny Hoyer.

Hoyer did make the point that the Democrats still have a way to go before fulfilling all the promises they made going into the year.

"We didn't stop the war yet," said Hoyer. "The left is mad at us for that". And voters are "sort of perplexed by the fact we came in there with the New Direction, had this great Hundred Hours and passed these great things, and they're just not happening. You've just got minimum wage . . . that's it. Bush vetoed the stem-cell bill. We need to get things done." Hoyer said things move slowly in Congress, but he couldn't remember a more productive six months in his 30 years there. "Ultimately, what the public is going to make a judgment on with this Congress is, from a policy standpoint did we pass legislation that positively affects their families, the safety of their country, the economic growth and the opportunities for their children."

In an interview in May 2007, Pelosi herself was upbeat. She said things are moving forward, albeit more slowly than she would like, and that she has learned the value of patience in pursuing her legislative goals. She points out that the Presidio deal took 18 years; winning the House back took 12 years;

fighting AIDS is a continuing, 20-year struggle; and getting a woman into the leadership of the U.S. Congress took 200 years. She is a fighter who does not give up easily. "I have a serenity about the job," she said a few months in. "I know the policy because I was for many years an appropriator without any thought of running for leadership, not even the faintest thought. I know the politics very well and I understand the people here. Those three areas help shape how you go forward. When there's unease in our caucus about the issues, we try to find the best place to find our common ground. And no offense taken on disagreements after that. We just move on."

By late July, Pelosi and her lieutenants had broken the logjam some. In a flurry of of bill-passing during the last 10 days before their summer recess, Congress passed a final version of legislation implementing the recommendations of the 9/11 Commission; an expansion of children's health care; a major farm bill; and an energy reform bill that included new taxes on oil companies to fund investment in renewable fuels. Pelosi had to make some compromises to make progress: Increased fuel economy standards were dropped from the energy bill, and the farm bill didn't do much to dismantle the subsidies wealthy farmers and corporations receive from the government. But she claimed it was a start.

With careful tactical maneuvering, and the sacrifice of the two-year-prohibition against former members of Congress joining lobby firms, Pelosi was finally able to get a major rewrite of Congressional ethics and lobbying laws passed by the House, 411–8. The 83–14 Senate approval of the reform legislation on August 2, 2007, came just hours after a U.S. district judge in Miami sentenced former lobbyist Jack Abramoff, the poster boy of influence-peddling scandals, to five years and 10 months in prison on conspiracy and wire fraud charges. Bush has already signed the bill into law. Pelosi also passed an "Innovation Agenda" to develop new jobs through public-private partnerships.

All the ups and downs, bumps and bruises, firsts and lasts during Pelosi's inaugural session, however, were overshadowed by a single rancorous struggle, the defining issue of the day and an open wound that festered straight through 2007, stymieing progress on a host of other fronts in Congress. Despite Pelosi's legislative accomplishments, lack of progress on this one front sent approval ratings for Congress plummeting to lows equal to President Bush's. On Capitol Hill they call it the war over the war.

Iraq.

CHAPTER 12

THE WAR OVER THE WAR

America must be a light to the world, not just a missile.

—Nancy Pelosi

You can no more win a war than you can win an earthquake.

—**Jeanette Rankin**, the first woman elected to Congress, 1880–1973

T wo hundred and eighteen votes.

That's what Pelosi needed to change the course of the Iraq War and, in doing so, she believed, correct the course of the country. Now April 25, 2007, the day of reckoning, had come. She had been up past midnight in her offices in the Capitol the night before lining up her support, calling members of Congress and talking them through the vote. Chief of Staff John Lawrence had been there with her. They'd made 30, 40, 50 calls, maybe more. For days she'd been calling members, talking to them in the halls, holding pep rallies, listening to concerns, modifying the language of the bill to meet each individual lawmaker's concerns. She'd put off the vote twice to try to gather more support. Still, she wasn't sure how it would go.

If she couldn't stop the war just yet, she would make sure there was some accountability for its conduct in Congress. In her view, President Bush had been operating with a blank check for three years, with no real oversight in Washington. No one on Capitol Hill had significantly challenged Iraq policy legislatively since the war began. With a compliant Congress, and a tightly disciplined, insular White House, Pelosi felt Bush had become dangerously deaf to dissonant voices, too stubborn to readjust his strategy in Iraq to glaring new realities. The war was going badly, that was plain for all to see. She felt the president was in a state of denial.

Pelosi's strategy for ending the war was not just this one vote but many votes. She saw it all as a sequence, a gradual ratcheting up of the pressure on Bush and Republicans in Congress—and in the realm of public opinion—until American troops were redeployed. Because of the Constitution's separation of powers, which gives the president the authority to execute wars but Congress the responsibility for funding them, the House and the White House were embarked on what would be months and months of fighting.

But Pelosi was playing a dangerous game. She was operating with a majority of only a few votes, and many of the more liberal Democrats weren't happy that the funding bill wasn't tougher. Many Americans around the country who had voted the Democrats into power in Congress wanted funding cut off completely. If she didn't do something meaningful to bring the war to a close, other Democratic representatives were going to pay for it in their home districts. If Pelosi and the Democrats pushed too fast and hard, the president was going to veto bill after bill. If the Democrats didn't approve any sort of funding or support for the troops in the line of fire, the backlash might cost them the next presidential election. Republicans are now trying hard to recast the Democrats as the ones responsible for the problems in Iraq by not giving the troops enough time or support to accomplish their mission. In other words, if she cut off funds too quickly she's the one who might be blamed for *all* the failures in Iraq.

Pelosi was walking a balance beam four inches wide, but even if she fell off, she planned to get up again and again and again. She planned many more votes ahead, putting the war on an installment plan. Her strategy was to force Bush to show progress every few months. If that progress wasn't being made, she would start cutting funding—if she could get the votes, that is. When she began the session, she had a majority of 33 votes. But 35 votes belonged to moderate Blue Dog Democrats, many of whom were strongly pro defense. She had no real idea how she was going to get the 218 votes necessary to put the brakes on Bush's war, but she knew that the people who had put her into the Speaker's chair wanted something done. Protestors from Code Pink, an antiwar group whose members dress entirely in pink, surrounded her home in San Francisco and roamed the halls of Congress, accosting her and her lieutenants, lest she forget.

Pelosi had never bought into the Iraq War. She opposed the idea of it as a misuse of American power from Day 1. Unlike other Democratic leaders—Hillary Clinton, John Edwards, John Kerry, Richard Gephardt, Steny Hoyer, John Murtha—she has no vote on her record in support of the war. All the top Democrats, including Hillary, are on the same page now in calling for redeployment, but only Pelosi has been on that page from the get-go. Clinton, in fact, recently said, "If I had known then what we know now, there never would have been a vote and I never would have voted to give the president the authority."

Why did Pelosi vote against the war when so many other leading Democrats did not? Those close to her think it was because of her extended tenure on the House Committee on Intelligence. Before she became Speaker, she was the longest-serving member of the committee in the history of the House. Others on the committee say she paid close attention to what the reports were saying about the difficulty of both the execution of a war in Iraq and its likely costs. The intelligence had persuaded Pelosi—incorrectly as it turns out—that there were weapons of mass destruction in Iraq, but she also had access to reports that showed evidence of WMDs in many other countries, including Pakistan, North Korea, and Libya. Pelosi didn't believe the WMD rationale was enough of a reason to invade Iraq. More important, she saw nothing in the intelligence reports that persuaded her that Iraq had the rockets or other delivery systems that could be used to send such weapons against the United States. The only way such weapons could harm Americans, according to her reading of the intelligence, was if the United States invaded. So in Pelosi's view, initiating an attack actually increased the danger to the United States from Iraq rather than decreased it.

After classified briefings by national security adviser Condeleezza Rice and CIA director George Tenet in September 2002, just weeks before the vote, Pelosi said: "I know of no information that the threat is so imminent from Iraq. I did not hear anything today that was different about [Hussein's] capabilities." Richard J. Durbin, a Democrat from Illinois on the Senate intelligence panel, reinforced that view. "It would be a severe mistake for us to vote on Iraq with as little information as we have. This would be a rash and hasty decision." Pelosi thought the vote could wait until after the November elections and a new Congress was in place. She was probably banking on the hope that more Democrats would join Congress and give her enough votes to defeat the resolution, believing opposition to it would mount with time. But Bush wanted the vote by October. He didn't want to take his chances on the election. The White House had originally suggested that it was within its constitutional rights to act against Iraq without congressional approval. A senior administration official said the objective of the resolution "is to provide to the president the maximum flexibility to deal with the threat posed by Iraq."

"This is about the Constitution," Pelosi said at the time. "It is about this Congress asserting its right to declare war when we are fully aware what the challenges are to us. It is about respecting the United Nations and a multilateral approach, which is safer for our troops."

Her unwavering opposition to the Iraq War certainly was based in part on pragmatic assumptions about intelligence, but her approach to assessing whether war was worth the risk may have had deeper roots. "This is a vote of conscience, as war is for everyone," Pelosi said at the time. Pat McGuire, president of Pelosi's alma mater, said many women of Pelosi's era believe religious values and social justice go hand in hand. "They tend to be much more aggressive about opposing war. It's more a religious issue than a political one." The Catholic Church of which Pelosi is a member opposed the Iraq War from the start on the grounds that it did not satisfy the church's requirements for a "just war." The doctrine acknowledges that war and violence are, as a last resort, sometimes necessary. But it also insists on evidence of a danger to "the common good" as fundamental justification for a war—the "just" part of the "just war" tradition. Pelosi has said she never saw that compelling evidence. Her faith teaches her that any military action without that fundamental justification is absolutely, unequivocally wrong and immoral.

"The only reason you can ever kill somebody is self-defense," said George Wesolek, director of the Office of Public Policy and Social Concerns for the Archdiocese of San Francisco. "So the only reason you can go to war as a country is to defend the community. And that's why the Vatican and other theologians have declared the war we're in now is not really a just war because it does not fill that condition." Wesolek said he's fairly certain the priests in Pelosi's parish have preached against the war from the pulpit. "Around war, there is a whole series of things you have to do to in order to make this a justified war," he explains. "The means used, for example, have to be proportionate to the good that's being done. So in other words, you can't drop a nuclear bomb and kill 200,000 innocent people in order to achieve your objective. Then there's a whole series of things you can't do when you're in a war. Killing innocent combatants. A lot of moral theologians have been talking about these issues regarding this war."

Not only was Pelosi's church strongly opposed to the resolution authorizing war, her constituents in San Francisco were dead set against it. She received 12,000 calls about the war from constituents in the three weeks before the vote, with only 20 of those supporting the resolution. Pelosi's home district was sending her a clear message: Vote no.

Ten days before the vote authorizing the war, the Bush administration delivered a classified, 90-page report to Congress detailing what was known and what was not known about weapons of mass destruction in Iraq. After reading the report, Senator Bob Graham of Florida, the chairman of the Senate Intelligence committee at the time, decided the evidence was weak. He urged Pelosi and other colleagues to read the full report, which he felt contained much more information than the unclassified summary the administration had made public. It's unclear how many members of Congress actually read the full report. But Graham, like Pelosi, voted against the authorization as a result of it and other information he had access to that the public didn't.

Although most Democrats followed Pelosi's lead, the resolution still passed the Republican-controlled House 296 to 133 on the afternoon of October 11, 2002. The Democratic-run Senate followed at 1:15 a.m. with a 77 to 23 vote. The resolution authorized President Bush to use the armed forces "as he determines to be necessary and appropriate" to defend the nation against "the continuing threat posed by Iraq."

In a meeting with President Bush, Pelosi tried one last time to air her objections to the war before it started. It was Wednesday, February 5, the day Secretary of State Colin Powell planned to make his case before the United Nations that a war against Iraq was necessary. Bush had called 20 key members of Congress together for a classified briefing in the Cabinet Room of the White House.

Pelosi asked Condoleezza Rice, who was there with Bush, what would stop a new regime in Iraq from developing weapons of mass destruction. "Can we conclude that the threat is best eliminated by going to war now? Any fissile material Saddam Hussein gets is from the outside. It's a global problem, and we don't have a global solution." She pushed for some sort of consistent policy for dealing with both Iraq and North Korea. "Is war the best way?" she asked. Rice explained that the United States had tried sanctions, limited military options, U.N. resolutions, and that now war was the only viable option.

After the meeting ended, Republican Senator John Warner, the Armed Services Committee Chairman, warned an administration official that if they didn't find weapons of mass destruction they were going to have a problem.

Shortly after the meeting, Powell made his televised presentation, which was aimed at persuading the American people of the need for war as much as the United Nations. In the next month the might of the U.S. military was hurriedly assembled in Kuwait for the attack. Forty five days after Pelosi's meeting with Bush, the U.S. began bombing Baghdad. The minority leader's newest battle was joined and her newest role assumed, that of the lonesome dove.

It was a Monday, Jack Murtha remembers. Democrats were all over the map in 2005, a chorus of conflicting voices as the war dragged into its third year. "There is no one Democratic voice . . . and there is no one Democratic position," Pelosi said in an interview with *Washington Post* reporters and editors. The voices of the antiwar left had coalesced behind Howard Dean's presidential campaign in 2003, but he self-destructed in early 2004 and the antiwar movement's cohesion dissipated. John Kerry, the eventual nominee, was vocal in his criticism of how Bush was conducting the war but still supported the occupation. Such was the pressure to show patriotism in the country and support for the commander in chief in the war's early days. Pelosi assumed a lower profile for a time, deflecting press questions about the rightness or wrongness of the war. "She has been personally very skeptical of Iraq from the get-go and I think in the interest of the broader caucus has put aside her own strong views and tried to keep the caucus unified," said Adam Schiff, a moderate Democrat from California. Thomas Mann of the Brookings Institution warned in 2004 against overreacting to the divisions in the party at the time. "It's awkward now, but can you imagine anything else?" he said of the relative silence of Democrats, including Pelosi. "It would be quite inappropriate to attack the president." Nobody felt comfortable speaking out against the war at first, except perhaps the Dixie Chicks and filmmaker Michael Moore. Moore was drowned out by boos and catcalls at the Academy Awards in 2003 when he criticized Bush. And radio stations stopped playing the Dixie Chicks after they disowned Bush's policies during a concert, and the three singers received death threats.

After the war passed its first year, Pelosi went back on the attack. In an interview with the *San Francisco Chronicle* in May of 2004, Pelosi let loose her sharpest critique of the president ever: "Bush is an incompetent leader. In fact, he's not a leader. He's a person who has no judgment, no experience and no knowledge of the subjects that he has decided upon . . . . Not to get personal about it, but the president's capacity to lead has never been there. In order to lead, you have to have judgment. In order to have judgment, you have to have knowledge and experience. He has none." When asked why Pelosi was so sure Bush was wrong about the war, John Burton one of her closest advisors responds: "Because the war is all fucking bullshit. We haven't been involved in a legitimate war since World War II."

By that time Pelosi had heard from a lot of progressives from California and within the caucus about the need to be more aggressive about pushing for the end of the conflict and bringing the troops home. Two years of unpopular opposition were beginning to harden Pelosi's resolve. In June 2005, California representatives Maxine Waters, Lynn Woolsey, and Barbara Lee formed an Out of Iraq Congressional Caucus made up of 50 liberal Democrats. "We have been too quiet, we have not challenged our caucus to adopt a position on the war and we have not spoken out ourselves because we have been waiting, and hoping that we could all do it as one," said Waters. The formation of the caucus coincided with Pelosi's introduction of an amendment to the defense appropriations bill insisting that the Bush administration provide Congress with a "strategy for success."

It was in this context that Pelosi went to Murtha and asked him to come up with a coherent policy on the Iraq War that all the Democrats could adhere to. Murtha's rapport with the military rank and file was exactly the reason Pelosi asked him to take command of the party's Iraq strategy. He had street cred.

Murtha was already angry about the situation in Iraq by the time Pelosi approached him. He'd been making noises about the problems there for a few months.

"Two or three days I sat down and thought about it," said Murtha. "For a year and a half I'd been sending letters and talking to military leaders, visiting bases, listening to the little bit of the hearings we had. They had four or five hearings in those days. Hell, I had written to the president and didn't get a reply for seven months," said Murtha. "You know, goddammit. Things like that, this administration is so secretive, so arrogant. I was in the minority; they didn't need me. And I understand that. But the point was here's an experienced person who used to talk to [Former National Security Adviser Brent] Scowcroft three or four times a week, used to talk to [Vice President Dick] Cheney every day . . . this was three years ago! I said you got to internationalize, you got to energize, and you got to Iraqitize. That's the three things I said." Generals were telling him the same thing, but generals don't break ranks with the commander in chief.

"I got to feeling that the military was so upset about what was going on that even though they weren't speaking out publicly . . . they needed a voice. They needed to hear somebody in Congress speaking out."

"People respect his views," a Democratic aide told *Roll Call* in 2005. "He's considered a hawk and an expert and if he changes his mind, that is going to have an impact on the caucus."

Murtha told Pelosi that because the members of the Out of Iraq caucus were so progressive, nobody was paying attention to them. After talking to commanders and soldiers and generals, however, he found himself agreeing with the caucus on how bad the Iraq situation was. "So I went to Nancy," said Murtha. "And I went much farther than they went. I said: You need to redeploy as soon as practical."

Murtha's about-face was a little like Charlton Heston deciding he's for gun control. According to aides who were privy to a conversation between Murtha and Pelosi in the week before he planned to announce his change of heart, Pelosi warned that "this is going to be a huge deal" and people would "come after him." Murtha's reply: "I can handle it. I'm ready for anything."

At a morning press conference on November 17, 2005, Murtha stood in front of seven American flags and a photo of John F. Kennedy. Then he stunned the Capitol by calling for an immediate pullout from Iraq. "Our military's done everything that has been asked of them," Murtha said. "The U.S. cannot accomplish anything further in Iraq militarily. It's time to bring the troops home."

He read a seven-page statement explaining his conversion. Near the end, he stopped to describe some of the wounded vets he had visited. He told of a father stroking the hand of his comatose son, and the soldier who lost both hands but couldn't get a Purple Heart because he had been injured by friendly fire. Murtha choked back the emotion as he finished his story. "I met with the commandant," he said. "I said, 'If you don't give him a Purple Heart, I'll give him one of mine.'"

There was a long silence afterward as journalists contemplated the seismic shift that had just occurred. Many reporters thought Murtha had just ended his career. Finally, someone had the guts to ask if he was advocating a cut-and-run. "This is a flawed policy wrapped in an illusion!" he roared, pounding the podium as he spoke.

Although Murtha got a "standing ovation" when he announced his position to the caucus the morning before his press conference, publicly he stood virtually alone afterward. At an afternoon press conference, Pelosi said Murtha "speaks for himself." When she was asked "But do you agree with the call for immediate withdrawal?" she answered: "As I said, that was Mr. Murtha's statement."

In an interview in his Capitol Hill office, Murtha said that Pelosi didn't back him right away because he'd asked her not to. "She supported it from the very start," Murtha said. "But she was so careful in the way she handled it. I said, 'Now I want to do this myself. I want to go out and make this statement myself.' I said, 'Because if I don't do that, I don't want you to necessarily get involved because you're at that position anyway. And it doesn't have the same impact.'" If Pelosi appeared with him, Murtha was worried that people would think the liberal from San Francisco had ordered him to back a pullout. "I think with my background and conservative credentials, if she'd have been out there, it'd of looked like she convinced me to do something I didn't want to do," Murtha said. "I went to the caucus first, and a lot of people wanted to go out with me" at the press conference. "She kept them from going out." Pelosi was attuned to the stagecraft of the moment. She wanted the full impact of Murtha the war hero standing alone and saying what he was saying. And impact she got.

White House spokesman Scott McClellan said Murtha was advocating a "surrender to the terrorists."

Republican House Speaker Hastert accused Murtha of delivering "the highest insult" to the troops. "We must not cower," Hastert commanded.

House GOP leaders hastily drew up a watered-down version of Murtha's withdrawal resolution and made Republican lawmakers stay in town for a Friday night session to vote it down. The debate on the House floor got ugly fast.

"A few minutes ago, I received a call from Colonel Danny Bubp," said freshman Republican congresswoman Jean Schmidt, who'd been in Congress all of 100 days. "He asked me to send Congress a message: Stay the course. He also asked me to send Congressman Murtha a message: that cowards cut and run, Marines never do." The Democratic side of the chamber exploded in boos and catcalls at the insult, and within minutes, Schmidt had sent a note of apology to Murtha. The resolution, however, was quickly voted down by a majority of both Republicans and Democrats.

"I got a lot of criticism," said Murtha. "President Bush, Cheney, you know people like that criticized me. They backed off eventually. Still, Rove and those guys never backed off. They kept criticizing me until recently."

But the reaction outside of the Beltway was different. "When I spoke out I got 18,000 communications in two weeks," Murtha said. "They were all positive. The negatives couldn't get through because it was such an overwhelming response to what I was saying. The public was way ahead of me."

But that still didn't bring a lot of Democrats along. "I mean, people were very cautious," Murtha said. "We were in the minority. You got a Republican president." And the shadow of September 11 still loomed. A few days later, Pelosi predicted that Murtha's statement would become a "watershed event for our caucus, for our Congress and for our country."

"Everything I predicted came true," said Murtha. "I measure stuff by what I know is a legitimate measurement. Electricity below prewar level. Oil production below prewar level. Unemployment as high as 70 percent, according to a former intern. Incidents going up steadily. Any way you measure it, it's not going well. No question about it. Iraqis want us out of there. It's worse that we're in there. They know that we're the enemy. Overwhelming force saves American lives, but it kills Iraqis and that makes enemies."

Mutha was just as angry that the Pentagon, in his view, wasn't being forthright about the problems. "They were dishonest about it," he said. "That's what's so frustrating. I spoke to the War College kids yesterday. I said folks, you gotta restore honesty to the Pentagon. You're at the point where you're so intimidated by the White House you're not being honest with the American people."

Pelosi was criticized for her silence in not backing Murtha right away. What no one realized was how much the whole thing had been orchestrated by the two.

"Matter of fact, I had to go out to her biggest fundraisers who wanted us out of Iraq in the worst way, and talk to them and tell them where she was, and that she supports me, because they were up in arms about her," said Murtha.

The Out of Iraq caucus was also furious with her for not publicly supporting Murtha and a call for withdrawal. "She was able to look them in the eye and convince the Out of Iraq people that she was against this war and was committed to ending the war," said Burton. "And they believed her, because she is a believable person."

"She was careful," said Murtha. "It took two or three weeks before she would even endorse what I said. It wasn't that she didn't support it. It's just that she adhered to what I requested and how she would wait until it was appropriate. And ever since then, of course, she's been for the policy. She hasn't been ahead of me, but she sure has been for the policy."

On November 30, exactly two weeks after Murtha's press conference, Pelosi became the first congressional leader to back a withdrawal of the 160,000 U.S. troops from Iraq. Pelosi said she was not speaking for the Democratic caucus but that "clearly a majority of the caucus supports Mr. Murtha." She later revised that estimate to half the caucus.

One of the Democrats who was not in her corner was her second in command, House Minority Whip Steny Hoyer. The day after Pelosi's announcement, he issued his own statement warning of a national security "disaster" if U.S. troops exited too quickly. DCCC chairman Rahm Emanuel and Hoyer worried privately that Pelosi's statements could backfire on the party, costing them votes. "We have not blown our chance" of winning back the House but "we have jeopardized it," a top strategist to House Democrats told the *Washington Post*. "It raises questions about whether we are capable of seizing political opportunities or whether we cannot help ourselves and blow it" by playing to the liberal base of the party.

But Murtha and Pelosi had been right: The public was ahead of Congress in its turn against the war. A *Washington Post*-ABC News poll a month later showed Bush's popularity had dropped to 42 percent, the lowest approval rating of any postwar president at the start of his sixth year except Richard M. Nixon. The poll also showed that the public preferred the direction Democrats in Congress would take the country as opposed to the path set by the president. By the November elections in 2006, Pelosi's and Murtha's tough stand actually won voters over to the Democratic side, as Americans grew increasingly disillusioned with the conduct of the war.

THE FIRST STEP

Fast forward to early February 2007, a little over a month after Pelosi's swearing in. Pelosi, Murtha, David Obey, and Ike Skelton are orchestrating the Democrats' Iraq policy. Rahm Emanuel and Steny Hoyer are responsible for getting the votes. They all decide to bark before they bite. War opponents in the Senate had tried to bring to the floor a 1,700-word resolution opposing Bush's new plan to "surge" 20,000 more troops into Iraq to help quell the violence there. But Senate Republicans used procedural measures to prevent the resolution from coming to a vote. Pelosi's leadership team took a different approach, crafting a simple, 10-line resolution that condemned the surge and supported the troops. They decided not to include language about a withdrawal yet. Despite objections from Republicans, Pelosi and other Democratic leaders also decided not to allow the minority party to offer any alternatives. They didn't want their resolution to get bogged down like the parallel resolution had in the Senate.

On February 13, 2007, they introduced their 97 words on the House floor, launching a historic bipartisan showdown between Congress and the White House, the first over the Iraq War since it began nearly four years earlier. It was Pelosi's "first step." The short two paragraphs were debated for three emotional days, during which 393 of the House's 434 members—221 Democrats and 172 Republicans—spoke on the floor. The angry, grueling debate lasted 44 hours and 55 minutes.

Democrats on the floor argued passionately that the war had been illegitimately launched and badly managed. Thanks to the recruiting efforts of Rahm Emanuel, three of the newly elected Democratic lawmakers who were on the floor had served in Iraq.

"We stand together to tell this administration that we are against the escalation and to say with one voice that Congress will no longer be a blank check to the president's failed policies," said freshman representative Patrick J. Murphy of Pennsylvania, who had been a captain with the 82nd Airborne Division in Baghdad. "The president's plan to send more of our best and bravest to die refereeing a civil war in Iraq is wrong."

Pelosi herself said: "In order to succeed in Iraq, there must be diplomatic and political initiatives. There has been no sustained and effective effort to engage Iraq's neighbors diplomatically, and there has been no sustained and effective effort to engage Iraqi factions politically . . . . President Bush's escalation proposal will not make America safer, will not make our military stronger and will not make the region more stable. And it will not have my support."

On the other side of the aisle, Republicans argued that the resolution would send a message that America can be cowed. Representative Don Young of Alaska claimed he was quoting Abraham Lincoln when he declared: "Congressmen who willfully take action during wartime that damage morale and undermine the military are saboteurs, and should be arrested, exiled or hanged."

Representative Duncan Hunter, the ranking Republican member of the Armed Services Committee, said: "This resolution by the Democrat leadership sends a message to three parties: America's enemies, America's friends, and America's troops. And I think it's going to be received by friend and foe alike as the first sound of retreat in the world battle against extremists and terrorists . . . . It's the wrong message, because this nation has been for the last 60 years involved in spreading freedom."

On the day of the vote, February 16, Pelosi kept 229 of her 231 Democrats in the fold, and 17 Republicans joined them. The resolution passed, 246 to 182. Republicans quickly warned that the resolution would embolden Islamic terrorists. Democrats heralded it as the beginning of the end of the Iraq War. Critics on both sides dismissed it altogether as a largely symbolic waste of time. The president was silent. Because it was a nonbinding resolution, it wasn't something he could veto.

"What the president cannot veto is the opinion of the Congress of the United States, the judgment of the Congress of the United States, the counsel of the Congress of the United States," Hoyer said after the vote, pounding on a lectern. "Let us hope that the commander in chief hears this counsel."

The vote was hailed by supporters as Pelosi's second triumph in two months, the first being passage of the Hundred Hours agenda. But it was a triumph bookended by personal tragedy for her. Four days before the vote, Pelosi had attended the funeral of one of her greatest mentors in California, former Lieutenant Governor Leo McCarthy. And then, just five days after the vote, Pelosi lost her brother Franklin Delano Roosevelt D'Alesandro, "Roosie," to cancer.

THE SECOND STEP

Before the first vote was even over, Murtha announced offhandedly during a National Public Radio interview that the resolution wasn't "the real vote." His timing probably cost Pelosi some Republican votes on the resolution— why bother if it wasn't a "real vote"? Murtha said the real vote was the second step of the Democrats' plan, and it would put strict conditions on any further money for the war before it was approved by Congress. Essentially his vision of the second bill would allow Congress to micromanage the war from Capitol Hill. Murtha wanted to attach language to the upcoming war funding bill that would require military personnel to receive specific levels of training and rest between deployments. "They won't be able to deploy troops unless they extend troops overseas. And if we limit the extension, then it'll be very difficult for them to continue this surge, which the American people are against and the Iraqis don't want," Murtha said on NPR. The Democrats also intended to shut down the military prisons at Guantanamo Bay and Abu Ghraib, where American guards had abused prisoners early in the war.

Republicans went ballistic. They said Murtha was trying to tie the commander in chief's hands, or, worse, that Murtha was trying to take over as commander in chief. Moderate Democrats thought Murtha had gone too far, as well, and rebelled. They thought any specific readiness requirements dictated by Congress were meddling in the army's business. At the same time, the Out of Iraq Caucus demanded *more* specifics than Murtha had proposed: Its members wanted a bill that included a timeline for withdrawing U.S. troops. For the first time, on February 27, 2007, a *Washington Post*-ABC poll found that a majority of Americans favored such a deadline for troop withdrawals. Pelosi felt like she had to go back to the drawing board, giving Representative

David Obey, head of the appropriations committee, a greater role in forging Iraq legislation and in effect watering down Murtha's role after his outburst on NPR. Murtha oversees defense dollars, Obey all spending by the House. The two old bulls had often clashed in the past, but found common ground as Pelosi's co-warriors against Bush's war policy. At the beginning of March, Pelosi, Murtha, Skelton, Obey and members of their staffs huddled for several days to come up with a new plan.

On March 8, while a bill was still being drafted, Pelosi announced in her office that the Democrats would propose legislation requiring Bush to withdraw U.S. forces by the end of August 2008. The bill would also impose some of the standards of rest and readiness proposed by Murtha and establish benchmarks the government of Iraq had to meet to continue receiving U.S. support.

That afternoon, 35 to 40 angry antiwar Democrats who wanted the war over sooner gathered in Pelosi's suite. From 1:30 to 4 p.m., they debated the legislation with Pelosi, Obey, and Miller. Pelosi argued that it was better to get behind an imperfect bill than to let the opposition thwart any effort to set conditions on Bush. A piece of pie is better than none at all. Miller warned that if this bill failed, Democrats would have to offer a bill to fund the war with no restrictions at all. At one point, three of the most liberal lawmakers in the group walked out while Pelosi was still making her pitch and staged a press conference announcing that they would only back a bill that called for a withdrawal by the end of 2007. The afternoon became known among antiwar Democrats as Bloody Thursday.

On March 10, Obey exploded, in a moment that was caught for all to see on YouTube. Tina Richards, an antiwar activist and mother of a Marine, asked Obey why he was supporting the supplemental war appropriations bill. She wanted to know why Congress couldn't just stop paying for the war.

"We can't get the votes!" Obey shouted. "Do you see a magic wand in my pocket? We don't have the votes for it."

On March 11, Code Pink protestors surrounded Pelosi's home in San Francisco complaining that now she wasn't doing enough to end the war. They erected Camp Pelosi for a few weeks, staging afternoon teas and even an Easter egg hunt in the Speaker's front yard. They marched on her sidewalk wearing pink Statue of Liberty crowns, pink shoes, pink hats, and calling members of Congress on their pink cell phones.

"San Francisco has a strong progressive element," said Alex Clemens "And the people who say she's not being a strong enough voice against the war are the same people who have always been critics of hers from the left. I don't think she's changed who she is but she recognizes and respects her new role as counterpoint to President Bush."

"The most progressive voices in the city want her to do more and faster and be out there," said Corey Cook, a politics professor at the University of San Francisco. "A vast majority of San Franciscans in the Bay area would want the war to end now. They want the funds cut immediately."

"I think the activists are completely unrealistic about what Democrats can actually do," said Larry Sabato. "I live in a university. Ninety percent of the people here oppose the war, and think it's outrageous that the Democrats haven't put their foot down and stopped it. They know nothing about the process. It doesn't work that way. Under our system, unfortunately, presidents run wars. And the Congress is almost an afterthought."

But Pelosi persisted. She and her lieutenants worked around the clock, person by person, vote by painstaking vote. She tweaked and tailored the bill repeatedly to satisfy concerns of individual lawmakers. After hundreds of phone calls, meetings, lobbying sessions, and caucus pep rallies, she had rounded up 200 votes. She needed 18 more. She pursued her colleagues relentlessly, in the hallways, on the House floor, but a small group of liberal lawmakers held fast. She had to postpone a floor vote twice. On the night before the scheduled vote, Pelosi met with the antiwar lawmakers again, this time in the basement of the Capitol, and pleaded for 4 more votes. It was at that meeting she got the 218. She had it. She the 218 votes she need to pass the first legislation to ever set a withdrawal date for U.S. troops in Iraq. The measure passed on April 25, 2007, 218 to 210.

"She was the general here, and there wasn't a stone left unturned, a person left uncontacted or a member whose position was left unknown," Representative Jan Schakowsky of Illinois, told the *Los Angeles Times*. "It was a brilliant campaign." Some credited the personal relationships the Speaker had with each member, while others said her credibility as a longtime opponent of the war won the day. Others said it was her steely spine and refusal to quit until she had the votes. Whatever it was, it worked.

THE THIRD STEP

The Senate passed its own version of the timeline bill the next day, April 26, when 2 Republicans joined all 48 Democrats in approving it. A conference committee hashed out the differences and sent it to Bush's desk, but because it had a timeline for withdrawal, the president summarily vetoed it. He said he would never agree to a bill with a timeline. Pelosi said she would never agree to a bill without one. Stalemate.

"They should have signed the bill," said Murtha. "Hell, there was no reason he couldn't have signed the last bill. The president's destroying the Republican Party." All that work, and no bill to show for it. Still, every time Congress voted on Iraq in 2007, Democrats gained a bit more support for timelines both publicly and within Congress.

"Democrats are trying to get members on the record, particularly Republicans in swing districts," said Matthew Green. Their long-term goal: force members to cast votes in favor of Bush's Iraq policy, with the assumption that will be an electoral liability. Their strategy was to continue to increase the pressure on Republicans in Congress until their constituents demanded they split with the president. Team Pelosi was back to square one, and the war effort was running out of money, but momentum was on her side. She promised to approve some kind of war funding bill by Memorial Day.

Four days before the Memorial Day break, after weeks of fruitless negotiations with Bush, Pelosi and the other Democratic leaders gave up on their insistence that the war funding measure set a deadline for withdrawing troops from Iraq—for the moment. She didn't have the votes to override another Bush veto, and she didn't want the Democrats portrayed as unsupportive of the troops. Bush had said, however, that he would pass a bill that included benchmarks the Iraqis had to meet in order to continue receiving funds. In the overall step-by-step scheme of things, that was forward motion. The requirements that Iraq show progress on improving security and unifying the country politically meant that Bush, for the first time, was allowing Congress a voice in the conduct of the war. But to Pelosi and many of the antisurge Democrats, it was a setback.

On Wednesday, May 23, Pelosi gathered the members of the 72-member Congressional Progressive Caucus that had opposed President Bush's surge in the Capitol and told them the bad news. The next day, there was an undertone of disappointment in her voice when she talked about the day's vote during an interview in her office.

"I don't like this bill today," she said. "And when people call it a compromise, it's not really a compromise. We allowed it to come to the floor, but it's not as if we split the difference on the policy. The president, though, is having to accept accountability at least on the benchmarks that are there, so that's a step forward, and I do believe this represents a new direction. It's a small step."

In a kind of political jujitsu, Pelosi had decided to allow the bill to come to the floor but not vote for it herself. "I'm not going to support the bill, because

I think it's a missed opportunity and we should be doing much more. But at the White House they really didn't want to do this." Pelosi was keeping her promise to never support a bill without a timeline, but decided to allow it to be brought to the House floor so money to the troops would not be cut off. The Democrats will live to fight another day, she decided. It was another example of her separating her personal politics from the politics of running the caucus.

On the day that culminated her three-and-a-half-month facedown with the president, Pelosi took the long view.

"It's all a sequence," she said. "We started with a big vote against the escalation. Then we sent our bill with the timeline that nobody ever thought that we would have had a majority in the House for, and then we sent another. But the Senate did not take that bill up, they sent us back their version, which we are acting upon today. But this is all a piece of taking us closer to a place where I think the days will be numbered for this war."

The face-off between Bush and Pelosi continued throughout 2007 and the early days of the 2008 elections season. Personally, Pelosi said she respects the president and the office he holds. Her daughter Alexandra, who originally introduced the two when she was shooting a documentary about Bush during his first presidential campaign, said the leaders actually have a lot in common. They both grew up in political dynasties, both got into politics late in life, both are devoutly religious. And people have made the mistake of underestimating both of them during their careers. "On any occasion that I have seen them together in private, they have appeared to be the best of frenemies—campaign-trail speak for politicians who keep their friends close and their enemies closer," Alexandra wrote in Time magazine. "I believe that Bush respects Nancy Pelosi," said Anna Eshoo. "I know that she respects him. They're both pros. I think they generally stipulate to the fact that she has to do what she has to do, and he has to do what he has to do. I genuinely believe that in some ways he gets a kick out of her. I think he admires her."

But others in Congress don't think Bush does much to engage Pelosi, or anyone on Capitol Hill. "I don't think there is much of a relationship," said Representative Bart Gordon. "They're two different styles. Where he is 'Hey Nany, how ya doing?' she doesn't do that. She's more professional."

Eshoo also points out that Pelosi is not easily thrown off her game, as many politicians are, by the atmospherics in the White House. "It's rarefied air. Nancy is not sucked in by that. She doesn't lose her head. She doesn't get dizzy at that high level." Professionally, Pelosi said she doesn't understand what the president's plan is. She knows what her next plans are for bringing the war to a close, but she has no idea what Bush's are.

"What I will do, I will have a goal, and that's where the president and I differ," said Pelosi. "I'm more goal-oriented than he is, and I keep saying, why can't you even support a goal? What's the matter with a goal? A timetable? Milestones by which to judge our progress?"

Pelosi said that she will find other ways to manifest her disagreement with the Iraq War. "That would be an appropriations bill, in two forms, the supplemental and a new supplemental, and legislation that we will call up, whether it's to reauthorize the war or redeploy the troops, change the mission. We've had a number takes on it." She said at heart she's a constituent pleaser and always has been, and now her constituents are the American people. All of them. "It's not about us, it's the American people and how we represent the lack of confidence they have in President Bush's conduct of the war."

Mann, editor of the book *A Question of Balance: The President, Congress and Foreign Policy*, believes Pelosi's strategy will be effective. "She's managed to keep Iraq alive, keep her caucus together to continue to ratchet up the pressure on Iraq. The strategy is to build pressure on the Republicans in Congress with vote after vote so that eventually their support for the president collapses and they join Democrats . . . . I think it's a very intelligent strategy. They've been able to keep some of their members who are really cautious about any kind of timetable, and the Out of Iraq Caucus, who are adamant about not compromising, she's managed to keep them together."

The day after the vote, senior administration officials told a reporter at the *Washington Post* that the Bush administration is developing what are described as concepts for reducing American combat forces in Iraq by as much as half in 2008. Pelosi's incremental approach appeared to be having some impact over the summer, when several prominent Republican senators broke with Bush's Iraq policy and demanded some sort of timetable or benchmarks or pullout. Among the defections were: John Warner of Virginia, Richard Lugar of Indiana, Pete Domenici of New Mexico and George Voinovich of Ohio.

Speaking of the long view, Larry Sabato said he's old enough to remember the process during the Vietnam era. "It took *years* for Congress to have an impact in ending the war. And I predict quietly that a Democratic Congress eventually will have a major impact in ending the Iraq war. But it's going to take time. Probably years. It could take a couple Congresses. It could take a new president. They don't have the votes."

Murtha sees one big difference between today and the Vietnam War, which he fought in. "When I came back from Vietnam, the reaction was just, what the hell, where have you been? It was just one of those things where it was no big deal. But as the war became more unpopular, the troops became unpopular. I have a brigadier general in my district who still has headaches from Vietnam and he said they spit on him when he came home. People in ROTC wouldn't wear their uniforms during that period of time. So there's a big difference today. People understand that there's a difference in policy with the White House, but everyone recognizes that the troops aren't the ones that should be blamed for this. And I think that's where it should be."

Murtha thinks that the Bush administration tried to paint Democrats as anti-troops. "They tried to say for a long time, the White House did, to say that if you were against the war you were against the troops. It didn't fly. People know better."

Murtha is confident that his efforts and Pelosi's efforts to hold the Bush administration accountable on the Iraq War will bear fruit over time. "Through hearings, and through monetary accountability, we're going to force them to recognize that we need to get out of there. Now, it's not going to happen overnight. It's going to take time. She works at it diligently. Pushing back, pushing back against the president when he says something. And we know we can't override a veto yet. I predicted the Democrats would come along when I first spoke out. They're coming along. Obama finally came along. Hillary Clinton finally came along. The Senate's coming, so it's a slow process. It's political pressure exerted by a majority. And if you didn't have a majority, none of this would be happening. I think the most important part is accountability. I think that's the most important thing she's taken on. It's gonna have a real impact in the long run."

Out loud, Murtha reads a letter he received in 2007:

Dear Congressman,

I would very much like to ask you to accept my apology for the unkind thoughts I had.

You and I have never met. I am not a public figure. I do not have a platform for which I speak. My personal feeling: when you came out against the war in Iraq, my thoughts and feeling toward you were less than charitable. Now further down the road, the more I realize how right you were all along.

Pelosi pulled a few tricks out of her bag on the day of the vote on the spending bill. Before the day was over, she managed to get a lobbying reform bill through the House and a minimum wage increase approved by Congress. In another bit of political origami, she and her lieutenants divided the war vote into two votes on the floor. One provided the war money in the watered-down version of the bill that has benchmarks but no timeline, and a separate bill featured pieces of the original appropriations bill that were more popular with Democrats: the minimum wage increase and $17 billion more than Bush asked for in military and domestic spending. In a historical rarity, the funding bill passed but a majority of Democrats, including the Speaker herself and the man who drafted it, David Obey, went on record as opposing it.

"We knew that we wanted to pass the emergency domestic side of the bill," said a senior Democratic staff member. "And we didn't want our members to be put in a situation where they had to vote for the Iraq money without the kind of accountability provisions we were insisting upon, and explain that, or vote against that, and vote against all these other priorities. So we devised this two-vote strategy and found a way to do it. We were going to be in a situation where we couldn't have passed anything if we hadn't done it that way. And we knew that a number of our people were going to vote for the Iraq money. She doesn't like to twist arms around those war and peace issues. She really sees those as a conscience vote. But we also knew there were an awful lot of people who did not want to be in a situation of having to vote against these other things they wanted to do because they were attached to the Iraq money."

The war over the war will likely drag on until President Bush leaves office. "I don't think Congress ought to be running the war," he said in a July, 2007, press conference. "I'm certainly interested in their opinion. But trying to run a war through resolution is a prescription for failure, as far as I'm concerned, and we can't afford to fail."

Still, Pelosi takes pride in the fact that the debate in Congress is now over when troops will come home, not if. "We changed the debate in Iraq," she said. "We put a bright light on what was happening on the ground in Iraq."

Julian Zelizer, a professor of history and public affairs at Princeton, believes Pelosi is right. "They really reshaped the debate on Iraq," Zelizer told *The Politico*. "It is now about an exit strategy instead of simply supporting what the president has done. The exit strategy debate would have been almost unthinkable just a few years ago."

"If she could end the war in Iraq tomorrow by saying after the war you can have my speakership, she would do it," said John Burton. "She's as committed as anybody in the country to ending the war."

WOMAN OF THE HOUSE

Men and women are like right and left hands; it doesn't make sense not to use both.

—Jeanette Rankin

Is there a third act in Pelosi's future? She's been asked several times whether she might like to try to move up from the third most powerful job in the country to the second or first. But the 67-year-old Pelosi usually answers such queries with a courteous quip about how wonderful it would if two women shared the podium during the State of the Union address: Pelosi as Speaker and Hillary Clinton as the first woman president.

Pelosi has never indicated any interest in the president's job herself, and she's still officially neutral about whom she will back in the 2008 presidential race. In years past, pundits and party insiders have mentioned Pelosi several times as a possible vice presidential candidate. Such talk has never gotten very far because of the long shadow of Geraldine Ferraro's unsuccessful run as Walter Mondale's running mate in 1984. Male voters shunned the ticket in large numbers that November, giving Ronald Reagan a landslide victory, and presidential candidates from both parties have shied away from women running mates ever since.

But Pelosi certainly has the bona fides for higher office. She's got a better resume than most of the current presidential candidates and has done more for her party than anyone currently running. She's got a great political pedigree and bicoastal pull, as well, given her Baltimore roots and California connections. Any presidential candidate hoping to win California would be silly not to consider her ability to corral the country's biggest electoral prize for the ticket. If a man had returned his party to power in Congress after a 12-year drought, had kept his party more unified in Congress than any other leader in the last 50 years, had overcome 200 years of cultural bias to assume the leadership of the House, had restored congressional checks and balances on the executive branch that even many high-level Republicans now say were dangerously lacking, had gotten the first minimum wage increase in 10 years passed, had helped forge an energy bill that taxes oil companies to pay for alternative energy research, had put global warming on Washington's agenda for the first time, and had steadfastly opposed the now widely unpopular Iraq War since its inception, it's hard not to believe he'd be right at the top of the list of Democratic presidential candidates, let alone vice presidential candidates.

On the flip side, Marie Wilson makes the case that none of the current crop of male presidential candidates would stand a chance if they were women. "I think what we don't realize all the time is that there's not a man in the race that were he a woman would be in the race," she said. "There's really a difference in criteria for women. You wouldn't be that old, as [John] McCain. You wouldn't be as many times married as [Rudy] Giuliani. And I don't care how much your husband begged you to keep running if he had cancer; if you did it you would be vilified as a woman if you were [John] Edwards. The double standard is there."

When Pelosi is asked if she'd consider running as vice president on the Democratic ticket if the nominee came calling, her response is immediate. "I wouldn't have the faintest interest. Not the faintest. I'm not interested in Number Two." She said her relatively secure congressional seat means she doesn't have to focus on advancing herself, which allows her to focus on her colleagues in Congress, who have become in a way a new set of constituents. "One of my strengths is my colleagues," she explains. "They know I'm not interested in anything else. I'm not interested in any other electoral thing, appointed thing, nothing. What decisions are made are about them, and for them."

A senior Democratic staff member seconds the notion. "She really does see the members as her constituents, not replacing her other constituents, but she's responsible to them, and of course she calls upon them, to do things. She calls upon them more out of loyalty to the issue rather than she does out of loyalty to her. She doesn't say you do this because I'm telling you to do this. She already has that relationship."

Pelosi also points out a Washington reality that few beyond the Beltway understand: the Speaker of the House has far more power than the vice president to affect daily lives. "There is nobody short of an actual president who can actually do more for people," said John Burton. And the president doesn't make laws, he enforces them. It's Congress that makes the country's laws. Besides, Pelosi said, being the first Speaker of the House is more than enough for one lifetime. "I never expected such a thing, so I'm very honored to have that position."

So if not higher office, what does come next for Nancy Pelosi? The answer, like Pelosi herself, has two distinct sides. The public Pelosi—the one who stood up on the podium with all her grandkids on her first day in office, which is the image the vast majority of Americans are familiar with—is already in the history books. Her lasting legacy as the first woman Speaker of the House is assured. For the behind-the-scenes legislator, however, her legacy is a more open-ended question. Has Pelosi, in her first term, begun to fulfill her pledge of civility and partnership in Congress? Will she leave a legacy of accomplishment to match her history-making feat? Will she succeed in getting the country out of Iraq, a legacy that could vary well come to over-shadow her pioneer role, just as Jeanette Rankin's vote against war eclipsed her achievement as the first woman to win a seat in Congress? And what will her impact be on the 2008 election? Or has Pelosi already peaked, and the rest is just placeholding?

A glimpse, then, into the future to contemplate how history might remember Pelosi as a public figure, and as a politician.

PELOSI THE PUBLIC FIGURE

"She's established her place in history; her obituary is more than written," said congressional pioneer Pat Schroeder. She will forever be an inspiration to legions of young women, especially women in politics, for whom she has paved the way. Woman historians and activists say the 'power of the mirror' is enormous. What women see, they believe they can become, and Pelosi is a possibility mirror for the whole country. Women have long since broken many ceilings in other areas—business, the media, academia, and sports. But the Capitol is America's court, where we all look for our idealized versions of American men and women, our own princes and princess, kings and queens, even those of us who like to pretend a democracy doesn't need those sort of touchstones and paragons.

"People do realize how much of our success is wrapped up in the excite-ment about her," said a senior staff member. "And I guess part of that goes to the fact that she is the first woman Speaker, and we don't try to deny that."

"She's played the public part of it exceedingly well," said Larry Sabato. "The history-making aspect of it. And yes, she has a partner in the media there, because the media's oriented just as universities are to diversity, and making history." The news media favors *the new*, in other words—firsts and breakthroughs and never-befores. "That has bought her some wiggle room," adds Sabato. "I think her personal image is still fairly positive, even if the job performance has fallen, along with Congress's."

Sabato thinks Pelosi's image, her gender, her history-making achievement all help the Democrats in the PR battle for voters. "As a Speaker, she probably ought to be doing more Rose Garden strategy, if you can call it that," said Sabato. "They don't have a Rose Garden in the House, but maybe they ought to create one. Right outside of her office. She can come out and kiss babies. Give the blessing to elementary school kids. It may be the only thing she can do to buy more wiggle room. You get some PR points, and it enables you to survive a controversy."

"Speakers have become more high profile over time, but over a long period of time," explained Matthew Green. "Starting in the '70s, Speakers started using the press more and started drawing attention to themselves." They became players on the media stage by necessity once that stage began replacing the congressional floor as the place where the country's toughest issues are hashed out. That displacement has accelerated with the ubiquity of blogs on the Internet.

Inevitably, visitors to the House chamber are disappointed these days when they watch Congress in action. Even with the five-day workweek instituted by Pelosi, it's a rare day when a visitor can see an actual debate taking place on the floor. Often the room is empty except for the presiding officer, a few clerks recording the proceedings, and one or two of the 435 representatives arguing their points passionately to the C-Span cameras. Deliberation is done by press conference now, and the speakers are no different from any of the members. After the telegenic Ronald Reagan won the 1980 election, Tip O'Neill brought a young person into his press office named Chris Matthews who helped him get comfortable in front of TV cameras. Matthews is now an omnipresent TV commentator for MSNBC's *Hardball*. "Chris Matthews turned it around," said John Murtha. "Chris Matthews understood how you speak at only certain times and that you know exactly what you're gonna say. He would do that. He would only say things when it was relevant." It was the beginning of the modern Speaker as major public figure in the great American debate.

Pelosi is in the public eye constantly, holding press conferences, making speeches, giving interviews, attending conferences, delivering graduation addresses, headlining fundraisers, participating in power lunches, hosting party pep rallies, and generally staking out a high profile. Part of her reasons for doing so is a firm belief that government should be transparent, and part is a deliberate effort to counter the PR machinery of the president's office.

"Now today, Nancy realizes every time the president speaks, you gotta say something," Murtha explains. "Every time that there is a spin from the Republicans, she has to use the same spin. I don't like to govern that way, but I know it's the way it is today. There's so many blogs out there, there's so many of these damn things that come up every day. And she responds to that. She deals with the blogs. She deals with the members of Congress. She works tire-lessly day after day, meeting after meeting, Jesus Christ, I go to a lot of meet-ings, and I go to a lot less than she does and a lot less than she would like. It's a pain in the ass!"

And her public image, despite all the laments by women's groups and some pundits that too much is made of it, has undoubtedly played a role in her political success and in redefining the Democratic Party. "This is not Bella Abzug," said Sabato. "That would be a problem for the Democrats." Abzug was the radical Congresswoman from New York who became *the* poster girl for progressives in the early 1970s. "This woman's place is in the House—the House of Representatives," she said frequently during her 1970 campaign. Politically, Pelosi and Abzug really aren't that different. Stylistically, however, the two pioneers are worlds apart. "Bella was the image of the Democratic Party that people have come to dislike," said Sabato. "A left-wing, crazy, wild feminist. That is not the way Pelosi comes across at all. She speaks to the sub-urban professional woman. Look, she looks great. I mean, this sounds like a sexist comment, but she looks terrific for somebody that age. She wears those designer suits, and she's filthy rich."

Pelosi's wealth is certainly part of her style and appeal. A millionairess woman of the people, quipped National Review's Lisa Schiffren. The couple's net worth, thanks to her husband Paul's investments, is listed on their most recent financial disclosure statements as somewhere between $25 million and $102 million, with liabilities of $6 million to $31 million. That range places Pelosi among the 10 richest people in the House. Her marble and gold pent-house overlooking the Potomac River in Georgetown has become one of the prime gathering spots for Washington society, much the way former Washington Post publisher Katherine Graham's home was in her heyday.

Pelosi also likes to get away with colleagues and friends to the family vineyard in Napa Valley. (Those who have visited say the view from the infinity pool overlooking the vines is to die for.)

And Sabato is not alone in commenting on what an attractive figure Pelosi cuts personally. Friends say it, enemies, colleagues, fashion columnists, Democrats and Republicans. It came up time and time again unsolicited during interviews for this book. She's made *Roll Call*'s annual list of the "Ten Best-Dressed Members of Congress" dozens of times, and often as the only woman on the list." "She was *glamorous* in her early days, more than just being attractive," said one Congressman. "And I think that was a detriment. I think there was an idea early on that she was too pretty to be smart. I think she resents that. It makes you work harder and do more. It makes her strive more to show that's not the case."

In discussions about Pelosi from a policy perspective, of course, her image is immaterial. But when the discussion is expanded to include her role as a public figure and what people around the country project onto her public persona, it's probably unavoidable. Women comment on her appearance as much as men, maybe more so.

Pelosi's attentiveness to appearance suggests she understands that image does matter a great deal in modern politics, even if it shouldn't. Her Jimmy Choo pumps and $8,000 South Sea Tahitian pearls and Armani pantsuits certainly accentuate an overall impression of polish and taste. (Though *Washington Post* fashion writer Robin Givhan says not obsessively so. It is her husband, after all, who buys those suits for her.)

Washington is still sometimes referred to as Hollywood for homely people, but it's an outdated adage. Hollywood's emphasis on image took over the Capitol a long time ago, probably as far back as the historic debate between Richard Nixon and John F. Kennedy in 1960. Nixon wore no makeup for the show, and had on a gray suit that didn't contrast with the background very well. He was recovering from the flu at the time and had lost weight. Kennedy wore a dark suit and makeup, and he was coached on how to present himself on television. Ever since, image has been an integral part of politics, especially in states like California, where the races are played out almost entirely in the media.

How important are the politics of beauty? Lee Sigelman, a political scientist at George Washington University, has actually studied the impact of "attractiveness" on political campaigns. In research he did in 1990 at the University of Arizona, Sigelman hypothesized that, despite an advantage in voter registration, Democratic candidates were falling behind nationally because of a "beauty gap." His research found that of the 26 least attractive candidates for governor and Congress, 25 were Democrats.

Sigelman believes Democrats paid more attention to the attractiveness of their candidates in the last election, and that helped them win back Congress. "There has been an arms race, perhaps a face race, where neither side gains the advantage, but where one side might be disadvantaged if it failed to play along," Sigelman said. Democratic operatives privately acknowledged to a *Washington Post* reporter that they did notice that some of their best prospects for candidates last fall were quite attractive. Among the "good-looking" candidates who won their races are Heath Shuler of North Carolina, the former Washington Redskins quarterback; Michael Arcuri of New York; Brad Ellsworth, a macho former sheriff from Indiana; and 37-year-old businesswoman Gabrielle Giffords of Arizona, who likes to ride a motorcycle.

When you look at the Democratic leadership team—Pelosi; Majority Leader Steny Hoyer; Chris Van Hollen, chair of the DCCC ; and even Rahm Emanuel, who has a smoldering kind of bad boy appeal, according to sources who wished to remain anonymous—it's hard not to concur that this is the best-looking bunch of Democrats since the Kennedy days. The only good news in all of this is the easing of the appearance double standard for women and men. For years, in highly visual public roles, women had to look like Jackie Kennedy to succeed while the men could look like Al Franken. Now the men have to be attractive as well.

Pelosi herself generally ignores the whole discussion. When told by an interviewer that several of the men in Congress had said she was "an attractive lady," Pelosi replied: "Well, they spoke more eloquently with their votes."

By all accounts, Pelosi has grown more comfortable over the years fulfilling the public demands of her role, especially in the last year, observers and aides say. "She's actually getting better in some of the public speaking parts of it," said congressional scholar Thomas Mann. "That was always her weakest side, and she's getting better at it. As Bush gets angry, she sounds more motherish. 'Come come, now, we're all together in this. The first branch of government has a role to play. Instead of screaming at each other we need to talk to each other, and as responsible adults we need to work this out.' And I think that plays well."

"I think when she first got to be minority leader she was terrified of public speaking," remarks Berkeley's Robin Lakoff. "There was something in her eyes and a kind of frozenness in her manner. . . . You didn't see much warmth when she was talking to the cameras. She used to look like she was just a poor weak woman. Clearly that was an underestimate." Gone are the early days of the frozen smile and the awkward, bumper-sticker recitation of Democratic talking points. A number of people interviewed for this book think Pelosi has gotten better and better in her public role, especially since she took over as Speaker. "The fright in her eyes is gone," said Lakoff. "She smiles. She has a warm tone of voice. And it seems like she kind of likes it."

Pelosi said she's naturally reticent, more of a behind-the-scenes person, and has had to force herself into the limelight more as the Speaker's role demands it. Pelosi is still a quieter speaker than most of her predecessors. Newt Gingrich, for example, held 33 press conferences in his first three months; Pelosi conducted half that. And she usually shares the spotlight with other lawmakers, something the bombastic, charismatic Gingrich never did. A former Gingrich aide told The Politico he thinks Pelosi's low-key image has hurt the Democrats. "She's taking a lower profile for longevity," the former aide said. "But at the end of the day, do you want to have stuck around for a long time, or do you want to have accomplished something?"

Certainly Pelosi's easy-to-like image has helped in the public piece of her job, though. It may also greatly have aided her rise within the halls of Congress. Lakoff thinks Pelosi has taken advantage of her image as an attractive woman, mom, and wife to put her colleagues at ease. "She's saying 'I'm a woman, therefore you can trust me. I'm not going to try to hit you over the head. I'm a mother of five. I love chocolate. I'm like your wife, and I'm like your mother, and I'm like your daughter and these are all people that you trust.'" It may have been essential to Pelosi's rise that she wasn't perceived as threatening to the male congressmen around her. Ironically, her wife and mom credentials may have been the key to her attainment of power not because, as she so often said, they gave her the right skills for the job, but because they fit more neatly into a stereotype for woman that was easier to swallow for the largely traditional men of the House. One psychologist said men in Congress probably see her as the attractive, together mom next door, an archetype they're completely comfortable with.

Because there is not an abundance of women in high public office yet, both Pelosi and Democratic presidential candidate Hillary Clinton get slotted into female stereotypes by many Americans. Since Pelosi didn't run for political office until she was 46, her identity is formed around her early life as a wife and mother, a relatively typical American style she tries to emphasize at every turn.

"She kind of learned that wife-and-mom style," said Lakoff. "Whereas Hillary has always been in politics and that was her first identification, and she plays power politics." Hillary "is more of a masculine model. She's very precise. She has clear-cut outlines. She really has a much more edgy style."

Hillary has long been a magnet for strong feelings, good and bad, about women's choices and roles. A 1993 cover story in *Time* described her as "the medium through which the remaining anxieties over feminism are being played out." Pelosi is not the lightning rod that Clinton is because she was largely pregnant during the height of feminism. At the stage of gender politics America finds itself in in 2008, it may be that voters aren't worried about whether Hillary is man enough for the job but whether she's woman enough for it.

"The question is, can a woman play that game at the presidential level and be successful?" Lakoff thinks the answer is no. "It arouses too many kinds of uncertainty. I think she makes some people nervous because she sounds too tough. She sounds like the B-word." Pelosi is somehow different, observers say. Somehow she pulls off being tough without seeming bitchy. "She's able to be a "good woman" and a powerful person at the same time," said Lakoff. "It's a remarkable thing. I wouldn't have thought it possible."

"Because of Hillary's famous war vote, people decided there are a lot of differences between them on the issues, but there's not," said Marie Wilson a champion of women in politics. "But they're very different women. Hillary feels like a much more public woman. I don't feel like Hillary has ever had to lead from the foot of the table. Ever. She was a leader from the get-go. Pelosi may have led in lots of ways, too, but Hillary got into politics from a position of authority. She had authority from her husband first. Then she ran on her own. She was a leader. But she hasn't had to build as much of a posse."

Ellen Malcolm thinks Pelosi's swearing in reminded women how exciting and important it is to break through gender barriers at the highest levels of politics, generating more interest in Hillary's run. "I think that Nancy has proven to the country that women know how to lead. If anything it's helpful to Hillary. Every time we break women through the barriers, they go through this process." Malcolm has seen the same reactions come up again and again each time a woman reaches a new first. One of them is: she can't win. Another is the gender stereotyping in the media, like all those stories on Nancy's boots and dresses and her pearls. Another issue that always gets raised: can a woman actually do the job?

"When Nancy shows that women know how to lead in effective ways, it's one sort of extra piece that helps Hillary Clinton make the same case she knows how to lead and will be an effective president."

Lakoff, however, believes the United States has already had its first woman president. "Bill Clinton was our first woman president," she posits, referring to the traditionally feminine character traits such as emoting and empathy he often displayed. Recall his famous line "I feel your pain." Lakoff said Hillary and Bill Clinton crossed accepted gender roles, and that confusion may be at the subconscious root of much of the unease people have with Hillary Clinton.

"They drew outside the lines," she notes. "I think that is one reason why people really, really hated them or were afraid of them. What we like the president and the first lady to do is be really good, ideal versions of the male and the female American. Sort of like Bush plays like and Laura plays like. The Republicans play this game much better."

The reversal of some traditionally male and female personality traits in the Clintons makes a lot of people antsy because it questions their own comfort and their own gender roles. We tend to look at the president as a sort of idealization of ourselves. It's a subconscious thing, one psychologist said. Most people don't even really understand what they're reacting to. Often people are critical of Hillary Clinton for her stand on the war or her handling of universal healthcare, but what they are really saying is that they don't like how she makes them feel. As a result, Clinton has been playing up her maternal and matriarchal side, her soft side, just as Pelosi did at her own inauguration. In her first appearance as a presidential candidate, Clinton held hands with a young girl and argued passionately for children's health insurance. In the video that announced her campaign on her Web site, she was sitting in a cozy living room and speaking to America from a billowy couch. She's purposefully embodying a kind of retro stereotype for women, something that drives old-school feminists nuts.

Wilson thinks just the fact that there are several women in prominent public roles helps broaden what people accept and expect from women in leadership roles. "Numbers matter, and if there's only one person, one woman, who's an outsider being focused on, then she has to be man enough for the job, she has to be the good girl, she has to be everything. As long as you have Pelosi and these other people, it takes the pressure off Clinton. It spreads it around so that you get a little more agenda rather than gender."

Lakoff agrees: "The more women there are in Congress and the government, the more normal it will be for women to be in those positions. They'll have more freedom. Just the way male Congress members have a certain amount of freedom in their self-presentation. There's a whole spectrum of ways that you can be. The more boys and girls growing up can see that there is a wide spectrum of ways you can be male and ways you can be female and get respect, no matter what, the easier it will be for people who want to play unconventional roles. But also the more you have different kinds of representation with different kinds of styles and different interests, the more interesting ideas can come out."

Most politicians and Washington watchers contacted for this book believe Pelosi's high profile as Speaker will have a positive impact on Hillary Clinton's presidential run. One person close to the campaign said Pelosi is "conditioning the country" for Hillary.

Pelosi herself said: "I don't think it will have any effect on Hillary Clinton. She's a force, in her own right, well known to the American people. They will make their own judgment."

Senator Barbara Boxer agrees to a point: "I don't think the connection is that logical or conscious, but I think every time you see a woman break through the barrier, and do it well and do it with great courage, intelligently, it helps the next woman. No question in my mind. And of course because I think she [Pelosi] is doing it with grace and with courage and with intelligence and focus, I think it definitely helps Hillary."

Larry Sabato, however, thinks even if Pelosi is enormously successful between now and the election, she still may hurt Hillary. "Let's be honest. There's still a very strong sexist element in our society. I can still see some voters saying, hmmm, *they're* getting too much power. The president and the Speaker and what's next? They're going to run everything." Some voters will interpret that as a threat, Sabato believes.

A Democratic strategist put it this way: "Pelosi could become the poster child of a left-wing woman politician—and Hillary gets put into the same basket, especially since people already suspect she's too liberal."

A Republican critic was even more certain of the negative impact. Pelosi's "shrill yet glib and often emotional performances could collaterally damage Hillary's chances in '08 because there would not be room for two such women on the national stage," according to GOP pollster Kellyanne Conway.

Sabato points out that Republicans already get a disproportionate share of the male vote. "Everybody focuses on the women side of the gender gap equation, and it's true Democrats are going to win women by X percentage points, but even if women are going to be 52 to 53 percent of the electorate, if men go even more heavily Republican, they'll carry the election for the Republican candidate. It happened with Ferraro, it happened with Bush-Kerry. Kerry won women but Bush won men by such a large majority that he actually won the election."

Berkeley's Bruce Cain sees it differently. "Women are beginning to realize that this is an historic opportunity," Cain said. He thinks Republican attempts to target Pelosi in ad campaigns will backfire in the presidential race. "Trying to villify Pelosi in that context is going to be problematic. If more educated women voters are engaged, targeting another woman is not going to be received well by them." Cain believes Pelosi's high profile and relative success so far have already helped Clinton. "Many Democrats had been saying that they couldn't win with Hillary. It's too risky to run a woman when they have such a golden opportunity. They seem to be starting to think it's possible. Her lead is widening."

What if Hillary wins the election and Pelosi remains speaker? For that matter, what if Congress actually represented the country, and 51 percent of its members were women, just as 51 percent of the country is? What would it be like if women were in charge?

"First of all people would sit down and figure out a solution to health care," said Malcolm. "I mean if there is one issue that is a concern to women in this country it is health care. I think if the Congress or White House were dominated by women we'd sit down and figure it out."

There'd also be more emphasis on education and fixing the schools, Malcolm believes.

"I think there would be a real effort to help families," she said. "We as a society have done a pretty poor job of dealing with the pressures of two-working parents and how do you take care of the kids."

Pelosi and Clinton are more rivals than compatriots, according to one aide on the Hill. They don't do many photo ops together. But Wilson thinks they are way too smart to get into any kind of public rivalry. "They're not going to get into any catfights. They're both party people. They're going to do whatever needs to be done whether they agree with each other or not. What matters to them most is party. And where that party goes."

Pelosi continues to work hard at maintaining her public image, at creating the picture of the perfect woman Speaker. She has said in private to friends that she's well aware of her responsibility to younger women to remain a kind of good example and icon. As a result, meeting her in person is a bit like visiting a monument: there's always a grandness, a polish and an aura of pomp and circumstance about Pelosi. She's a strong believer in the continuity and uplift of ritual, as is the Catholic Church she grew up in.

Of course, Americans hungry for a real greatness, a real humanity and authenticity in their leaders want there to be something more than packaging and marketing, stagecraft and scriptedness. They want Pelosi to be better than politics somehow, to transcend Washington, to change it just by the mere fact of her gender, her newness, her originality. Americans were so sick of Washington and its ways in 2006 they wanted to rearrange the whole picture as radically as they could. Five years after 9/11, mired in an ugly war with no end in sight, Americans craved some bright spot in the dark times, something to believe in and get excited about. They were longing for a return to a kind of politics that had some nobility and class about it. The zeitgeist was beyond ready for a leader like Pelosi, in other words; America was hungry for someone who was somehow so anti-Washington in her physical appearance she could reinvent the place overnight.

Those impossibly high expectations for the first woman in high public office may be responsible for some of the disappointments some people have felt. We as a country may have been too desperate for a competent mom figure, a rescuer who could save us child-citizens from the dark times and make the country whole again. Who do we really want when times get bad? We want our mommy.

If Pelosi outlasts the initial wave of great expectations and the trailing trough of great disappointments, however, she'll probably remain forever in the American imagination as a profound positive influence, a kind of late-to-the-party founding mother. As one of Pelosi's daughters said after mom won the job, "What the hell took so long?"

PELOSI THE POLITICIAN

Those closest to Pelosi say the legacy she really aspires to live up to, as a politician, is that of legendary Speaker Tip O'Neill. "Tip is the person who is like the ultimate Speaker to her. Her model. And she's close to the family," said Lemons. At the beginning of her tenure as Speaker, Pelosi agonized over whether to give up her office, which was Tip O'Neill's old office, and move into the more expansive, more luxurious suite of offices that recent Speakers have used on the second floor of the Capitol. She only did so because Caitlin O'Neill, Tip's granddaughter and one of Pelosi's aides on the House floor, finally gave her the go-ahead. Pelosi also counts Kip O'Neill, son of the late leader, as one of her closet friends in Washington. O'Neill, a lobbyist at O'Neill, Athy and Casey, said he and Pelosi share "a kindred souls sort of background."

Friends say what Pelosi most wants is to go down in history as one of the best Speakers ever, not just the first female Speaker. "I think she has certainly found her niche in this job, said Barbara Boxer. "She was meant to be Speaker," said Lemons. "I absolutely believe that in watching her over the years and seeing how she conducts herself, how she manages the business of the House, everything else. This is where she wanted to be. This is where she landed and intends to be and do a really great job." At 67, Pelosi thinks she's still got plenty of time to make her mark. "She wants to make her case," said Pat Schroeder. "And she would love to have a president and administration she could work with. If she could do that, I think she'd stay another eight years after that."

Colleagues and observers see some parallels with Tip. "He respected vision, she respects vision. He understood things had to be done," said Murtha, as does Pelosi. But Murtha, who was mentored by Tip, said it was a different era, that Pelosi's job is much harder than Tip's was. "Tip couldn't be the Speaker today because the way he operated was so different. Remember, he came up through the ranks being in the majority the whole time he was in Congress. She came through the ranks opposing everything that happened. So she had a terrible transition that she had to get through."

Tip didn't have to raise more money than everybody else, or take in so many other views before deciding important issues. "Now, Tip didn't need to do those things because we had 290 some votes," said Murtha. "We had a two-to-one majority. So he didn't need to have every vote every time. And she knows she has to. So there are similarities of tradition and history but there are also differences in the way you rule. Nancy knows the spin today is everything."

"I think the differences between her and Tip are the differences between her and other Speakers," said a senior staff member. People like Tip were strong Speakers in a system that was very much a committee chairman-dominated caucus. She is a strong Speaker who personally views the caucus as the bedrock of the Democrats in the House." Pelosi informed all the chairmen at the time of their election of this view so they would share it as well. "And so she has probably been far more involved in helping chairmen set some of their legislative agendas than Tip was . . . he gave great latitude to the chairs, the staff member said. It's different now because you need more discipline to set up objectives and achieve objectives." If you have a big vote margin like O'Neill had, and the next election is really just a signpost the party is driving past, then it's a whole different ball game.

Brian Green points out that Tip O'Neill initially got serious criticism for some of the mistakes he made as Speaker, as Pelosi did. "But now we look back at his Speakership and say that he was clearly an effective Speaker."

Murtha believes there was greatness in Tip and there's greatness in Pelosi. "She's as good a political mind as I've ever seen . . . With a Republican president who has dominated Congress, for her to change it around and to have such an influence in such a short period of time, is exceptional. The way she's handled her job, the favors she's done for members, the consideration she's given to different members she's put the on committees and so forth."

All that has given her enormous influence, Murtha said. "And she's very fair about it. She very seldom criticizes anybody or embarrasses anybody. She works very quietly on these things. It's a combination of all that." Other politicians who have worked with Pelosi for years are equally as effusive, even those away from the House who have nothing to gain by singing her praises.

"She'll have a tremendous influence for many years to come because she really knows how to put together these coalitions," remarks Boxer. "She knows how to unite people. People really respect her and admire her. These are really qualities that Nancy has, that she has developed. And she's grown over the years in the House. I think people are very attracted to that combination because again, she's empathetic with you, she knows where you're coming from, and she's not going to ask you to take a big risk. If she does, she'll figure out a way to make it up to you. And that's really important when you have a slim majority."

Senator Barbara Mikulski believes Pelosi and other women in office have begun to change the tone in Washington, but it will take a while. "We women set the tone for civility and respect on Capitol Hill. We want to carry that tone of civility with us in an otherwise prickly institution. We're trying to create a new sound and the new sound has a female voice."

John Burton simply said, "She's the guts. She has the guts. I've got absolute faith in her. I've got friends in office that I love and occasionally I've had to call up on certain votes and ask 'What the hell were you thinking voting like that?' Never, ever ever had to think about making that call to Nancy Pelosi. Nothing like her in the world. Nothing like her in the whole world."

"In 1987, after Nancy was sworn in [as a congresswoman], there was a small party at a hotel," remembers Lemons. At the dinner, Pelosi's brother Tommy got up and spoke about their family heritage and their tradition and about their father serving in Congress. "Tommy used a term that was uncommon to describe a woman. He said: 'My sister is a Thoroughbred.' It took me a while to digest that. It didn't take me too long to realize working with Nancy, that, like a Thoroughbred, it's in her genes. That single description couldn't have been truer or a better use of that term in describing Nancy. And of course, she crossed the finish line. Phil Burton didn't. She's the Thoroughbred who crossed the finish line."

Those who have worked most closely with Pelosi say what is unique about her as a leader, and the primary engine behind her climb, is her left-brain, right-brain approach to the game. Over and over again, politicians who know her best said the secret to her success is that double-barreled ability to do both policy and politics. She can crack heads with the best of them in the behind-the-scenes, mechanical part of her job, and she can display a great deal of empathy and warmth in the public, campaign part of her job.

"She has an amazing combination of skills that are needed in that position," said Boxer.

"She clearly understands both the policy and the politics," said Representative George Miller. "This woman knows exactly what's going on in Iraq. She knows exactly what's going on in the intelligence community. She knows exactly what's going on in the appropriations committee."

One senior Democratic staff member thinks someone who can play both sides of the political coin well, the politics side and the policy side, is rare. "In this business, you very often find people who are good politically as tacticians, or people who are good legislatively, but not really interested in the political side particularly. The campaigning, the fundraising." But Pelosi excels at both. "You have these two sides of her personality that means that she can be more effective."

Representative Eshoo cites the same thing as Pelosi's secret sauce. "She's hugely effective because she's multifaceted. There are all different styles of leadership, and ingredients in leadership, but they usually manifest themselves in certain areas. There are some leaders who unify people by what they say, in their rhetoric. Some who are fabulous tacticians. Some, like the brilliant John Burton, one of Pelosi's most important mentors, who rub people like sandpiper but know how to win, to get things done. But Nancy is across the board."

Her most valuable asset may be a kind of preternatural people-smarts that, for some reason, many more book-smart politicians like Hillary Clinton somehow lack. She's able to sift through a great deal of information and make sound judgments much of the time, the very definition of wisdom. She hasn't tripped up yet the way Newt Gingrich tripped up, for example, when an insular kind of hubris overtook his ample intellect. Pelosi's actually widened her circle of influences since becoming Speaker, so that she is less insulated than she was as minority leader. She solicits more views than past speakers, especially opinions outside the Beltway. With all that added information, the more good judgment, steeped in principle, is essential. That said, the low ratings Congress is currently experiencing may be just another incidence of people underestimating Pelosi's political wisdom.

But Larry Sabato said it's still too early to judge whether Pelosi's political abilities and her positive public persona will be enough to survive the snake pit of modern partisan politics. "I think the partisanship is as intense as it was in the late '60s, early '70s," he said. "Thank goodness it's not as bad as it was in the pre—Civil War era. And people are not adversaries, they're enemies." He thinks a dark force has taken over all aspects of politics and that Pelosi is powerless to transcend it. "It's a dynamic that's bigger than any individual, even somebody in her history-making position who receives reams of positive publicity."

Iraq certainly aggravates the current climate, but Sabato believes it started with Bill Clinton's presidency in January of 1993. "We've had two consecutive two-term deeply polarizing presidents. We're probably headed for a third. And that's just the way it is. And Congress is partly a function of the partisan presidential impulse and it's also a function of the conditions that create the partisan presidency. In other words, they're elected by the same people for the same reasons on both sides, which means they can't get along."

Pelosi promised to be the Speaker of the whole House at the beginning of her term, but Sabato said it's just talk. "Everybody says that and it's absolutely meaningless. I have no doubt she meant it because everybody was coming up and congratulating her, including the Republicans. Remember when Dick Gephardt handed the gavel to Newt Gingrich when he took over. You would have thought they were kissing cousins. It doesn't matter. It doesn't mean anything. It never means anything. It's just Washington bullshit."

How does Sabato think Pelosi's handling the partisanship? "I'm a college professor. I give her an incomplete. You can only give a grade for a full term." And that's still a year off, Sabato points out.

Savato's critique echoes that of many Republicans in Congress, who are almost universal in their criticism. Among their complaints: she's ham-handed with those who aren't in her inner circle, she's a mediocre intellect, more lucky than deserving; and she's an unrepentant partisan warrior, who will never make the transition to stateswoman.

"They've wasted the first seven months by being excessively partisan and creating unnecessary, in my view, disputes with a pretty robust minority of 49," said Senator Mitch McConnell of Kentucky, the Republican leader in the Senate.

"The defining characteristic of the new Democrat majority in Congress has been failure: failure to lead, failure to communicate, failure to organize, failure to deliver," former majority leader Tom Delay wrote on his blog, tomdelay.com.

Many Republicans are confident that Pelosi's legacy as a politician will be a short one, that Americans will grow quickly weary of her leadership and put Republicans back in charge of Congress in the 2008 elections.

"The Democratic majority revealed it is willing to break any rule, trample on any precedent, and run roughshod over its own members to defend a left-wing, big-government agenda most Americans reject," House Minority Leader John Boehner of Ohio wrote in a memo to more than 200 House Republicans after a nasty floor fight in the summer of 2007.

A Washington Post/ABC Poll taken in July, 2007, put Congress's job approval rating at 37 percent, not much higher than President Bush's at 33 percent. But the 1,125 people surveyed seemed to blame the lack of progress on Iraq and other issues on the Republicans in Congress more than the Democrats. Forty-six percent of those polled said they approved of the Democrats' performance; 34 percent approved of the job the Congressional Republicans were doing.

In terms of keeping the House in 2008, history is on Pelosi's side. "If you look at American history, it's extremely rare to have a party flip-flop after just one term," said Sabato, whose "Crystal Ball" Web site is a popular political prognosticator. "It did happen once in the '40s and once in the '50s, but it hasn't happened since. And before then, it didn't happen very often in all of American history."

The reason: New members of Congress generally are very careful about what they do, and they pay close attention to public opinion, as the Blue Dogs are doing now. And they can also say, as presidents say for their first midterm, give us a chance, we just got in. "And that usually works with voters," Sabato said. If the Republican presidential candidates are honest, he said, they're going to admit that the Democrats will be in charge for at least one more Congress. "I mean, that's obvious to all of us who follow Washington. It's not even going to be close. When you look at the seats opening up, the money being raised, it'll be very surprising if the Democrats don't pick up seats in the Senate and don't hold a clear majority in the House. I have a hard time seeing how they lose the House. I really do."

Pelosi is already hop scotching the country again to raise money for the party and campaign for congressional candidates in the 2008 elections. Money will play an even bigger role in the 2008 campaigns than it did in 2006, several political experts predict, so Pelosi's skill as a fundraiser will be as important as ever. She already devotes a large portion of her weekly schedule to fundraising and campaign planning for the 2008 House elections. Spending on the presidential and congressional campaigns is expected to exceed $5 billion this cycle, which is nearly $2 billion more than in 2004.

Whenever possible, Pelosi turns an event into a fundraising opportunity. Tickets for a party at Washington's Union Station marking her twentieth anniversary in Congress ranged from $1,000 for cocktails to $10,000 for co-chairs. Four hundred people attended the event, the highlight of which came when longtime friend George Miller got up in front of the crowd and described Pelosi as "the California earthquake who came to Congress." When Pelosi stood to speak, suddenly a train underneath started rumbling. "The room began vibrating and everyone heard this rumble, rumble, rumble. It was hysterical," said Pelosi's former chief of staff Judy Lemons. "It was like, whoa."

The Republican strategy early in the game is to target all those races where moderate and conservative Democrats won in 2006 and tar them with a Pelosi brush, saying they're following Pelosi right off the left coast of the country. But Brian Wolff, Pelosi's political director, is more worried about the left at this point than the right. Pelosi's fiercest critics at the moment are the people who complain that she hasn't done enough to end the war. If she and fellow congressional Democrats don't show more progress on the issue by election time, candidates may face a backlash at the polls.

Pelosi faces a challenge in her home district from Cindy Sheehan, the mother of a U.S. serviceman who was killed in Iraq. Sheehan became the face of the antiwar movement in 2005 when she set up camp outside the president's ranch in Crawford, Texas, and demanded an audience with Bush. Sheehan wants Bush impeached and is running against Pelosi because she doesn't think the Speaker has done enough to end the war.

But Pelosi isn't much worried about losing the House or her own seat. Sheehan's candidacy may actually help Pelosi and the Democrats, some pundits believe. If the far left is angry with Pelosi, the rest of the country may see her as more mainstream than the liberal cartoon Republicans have been painting of her.

John Murtha, Pelosi's oldest, strongest ally, said that no matter how partisan things get and no matter how Pelosi does the rest of her job, she will be remembered always for returning checks and balances to Washington. "Her biggest accomplishment is to restore the integrity of the Congress, to restore the influence of the Congress, representing the American people," said Murtha. "That's the biggest thing that she's done. She's done it very well. I don't know if there's anybody else who could do it. She's the right person for this time."

Some high-level Republicans agree.

"I had a very senior Republican who was talking to me right after the election," said Sabato. "And he said all the logical things about Bush, Iraq, corruption, and so on. But he really surprised me. 'But the fourth reason is never mentioned,' he said. 'And we made a giant goof. When Bush was elected, we gave up the oversight function.' And that's exactly right," Sabato thinks. "If they had been performing at least to some degree the oversight function during the Bush administration, they might have been able to separate themselves more from Bush when he became unpopular. It might have made a difference. They had thrown that away, and they had shut down the checks on the executive branch. Now the test for the Democrats will come if there's a Democratic president in 2009. Are they going to make the same mistake that the Republicans made, and give up oversight? To me that's the real test. And they better not. They will suffer for it if they do."

Pelosi is keeping a keen eye on the 2008 election, but she has another eye focused farther down the road, as always, on the next generation. Repeatedly during our last conversation in her red-walled office, she returned to her favorite subject and central organizing principle. If Pelosi has a greatest cause, an overriding passion, a single thread that ties together her overarching outlook and her entire career, it's kids.

"We had a conference the other day on children. A children's summit," Pelosi said near the end of the interview. "It was absolutely fabulous. In fact, in my 20 years here it was probably my best day, because it was listening to what science knows about the development of a child, and then they were asking what we can do about it."

Pelosi's own children have already begun to follow in their mother's public service footsteps. Christine has worked as chief of staff for Representative John Tierney of Massachusetts, and campaigned across the country with her mom. Last year she published a kind of how-to book for answering the call to public service, *Campaign Boot Camp*.

Daughter Alexandra has made her mark in politics as a documentary filmmaker and author who has chronicled two presidential campaigns. Her 2002 film, *Journeys with George*, was an inside look at George W. Bush's first campaign, and *Diary of a Political Tourist* followed Democratic presidential candidates in 2004. Her most recent film, *Friends of God: Road Trip with Alexandra Pelosi*, was a quirky portrait of evangelicals around the country. She said she has documented much of her mother's career on film but has no plans to make a movie of it. She's also the author of *Sneaking into the Flying Circus*, a book about the media and presidential elections.

Pelosi's only son, Paul Jr., has taken up his mother's interest in the politics of the environment. He was appointed to California's Commission on the Environment by former San Francisco Mayor Willie Brown in 2003 and now serves as president. Daughter Nancy Corinne followed her father's path into business as a hotel executive, and Jacqueline apparently inherited her mother's uncheckable enthusiasm for kids. She runs an art school for children.

Pelosi believes it's the generation of her children's children, today's grade-schoolers, who will benefit the most from this particular moment in history.

"I think in your daughter's case it will all be different," she tells me after I mention that my first-grader is already contemplating a presidential run. "It's generational. I think by the time your little girl is old enough to vote . . . that whole attitude, I think, will be changed. I really do. I see the reaction to my Speakership . . . everybody knows who the president is, most people don't even know that a Speaker exists, or what that is . . . but I see the reaction across the country, traveling, just walking through airports, whatever, and it's really quite a phenomenal thing." Pelosi said women are very proud of where she is, but it's the fathers of daughters whose reactions have been the biggest surprise. "It's been an interesting phenomenon to me because they come and say 'Thank you for my daughters.'"

Representative Bart Gordon likes to tell a story about Pelosi and his six-year-old daughter, Peyton. "When she [Nancy] was sworn in, I tried to get Peyton to go with me. But she didn't. She watched it on television. When I got home she was jumping around like a cheerleader. She was saying 'M-S-P! M-S-P! M-S-P!'"

"I asked her what that stood for.

'Madame Speaker Pelosi! Madame Speaker Pelosi! Madame Speaker Pelosi!'" she shouted.

"We don't talk about politics at home," Gordon adds. "Being a woman Speaker—that role model penetrates more than people really know. And that will be a part of her legacy. Peyton knew that she was proud of her."

Pelosi has to rush off for another floor vote, so she graciously ends the interview with the recommendation that I bring my own daughter to the House floor sometime, just to show her that the "sky's the limit."

"Anything is possible for them," said Pelosi. "If you can succeed in this arena, then that really is a marble ceiling that is broken and they can just go right through it."

ACKNOWLEDGMENTS

First, I warmly thank Anna Ghosh and Russell Galen at Scovil Chicak Galen for making this book happen. Anna has been a literary agent, editor, voice of encouragement, and midwife for the manuscript from its inception. Without her hard work and Russell's faith in the idea of this biography, it simply wouldn't have been made.

Jake Klisivitch at Palgrave Macmillan edited the manuscript with a keen eye and kind words, not to mention an infectious enthusiasm. He is the engine behind the whole effort, the driving force responsible for seeing the potential in the book and bringing it fully to fruition. Yasmin Mathew and her copy editing crew at Palgrave refined and improved the book immensely, translating ungrammatical rough drafts of thoughts into actual readable English.

At the *Washington Post*, I'd like to thank Phil Bennett and Len Downie for their generous support for the book and for the time they gave me to complete it. I'd also like to give a nod of the head to my boss Ed Thiede, whose insistence and encouragement got me to take the first steps. After that, his enthusiasm and patient for the writing process never flagged, no matter how many days of work I missed. It sometimes takes a village to make a book, and my colleagues on the news desk provided the intellectual village that enabled this effort to thrive. They generously listened to and helped sharpen my ideas, and completely supported my year-long preoccupation with Pelosi. The story was further improved by several senior editors at the *Post* who generously allowed me to bounce approaches and pages off them, including Jill Dutt, David Broder, Tim Curran and David Hoffman. I also relied heavily on the research and writing of colleagues at the Post who know Congress much better than I, especially Jonathan Weisman, Juliet Eilperin, Lyndsey Layton, Lois Romano and Shailagh Murray.

I'd also like to thank Tom Cronin, Colin Simpson, Gene Robinson, Steve Coll, and Al Simpson for their encouragement and feedback.

I've mentioned all my generous sources in the source notes, but there are a few who took so much time and effort to help me with the reporting for this story I want to give them special thanks here. They are Leonard Boswell, Brendan Daly, Bart and Leslie Gordon, Judy Lemons, John Lawrence, Anne Pauley, Tommy D'Alesandro, Anna Eshoo, and Nancy Pelosi herself.

My children, Xavier and Zola, gave me the gift of their patience during the months and months I took time away from them while I was researching and writing. My mother and father, both journalists themselves, improved the manuscript immeasurably with their comments and suggestions, especially concerning the writing.

Last and foremost, my wife, Kelsey, acted as sounding board, chief editor, and idea maven for this effort. Her insights into the story from her psychologist's point of view were the start of many of the roads I researched and traveled in telling this tale. She also served as a one-woman support system from start to finish. Without her it's hard to imagine much of anything happening at all.

SOURCE NOTES

The bulk of this story has been gathered from extended interviews granted by: Tommy D'Alesandro, Mike Barone, Naftali Bendavid, Representative Leonard Boswell, Senator Barbara Boxer, John Burton, Bruce Cain, Anne Ceeley, Joan Clarke, Alex Clemens, Corey Cook, Vince Culotta, Representative James Clyburn, Brendan Daly, Representative Anna Eshoo, Sister Mary Fitzgerald, Representative Bart Gordon, Matthew Green, Representative Steny Hoyer, Robin Lakoff, John Lawrence, Judy Lemons, Ellen Malcolm, Thomas Mann, Leah Martin, Pat McGuire, Senator Barbara Mikulski, Representative John Murtha, Aimee Olivo, Chrissy Palmer, Anne Pauley, Nancy Pelosi, Cindy Simon Rosenthal, Larry Sabato, Gilbert Sandler, Pat Schroeder, George Wesolek, and Marie Wilson. Many other people provided short interviews, pieces of information, and background, and some of those people asked not to be named. Christine and Alexandra Pelosi also contributed insights via e-mail.

Paul McCardell at the *Baltimore Sun* provided invaluable information about Pelosi's early days from the newspaper's archives. The Library of Congress was a font of historical information and floor speeches relevant to Nancy's career, as were the Congressional Research Service and the *Congressional Record*. The collection of Tommy D'Alesandro's papers at the University of Baltimore's Langsdale Library provided much of the history of the D'Alesandro family in Baltimore. The *Washington Post's* archives yielded most of the newspaper articles and reporting cited in the book. Other relevant news stories were found in the archives of the *San Francisco Chronicle*, the *Los Angeles Times*, the *New York Times*, and *Time* magazine. Nancy Pelosi's communications director, Brendan Daly, also provided biographical material on her. Much of the information regarding Pelosi's finances and voting record come from Project Vote Smart.

These notes do not include the hundreds of newspaper articles read for this book, only the ones quoted directly. If a source is noted within the text of the book, it is not repeated in these source notes. Any quotes that are not mentioned in the notes are from the interviews mentioned above. If Pelosi has made a statement more than once in different venues, those quotations appear unattributed.

INTRODUCTION

The description of inauguration day was pieced together from eyewitness accounts by John Burton, Alex Clemens, Nancy Pelosi, Pat McGuire, and Pat Schroeder, from C-Span coverage of the event, speeches recorded in the *Congressional Record*, and articles by *Washington Post* reporters Lyndsey Layton, Jonathan Weisman, and Shailagh Murray on January 5, 2007. The idea to watch for outbreaks of color on the House floor was inspired by *Washington Post* writer David Finkel, who noted how little color there was on the floor of Congress in a May 10, 1992, *Washington Post Magazine* article, *Women on the Verge of a Power Breakthrough*. Representative Rosa DeLauro (D-Conn.), called Pelosi "the most powerful person in Washington" at a woman's tea on January 3, 2007, according to *New York Times* reporter Sarah Wheaton's blog item on the same day. Pelosi's remark about women helping other women comes from an Associated Press interview, January 3, 2007. Her comment about public service as a noble calling comes from her speech to Congress on January 4, 2007, after she was inaugurated as Speaker. Phil Burton's quote about making the universe a better place appeared in John Jacobs's *A Rage for Justice* (Berkeley: University of California Press, 1995). The remarks of Rahm Emanuel and Nancy Pelosi on inauguration day are taken from the *Congressional Record*. Pelosi's remark about ripping off faces appeared in *Time* magazine, August 27, 2006.

Congressman Edward Markey's comment about Pelosi appeared in Albert Hunt's Letter from Washington for *Bloomberg News*, November 5, 2006.

CHAPTER 1   THE FAMILY VOCATION

Much of the description of the St Anthony's festival is taken from an interview with Gilbert Sandler and from his book *The Neighborhood: The Story of Baltimore's Little Italy* (Baltimore: Bodine & Associates, 1974.) Tommy D'Alesandro and Vince Culotta also provided details. H. L. Mencken's quotes about Baltimore are excerpted from Fred Hobson's *Mencken: A Life* (New York: Random House, 1994). The descriptions of the Great Fire are an amalgam of Tommy D'Alesandro's descriptions and those found in *The Neighborhood*, including the account by Marie O'Dea and Harold Williams.

Additional details are taken from Williams's book *Baltimore Afire* (Baltimore, Md.: Schneidereith & Sons, 1954). The background about Nancy's ancestors comes from an interview with her brother Tommy D'Alesandro. The details about where Nancy's relatives lived in Little Italy appeared in a profile by Mark Barabak, *Los Angeles Times*, January 26, 2003. Pelosi's remarks about wanting to be a priest appeared in an interview by Joe Feuerherd in *The National Catholic Reporter*, January 24, 2003. The statistics about the number of women in political office appear in the *Almanac of American Politics* (Chicago: University of Chicago Press, 2006), by Michael Barone and Richard E. Cohen. Sandler's quote about the connection of people of Little Italy to their streets is from an article by Judith Valente, *Washington Post*, September 3, 1977. Pelosi's remark about working on the side of angels comes from her speech to Congress on January 4, 2007, after she was elected Speaker. The story of Tommy D'Alesandro's early years is largely based on his son's account but is supplemented by material from an unattributed article in *Time*, April 26, 1954. The history of the Piracci scandal comes from the same article.

The descriptions of D'Alesandro's early days in the state legislature and his fashion sense were recounted by his former press secretary, Tom J. O'Donnell, to Lynne Duke in the *Washington Post*, November 10, 2006. O'Donnell's retelling of D'Alesandro's encounter with Jimmy Hoffa is from the same article. All of Tommy senior's comments to Sandler appear in *The Neighborhood*, including the "paisano" quote. The details about the mayor's accomplishments were culled from D'Alesandro's papers at the University of Baltimore's Lansdale Library. His comment that he hadn't done everything right comes from *Time*, April 26, 1954.

The description of Tommy and Annunciata's wedding can be found in *The Neighborhood*. The story about the words on the bulletin board at the Institute of Notre Dame was reported by Michael Olesker for the *Baltimore Sun*, June 25, 1989. The "Profiles in Courage," tale is told by Elle Gamerman in the *Baltimore Sun*, November 14, 2002. Gene Raymor's recollection of Annunciata's funeral is from the same article. Mari Perry reported Pelosi's comment on independence for Capital News Service, October 28, 2005.

CHAPTER 2   THE SOCIAL GOSPEL

All of Pelosi's speeches at Trinity have been archived on the university's Web site, www.trinitydc.edu. Pelosi's comments about shuttling around to different churches were made to Joe Feuerherd of the *National Catholic Reporter*, January 22, 2003, as were all her quotes about the accountability of the individual later in the chapter. Alexandra Pelosi's remarks about Catholicism appeared in the *Washington Post*, January 21, 2007. Pelosi's votes regarding abortion come from Project Vote Smart data. The text of the House Democrats' statement on abortion can be found in the *Congressional Record*. Much of the history of social justice within the Catholic Church was explained to me by George Wesolek, director of the San Francisco archdiocese's Public Policy and Social Concerns Office. Father Maurice Ouellet's comments were cited by David DiCarto in an article for Catholic News Service on Jan. 25, 2007. Jon Meachem's comments are all drawn from his book *American Gospel* (New York: Random House, 2006). Much of the history of Jerry Falwell's rise is taken from *American Gospel* as well, including the direct quotes from Falwell regarding the separation of church and state. Pelosi's inaugural address appears in the *Congressional Record* for January 4, 2007. Pelosi's St. Augustine remark was made to David Rogers for an article in the *Wall Street Journal*, July 24, 2007. Kristen Day's comments about the incoming representatives were excerpted from Right Democrat, a blog for moderate and conservative Democrats, on Nov. 10, 2006. Pelosi's comment about being less visible on abortion was made to Feuerherd for the Jan. 22, 2003 article. Her comment about the pope reinvigorating the church was made in a speech to Trinity students in 2003. Professor Clarence Baruch's comments on the religious history of civil rights appear in an essay written for the June, 2006, issue of *History Now*, a quarterly online journal. All of the comments and stories from the Reverend Jim Wallis whose sources are not noted in the text have been excerpted from his book *God's Politics: Why the Right Gets It Wrong and the Left Doesn't Get It* (New York: HarperCollins, 2005). The data about the views of evangelicals from the Pew Study appeared in Alan Cooperman's article in the *Washington Post*, May 22, 2007. The e-mails and letters sent to Trinity President Pat McGuire appeared on her blog at the Trinity Web site.

The comments of Cardinal Theodore E. McCarrick, retired archbishop of Washington, were made to Patrick Zapor, Catholic News Service, January 5, 2007. Anne Pauley, vice president for institutional development at Trinity, provided the detailed description of the Mass at the Notre Dame Chapel. Sister Mary Clayton's remarks appeared in Amy Argetsinger's article on Trinity's makeover in *Washington Post Magazine* on April 7, 2002. The "Well Sing" was described in the same article, with further details supplied by Pauley.

CHAPTER 3   PELOSI'S FAMILY VALUES

The epigraph comes from an interview by Sally Jacobs that appeared in the *Boston Globe* on February 5, 2003. The school lunch ritual was recounted in the *Los Angeles Times*, January 26, 2003. Pelosi's "One of the things I insisted" quote is from an American Profile interview on C-Span, November 29, 2001. The "raise five children" quote is from the same article in the *Los Angeles Times*, January 26, 2003. Debbie Wasserman Schultz's comments appeared in article by Kathy Kiely, *USA Today*, May 10, 2007. Pelosi's quote about raising her children outside of embassies was reported by Robert Salladay, *San Francisco Examiner*, June 29, 1998. The story about Alexandra parching her tongue appeared in an article by David Von Drehle and Hanna Rosin in the *Washington Post*, November 14, 2002. The assembly line and "He's Got the Whole World" anecdotes were mentioned in an article by Marc Sandalow and Erin McCormick in *The San Francisco Chronicle*, April 2, 2006. Pelosi's "never marry a cheap man" advice was quoted in an article by John Powers for *Vogue* magazine, March 2007. Alexandra's cranberry comment appeared in the same piece, as did the story about Paul recording *The Daily Show*. Alexandra's comparison of the San Francisco and Baltimore households appears in a report by Ellen Gamerman in the *Baltimore Sun*, November 14, 2002. Pelosi was quoted in *USA Today*, May 10, 2007, as saying she had "no amnesia about how much work it was." The bagels and Jerry Brown story appeared in the November 14, 2002, *Washington Post* article mentioned earlier. The history of the campaign in Maryland for Brown was excerpted from the same article.

Pelosi's remarks after dropping out of the race for national party chair are quoted by Mary McGrory, *Washington Post*, February 5, 1985. The comments from party members in reaction to her dropping out, including the "airhead" exchange, all appeared in an article by Peter Kumpa, *Baltimore Evening Sun*, February 1, 1985. Pelosi's description of Paul as a good sport comes from the C-Span interview on November 29, 2001.

CHAPTER 4   BACK IN THE GAME

The descriptions of Sala Burton's deathbed request that Pelosi succeed her are drawn largely from John Jacobs's *A Rage for Justice* (Berkeley: University of California Press, 1995), though John Burton, Judy Lemons, John Lawrence, and George Miller all added details in interviews. Pelosi's "you must promise me" quote was taken from the American Profile interview on C-Span, November 29, 2001. Senator Gaylor Nelson's quote about Phil Burton is the epigraph of *A Rage for Justice*. Much of the history of Burton's career is from the book as well. The rest of the history is derived from a column by Harold Myerson, the *Washington Post*, January 20, 2007, including the detail about John Burton's uncertainty who Nancy was, and most of the list of Phil Burton's accomplishments during his 19 years as a congressman. The Burton interview with a conservation magazine is quoted in *A Rage for Justice*. The quote from Abner Mikava is in the book, too. Pelosi mentioned the "Get a life" line in a profile on NBC's *The Today Show*, January 4, 2005. The descriptions of the 1987 campaign are all from *San Francisco Chronicle* reports, unless otherwise noted. The amount of money Pelosi borrowed from herself is noted by Paul West, *Baltimore Sun*, April 5, 1987, as were "the legislator . . . or the dilettante?" campaign signs and Tommy D'Alesandro's quotes about Nancy fighting like a tiger. The description of the televised debate is Dan Balz's in the *Washington Post*, April 5, 1987. James Hormel's quote is from Balz's story as well. John Burton provided much of the anecdotal material about the election and campaign in an interview. The story about George Miller's chair appears in *A Rage for Justice*.

CHAPTER 5   A VOICE THAT WILL BE HEARD

Pelosi's first floor speech is taken from the *Congressional Record* for June 9, 1987. Much of Pelosi's early work on AIDS issues was culled from biographical information compiled by the Speaker's office. Charlie Cook's comments and the discussion about Pelosi as a candidate for vice president are recounted by Marc Sandalow in the *San Francisco Chronicle*, March 21, 1989. Pelosi's remark about a clash between Democratic values and new ideas was reported by John Nichols in *The Nation*, August 6, 2001. The thoughts of gay advocates on Pelosi's Speakership have been gathered from an article that appeared in *The Advocate* in January 2007, as was California assemblyman Mark Leno's quote about Pelosi as a champion of gay rights. John Murtha provided much of the background on the Presidio deal, but other details were drawn from John Jacobs's *A Rage for Justice* (Berkeley: University of California Press, 1995). Pelosi's protest in China is recounted by Robert Salladay in the *San Francisco Examiner*, June 29, 1998. Pelosi's floor statements on China appear in the *Congressional Record*. The history of Pelosi's battle against China over the years has been compiled from stories in the *Washington Post* archive.

CHAPTER 6   THE BOYS' CLUB

The history of the suffragist movement has been gathered from a Public Broadcasting Service documentary, *American Experience: One Woman, One Vote*. Much of the description of the Anita Hill hearings, including Eleanor Holmes Norton's remarks, come from a book by Eleanor Clift and Tom Brazaitis, *Madam President* (New York: Scribner, 2000). The description later in the chapter of the picture on Barbara Mikulski's office wall comes from *Madam President* as well. Pelosi's quote about the hearings can be found in the *New York Times*, October 8, 1991. Senator Barbara Mikulski's comments to her colleagues are quoted by Marjorie Williams, the *Washington Post*, October 9, 1991. Schroeder's "Times they are a-changing" quote is from the *New York Times*, October 8, 1991. Most of the profiles of women in Congress are based on information from the book *Women in Congress, 1917–2006*, published, researched, and written by the Office of History and Preservation in the House's Office of the Clerk. Profiles of the women who have run for president are excerpted from *Madam President*. Ellen Macolm's comments come from an interview with the author on July 27, 2007. Barbara Kennelly's comments about the most powerful women in Congress are quoted by David Finkel, *Washington Post Magazine*, May 10, 1992. Mary Rose Oakar's tale about the leadership meetings is recounted by Lois Romano, *Washington Post*, March 6, 1990. Anita Hill's "invisible lines" quote appeared in an interview with Patricia J. Williams in *Harper's Bazaar*, October 1997. Schroeder's "private club" quote is from *24 Years of House Work . . . And the Place Is Still a Mess* (Kansas City, Missouri: Andrews McMeel Publishing, 1998). Karen Foerstel and Herbert Foerstel tell Jeanette Rankin's story in *Breaking the Political Glass Ceiling* (New York: Routledge, Taylor & Francis Group, 2006). Her quotes are from the book as well. The aide's remark about Murtha shielding Pelosi from sexism appeared in an article in *Time Magazine* by Karen Tumulty and Perry Bacon Jr. on November 19, 2006

CHAPTER 7   THE GLASS CEILING

The reconstruction of the whip race comes in large part from Juliet Eilperin's "The Making of Madam Whip," *Washington Post Magazine*, January 6, 2002. The details of Pelosi's fundraising and her PAC to the Future are told by Marc Sandalow and Erin McCormick in the *San Francisco Chronicle*, April 2, 2006. Ken Boehm's reaction to Pelosi's fines and the details of McCarthy's defense are taken from Ethics Watch, a newsletter published

by the National Legal and Policy Center in the summer of 2004. Other
details were drawn from a story by Ethan Wallison in *Roll Call*, October 24,
2002, a press release issued by the FEC on March 6, 2004, and an unbylined
Associated Press story on February 11, 2004. Pelosi's quote about her large
base of supporters appears in Eilperin's article, "Madam Whip," as do the
details of Steny Hoyer's bid for the job. The vote count on October 8 is out
of a separate story by Juliet Eilperin in the *Washington Post*, October 9, 2001.
Pelosi's "How sweet it is" quote appeared in "Madam Whip." Edward Walsh
quoted Pelosi as saying "I didn't run as a woman" in the *Washington Post*,
November 15, 2002. Pelosi's first meeting as whip is described by Roxanne
Roberts in "Out and About," the *Washington Post*, February 11, 2002. Maxine
Waters's earthquake comment was quoted in *The Nation*, October 18, 1999.
The black leather whips were described by Juliet Eilperin in the *Washington
Post*, November 13, 2001.

CHAPTER 8   CHOCOLATE AND THE GAVEL

"The Chocolate and the Gavel" style was articulated by Katie Zernike, *New
York Times*, November 9, 2006. The details and remarks about Pelosi patching things up at the Democratic retreats are from Ed Henry in *Roll Call*,
February 5, 2003, as is Brendan Daly's remark about Democrats dancing
together. Pelosi made her kaleidoscope analogy in the American Profile interview *on C-Span, November 29, 2001*. The various estimates on the cost of the
Iraq war appear in an article by David Leonhardt, *New York Times*, January 17,
2007. Barton Gellman describes Clinton's four-day war against Iraq in detail
in the *Washington Post*, December 17, 1998. In the *Washington Post*, February
15, 2002, Walter Pincus reports all the information on the intelligence hearings that appears in the chapter, including Pelosi's quotes on the matter.
Follow-up stories by Dana Priest, Juliet Eilperin, and Helen Dewar provide
more of the details. All of Pelosi's statements on Iraq are from the
Congressional Record or press releases issued by her office.

CHAPTER 9   THE MARBLE CEILING

Pelosi's "no question I would win" remark was excerpted from an article by
Juliet Eilperin in *Washington Post Magazine*, January 6, 2002. The "never
again" statement appeared in *Roll Call*, May 14, 2003, in an article by Erin
Billings. The details about Pelosi's rising popularity are drawn from *Pelosi's
House Ascending*, an article by Marc Sandalow in the *San Francisco Chronicle*,
November 3, 2002.

Pelosi's ambitious travel itinerary is detailed by Sandalow in the *San Francisco Chronicle*, November 3, 2002. Donna Brazile's "bold strike" quote appears in an article by Adam Nagourney, the *New York Times*, November 9, 2002. Nelson Warfield's comments appeared in the same article. Billings also quotes Pelosi on "distilling that message" in *Roll Call*, June 27, 2007. In a different *Roll Call* article on October 5, 2004, Billings describes Pelosi's extensive travels and quotes Pelosi about fathers of daughters. Billings makes note of the 50,000 volunteers in *Roll Call*, September 27, 2005. Billings quotes Pelosi on taking Bush down in the same article.

Paul Begala's description of Rahm Emanuel appeared in an article by Steve Hendrix in the *Washington Post*, October 22, 2006. Pelosi's comments that Rahm was never a diplomat, and her "coldblooded" and "what is this conversation about" quotes come from the same article.

The remark from Emanuel about exercising more leadership is excerpted verbatim from Naftali Bendavid's *The Thumpin'* (New York: Doubleday, 2007). The description of election night at Democratic Congressional Campaign Committee headquarters comes entirely from *The Thumpin',* as well, as does the scene later that night at the Hyatt Regency involving Paul Pelosi. Christine Pelosi's quote about veterans outreach appeared in an article by Lisa Vorderbrueggen in the *Contra Costa Times*, September 15, 2006. Pelosi's 80-hour fund-raising trip was detailed by Juliet Eilperin in an article for *Atlantic Monthly*, October 1, 2006.

Pelosi's "take him down" quote appeared in an article by Erin P. Billings, *Roll Call*, June 27, 2005. The script of the NRCC commercials and Carl Forti's comments about it are reported by Hennifer Yachnin, *Roll Call*, October 3, 2006. Pelosi's "hard sell" comment was made to Brian Naylor during a *National Public Radio* interview, October 24, 2006. Brian Wolff was interviewed by Sandalow for the *San Francisco Chronicle*, November 10, 2006. Details about the celebration party at the Hyatt Regency were gathered from unbylined reports and video footage on *washingtonpost.com* on the night of November 7, 2006. Kendrick Meek's remarks at the party were taken from a *Congressional Quarterly* transcript for November 7, 2006.

CHAPTER 10   INAUGURATION DAY

The description of inauguration day is an amalgam of eyewitness accounts by John Burton, Alex Clemens, Nancy Pelosi, Pat McGuire, and Pat Schroeder, from C-Span coverage of the event, speeches recorded in the *Congressional Record*, and articles by *Washington Post* reporters Lyndsey Layton, Jonathon

Weisman, and Shailagh Murray on January 5, 2007. Lyndsey Layton provided much of the detail on what the day meant for women and the scene on the House floor in her sidebar in the *Washington Post*, January 5, 2007. Kathleen Hall Jamieson's comments appeared in the same article, as did Mike Murphy's. The Associated Press, the *New York Times*, and the *Los Angeles Times* all reported details of the day that are incorporated into the chapter.

The "transactional" versus "transformational" leadership argument is made by Judith Havemann in an article for *Wilson Quarterly*, in the Summer 2007 issue. The research of Jennifer Cliff, Nancy Lanton and Howard E. Aldrich is described in the same article, as is the list of books arguing that women are better leaders than men, and the *BusinessWeek* declaration of a new gender gap. Ruth Mandel's comment about women leaders was made to Kathy Kiely for an article in *USAToday*, January 3, 2007.

Pelosi's comments about women helping and inspiring each other are from an article by Peggy Lewis for *Trinity* magazine, fall issue, 2002. Jo Ann Davidson's observations on state legislatures were quoted by Julie Carr Smith in an *Associated Press* article, March 3, 2007. Ellen Malcolm's comment about opportunities for women appeared in an unbylined *Associated Press* article, January 3, 2007.

The results of the Rutgers study were detailed in a report by the League of Women Voters of the Fairfax Area Education Fund, March 2002.

CHAPTER 11   THE HUNDRED HOURS

The name "first hundred hours" is a play on former Democratic president Franklin D. Roosevelt's promise for quick action on the part of government (to combat the Great Depression) during his "first hundred days" in office. Newt Gingrich, the former Republican Speaker, had a similar 100-day agenda to implement the Contract with America. The number of Blackberrys, laptops, phones and parking places on Capitol Hill was gleamed by Lois Romano for an *In the Loop* column in the *Washington Post*, May 31, 2007. The quote by Representative George Miller about "the best three weeks of their life" appeared in an interview with the Associated Press, January 21, 2007. Pelosi's remark after the election about the minority party was also from the Associated Press, November 8, 2006. Henry Waxman's quote appeared in an article by Elizabeth Williamson, the *Washington Post*, April 25, 2007. Thomas Mann's statistical comparisons of Congresses appeared in the *New York Times*, August 26, 2007, on the Op-ed page. Norman Ornstein's observations on Congress appeared in a column he wrote for *Roll Call*, June 6, 2007.

The information about the Democrats hiring 200 investigative staffers was reported by Elizabeth Williamson for the *Washington Post*, April 25, 2007. The details about the types of investigations that were opened come from the same article.

Representative Barney Frank's comments about Pelosi and Hoyer appeared in an article by Jonathan Weisman and Lois Romano in the *Washington Post*, November 17, 2006.

The discussion of the Logan Act is largely drawn from a report done by the Congressional Research Service called "Conducting Foreign Relations Without Authority: The Logan Act," February 1, 2006. Representative Patrick McHenry's statements about Pelosi's "combative style, and his "needs to be done" quote are from an article by Betsy Rothstein in The Hill, January 9, 2007. The information about Democratic promises for open rules comes from a document compiled by House Democrats called, *A New Direction for America*, page 24. The document can be found on Pelosi's web site, www.speaker.gov/pdf/thebook.pdf.

CHAPTER 12   THE WAR OVER THE WAR

Pelosi's quote "I know of no information that the threat is so imminent" appeared in a story by Jim VandeHei and Juliet Eilperin, *the Washington Post*, September 11, 2002, as did Senator Richard Durbin's remarks on the subject. The same article mentions the White House's suggestion that it might act against Iraq without congressional approval. Hillary Clinton's "If I had known then what we know now" quote appears in Carl Bernstein's *A Woman in Charge* (New York: Knopf, 2007). Murtha's "I can handle it" conversation with Pelosi is reported by Shailagh Murray, *the Washington Post*, November 25, 2005. *The Washington Post-ABC News* poll results are described by Dan Balz in the Washington Post, *January 29, 2006*. Karen DeYoung and Jim VandeHei provide the specifics of the Iraq resolution in their report for *the Washington Post*, September 20, 2002. The reconstruction of Pelosi's campaign to get the 218 votes draws heavily on reporting done by Jonathan Weisman in *the Washington Post, March 11, 2007*. The February 5, 2003, White House meeting is excerpted from Bob Woodward's book *Plan of Attack* (New York: Simon and Schuster, 2004), pages 307–309. The description of Jack Murtha's press conference, his quotes during the event and the reaction to them are drawn from an article by Charles Babington for The *Washington Post*, November 18, 2005, and from *Washington Sketch* by Dana Milbank in the same issue of the *Post*.

Alexandra Pelosi's description of President Bush appeared in *Time* magazine, November 12, 2006. Pelosi's "changed the debate" remark was made to Charlie Rose during a *PBS* interview, June 6, 2007. Professor Julkian Zelizer's remarks appeared in an article by Martin Kady II and Josephine Hearn in *The Politico*, August 1, 2007.

EPILOGUE

The notion of a more attractive crop of Democratic candidates in 2006 was first mentioned in an article by Shailagh Murray for *the Washington Post*, October 14, 2006. Democratic Party officials made their private comments to Murray. Pelosi's comment about the eloquence of men's votes for her was made to Leslie Stahl in an interview for CBS's *60 Minutes*, October 22, 2006. Newt Gingrich's former aide was quoted in an article by Josephine Hearn for *The Politico*, June 27, 2007. The comparisons between Gingrich and Pelosi are all derived from the same article. The anonymous Democratic strategist's description of Pelosi as a poster child for left-wing women politicians was quoted by columnist Deborah Orin-Eilbeck in the *New York Post*, October 31, 2006. The quote from GOP pollster Kellyanne Conway appeared in the same article. The Kip O'Neill quote on "kindred souls" appeared in an article by Jennifer Yachnin and Tony Newmyer in *Roll Call*, January 22, 2007.

The *Washington Post/ABC News* poll numbers were reported by Jonathan Weisman for the Washington Post, July 27, 2007.

The description of the fundraiser at Union Station comes from Pelosi's former chief of staff Judy Lemons, who was there. The interview with Pelosi took place on in her office in the Capitol on May 24, 2007.

Mitch McConnell's remark was quoted in Carl Hulse's Congressional Memo in the *New York Times*, July 25, 2007.

INDEX